Praise for *Test-enhan*

Such a thoughtful look at an incredibly imp[...]
classroom teacher, I appreciate the deep dive into the research while also its accessibility to the classroom. *Test-Enhanced Learning* is a text all teachers, no matter their subject or level, can benefit from to improve instruction and learning in their classroom.

Blake Harvard, The Effortful Educator, advanced placement psychology teacher

In a power-packed compact volume, Kristian Still presents an extraordinarily well-researched guide to support teachers as they practically employ retrieval through quizzes, self-tests and other memory-stimulating activities. *Test-Enhanced Learning* is about how putting memory to the test can be applied in a host of learning situations. Through the use of an authentic teacher voice, case studies from a variety of contents and levels, and helpful summarisation points, Still manages to communicate a treasure trove of research in a way that educators can digest and readily apply.

Margaret A. Lee, educator, consultant, co-author of *Mindsets for Parents*

To say that this book is incredibly rich is an understatement. Written by a teacher, for teachers, Kristian Still has written a book that provides useful insights in multiple layers. In its entirety, the book eloquently distils significant amounts of academic research into accessible chapters for the busy teacher wanting to understand more about the science of learning, memory and testing. However, the book is also cleverly written in a way that moves beyond the research into day-to-day practical application. Each chapter ends with a bullet-list summary of its content and then a case study depicting how its content manifests in a real-life classroom. All of this, alongside well-placed honest reflections and enlightening anecdotes from the author's own exploits into test-enhanced learning. With so much to offer, why wouldn't you read this book?!

Jon Gilbert, Professional Development Director, The Two Counties Trust

This book is a fascinating exploration of the testing effect in practice. Finely balancing research and case studies, it will provide food for thought for any teacher or school leader interested in learning more about this important subject.

Kieran Mackle, teacher, author, host of the
***Thinking Deeply about Primary Education* podcast**

Still's *Test-Enhanced Learning* is the product of an intense three-year journey. Firstly, as an experienced educator, he has continued to adapt and hone his pedagogical practice in the classroom to study how testing, memory, spacing and interleaving can truly bring about the very best outcomes for his students. This has been paired with incredibly in-depth academic research on how we best study, learn, store and retrieve information. Still has presented some of these ideas before through his articles and presentations but having such a comprehensive overview of test-enhanced learning in this book is quite the achievement. Beyond the theory and research, Still also includes clear takeaways for the classroom and practical examples are explained through different case studies. This book is a must-read for any classroom practitioner who is keen to make the best use of test-enhanced learning and a testing routine to motivate their students to achieve.

Jon Wayth, MEd, Head of Upper School, El Limonar International School, Murcia

Retrieval practice is an essential topic for every teacher and school leader to understand. As it has gained in popularity (a quick Google Ngram search shows exponential growth in the use of 'retrieval practice' since 2000), educators around the world are looking to get their hands on no-nonsense, practical solutions for embedding techniques that harness the testing effect into their specific contexts. Still's *Test-Enhanced Learning* has provided educators with the primer and the blueprint for doing so. Through perceptive descriptions and illustrative case studies, Still takes readers on a journey through the research and related concepts of this powerful area of evidence-informed instruction. The result is a book that is accessible to both new and long-time enthusiasts of the science of learning. For a field that has often vilified testing while embracing fads, folk theories and other foolishness, this book is, if not a miracle, a giant step in the right direction.

Zach Groshell, PhD, instructional coach and teacher, blogger, author, host of the *Progressively Incorrect* podcast

This book is an accessible and enjoyable encyclopaedia of test-enhanced learning. Kristian explores all the facets of test-enhanced learning including the usual suspects in up-to-date detail plus feedback, motivation, metacognition, illusions of competence and more. Not only has Kristian done the reading, thinking and trialling in his classroom, he's also spoken to the researchers about their work and motivations. The result is a rich combination of their insights, providing suggestions for educators that they can use to guide their practice. This, in combination with practical case studies from exceptionally thoughtful teachers, brings the research to life. I'll be coming back to this book time and again!

Sarah Corringham, Associate Dean, Ambition Institute

This is a unique and long-awaited book. While it's been a few years now that schools have known about the top cognitive science teaching strategies, we've all been waiting for an in-depth analysis of their application in real classroom contexts by a practising teacher – one where the students' own psychologies, faced with a new and challenging about-change in how to learn, are noticed, developed and described. These are real field notes, backed by a comprehensive and interconnected familiarity with the relevant research.

Kristian Still's book is comprehensive, personal, analytical, practical and a positive validation of the impact of integrating and adapting teaching strategies to fit the context in which they are applied. I highly recommend this book and consider it to be a launch of a new era in which context and techniques are intelligently integrated.

Oliver Caviglioli, co-author of the Teaching WalkThrus books

Kristian has weighed, tasted and sampled the complex ingredients within the subject matter. The format in each chapter affords you the option of digesting the content as either a set menu or a mezze, in accordance with your bespoke needs and appetite.

Dr Sean Warren, co-author of *Living Contradiction: A Teacher's Examination of Tension and Disruption in Schools, in Classrooms and in Self*

Test-Enhanced Learning is illuminating, informative, applicable and actionable for teachers in all aspects of their job. Terminology, theories and concepts are clarified with concise explanations and examples. Readability and utility are enhanced with key takeaways and a case study at the end of each chapter. The signposts to one seminal paper per subtopic testify to Kristian's consideration for the time-poor teacher striving to be evidence informed. Refreshingly balanced discussion throughout protects against lethal mutations; Kristian does not shy away from conducting his negative controls!

Mitigating the desirable difficulties of testing, motivation is the golden thread running through the book; vital yet impossible to spontaneously or forcibly generate. Instead, it emerges along the learning journey only when preceded by success. Success leads to belief in the process, motivation emerges, engendering commitment from which achievement will follow, building confidence. And confident learners will not only reap individual benefits, they will enrich the classroom.

Dr Kerensa Ogbe, Assistant Head for Teaching and Learning, Clifton College

This well-researched book draws together so many elements related to testing and retrieval in an informative and insightful manner. The extensive range of relevant research from which Kristian quotes contains numerous pearls of wisdom as well as phrases that capture the essence of the argument that he presents, including 'the steady creep of improvement', 'the valley of disappointment' and how 'performance during learning is a poor predictor of future performance.' Kristian pulls together much of the thinking related to cognitive science that is currently popular but does so with depth and understanding and, crucially, practical application.

A most welcome book for the teacher looking to deepen knowledge and improve their teaching based upon detailed research and written in an engaging and informative style.

Dr Keith Watson, education consultant and coach

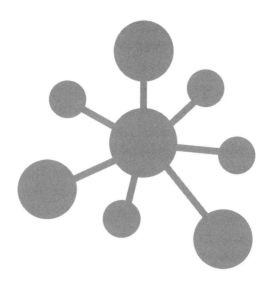

Test-enhanced learning

A practical guide to improving academic outcomes for all students

Kristian Still

Edited by Pete Henshaw

Crown House Publishing Limited
www.crownhouse.co.uk

First published by
Crown House Publishing Ltd
Crown Buildings, Bancyfelin, Carmarthen, Wales, SA33 5ND, UK
www.crownhouse.co.uk

and

Crown House Publishing Company LLC
PO Box 2223
Williston, VT 05495, USA
www.crownhousepublishing.com

Page 15: Figure 1.2, © Oliver Caviglioli, from https://static1.squarespace.com/static/58e151c946c3c418501c2f88/t/5c7e7bfe71c10be69b8ae6a4/1551793151262/Willingham+memory+model+diagram.pdf. Reproduced with kind permission.
Page 17: Figure 1.3, © Nigel Holt and Rob Lewis, 2015 from *AQA Psychology: A Level Year 1 and AS.* Carmarthen: Crown House Publishing.
Page 21: Figure 1.4, © Efrat Hurst from the blog post 'Reconsolidation: The life of a memory trace'. Available at: https://sites.google.com/view/efratfurst/reconsolidation?pli=1. Reproduced with kind permission.
Page 106: Figure 6.1, © K. E. Vaughn, J. Dunlosky and K. A. Rawson, 2016 from Vaughn, K. E., Dunlosky, J. and Rawson, K. A. (2016) Effects of successive relearning on recall: does relearning override the effects of initial learning criterion? *Memory and Cognition,* 44(6): 897–909. Reproduced with kind permission.

British Library of Cataloguing-in-Publication Data
A catalogue entry for this book is available from the British Library.

Print ISBN: 978-178583658-9
Mobi ISBN: 978-178583659-6
ePub ISBN: 978-178583660-2
ePDF ISBN: 978-178583661-9

LCCN 2022943015

Printed and bound in the UK by
CPi, Chippenham, Wiltshire

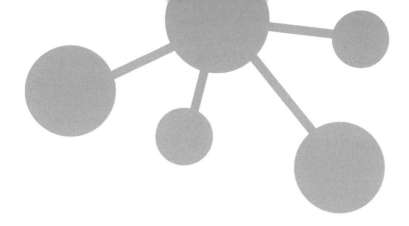

Foreword

Testing in education has a troubled history (Stobart, 2008) and there has been a regrettable mistrust and even aversion to testing in some quarters, including from many teachers. Tests have acquired an unfortunate association with damaging forms of accountability, including top-down, managerial forms of school leadership and heavy-handed, highly questionable use of data in schools. Many teachers even steer clear of the T-word, preferring to talk about quizzes, progress checks and assessments, or ensuring that it is accompanied by its less-threatening companion, 'low-stakes'.

This troubled image and history notwithstanding, countless teachers have come to understand the power of tests as an educational tool and adopted tests as a key component of their teaching pedagogy. It helps that the concept of assessment *for* learning (or formative assessment) is now widely understood - although it is quite demoralising to think that, after two decades of being part of the received wisdom and evidence base about effective teaching, 'formative assessment remains the exception rather than the rule in most classrooms' (Wiliam, 2022: 134). What has crept up on teachers, particularly in the last decade, is the idea of assessment as learning. Sometimes this term is used as a way of helping us better understand the relationship between assessment of and for learning within formative assessment (Earl, 2012); but there is a more fundamental sense in which assessment could and should be seen as learning. Over the last decade, a large body of literature on the benefits of testing (Roediger et al., 2011) has become connected with and articulated through the language and conceptual toolkit of cognitive science. The evidence is clear: testing raises pupil achievement (Perry et al., 2021; Yang et al., 2021).

Let us consider the current relationship between cognitive science and education. We have a mountain of strong evidence from cognitive science which provides robust and fundamental principles for learning and memory. I, like many others, am convinced that teaching and learning are unlikely to be successful if not in line with principles of memory and learning that are well-established in cognitive science. It is understandable, therefore, that teachers have been exploring the potential insights that cognitive science has to offer. Over the last decade, there has been increasing awareness of key results from cognitive science and a growing body of literature seeking to connect these to practice. Cognitive science is becoming a common focus for professional development, and many teachers are – individually and collectively – taking ideas and strategies from cognitive science and applying them in their classrooms.

These are exciting times, with a huge amount of innovation taking place and real optimism about the potential benefits of cognitive science in education. There is, however, a problem. The evidence suggests that we are still some way off realising the potential of cognitive science. There is presently a large gap between, on one hand, the laboratory and the controlled conditions of classroom trials and, on the other, the everyday reality of teaching. We have not yet created practical, scalable models of cognitive-science-informed professional development or school improvement that have demonstrable and sustained impact when tested in realistic conditions (Perry et al., 2021). Challenges also apply at a more local level. Teachers are still wrestling with conceptual and practical questions about how insights from cognitive science can be translated into classroom practice and embedded for lasting improvement. The gap between research and practice remains large.

It is in this context that Kristian Still's *Test-Enhanced Learning* picks up the challenge of bringing cognitive science to bear on our understanding of testing and its role in enhancing learning. If you are wondering about how you can help your classes 'remember more', and what the cognitive science evidence base *really* says about the role of testing in education, you are not alone. Happily, you have picked up the right book: it is a superb contribution to the current movement to realise the potential of cognitive science in the classroom. It connects a detailed and up-to-date understanding of the science to the complexity and nuance of classroom practice. It introduces and explains concepts, principles and evidence from across cognitive science, summarising a large and often technical evidence base with clarity and accessibility. Woven into this is a discussion of the implications and questions for practice, which is further reinforced by case studies of cognitive science in practice at the end of each chapter. Oh, and if all that wasn't enough, Kristian has taken all these insights about testing and cognitive science and built them into the RememberMore platform and app – which you can use, for free, in your own classroom. To connect research and practice in this way is impressive – and a lot easier said than done.

Allow me to comment a little more on the more general challenges of translating and embedding cognitive science in practice, and some of the issues that must be navigated. What has proved particularly difficult for those connecting cognitive science and practice is staying true to the research while relevant to the classroom. Many attempts have produced a compelling and practical account of what cognitive-science-informed practice should look like, but have lost sight of the science. Teachers are provided with a toolkit of strategies and principles that are ostensibly supported by an impressive evidence base but – while plausible – are filtered through the lens of the author's teaching philosophy and classroom experiences. In fact, the cognitive science does not provide much concrete detail on what classroom-ready activities and teaching and learning strategies should be. This is because the research has prioritised scientific control over realistic, everyday classroom conditions, and it has set up experiments that optimise rather than road-test classroom strategies in action. The research is, therefore, in many respects a poor guide to the practicalities of how cognitive-science-informed teaching and learning can be applied in typical classroom conditions.

To reap the benefits of cognitive science, teachers must understand principles of memory and learning and have a clear conception of what the research does and does not show. The research is not 'oven-ready' (to coin an infamous phase used by a former prime minister) and it is often difficult to see at what point scientific theory stops and teacher expertise must pick up. In this context, there are dangers of a too-reductive conception of cognitive science and an over-reaching conception of its contribution to pedagogical theory. Top-down and reductive accounts of the science can over-ride and undermine rather than enhance professional expertise. We still have some way to go until we can confidently say what cognitive science should look like in the classroom while remaining firmly grounded in the evidence. It is still worth teachers going back to the principles and evidence provided by the research to reach their own conception of cognitive-science-informed practice.

The opposing issue is that there are also many accounts of cognitive science that have remained true to the research while losing sight of the practice. Researchers have a tendency to underappreciate how much work and expertise is needed to put guidance into practice. Most jarring is how little cognitive science has to say about subject content, the individual differences of children and young people, the dynamics of classroom teaching, and other facets of high-quality teaching such as formative assessment, classroom management and fostering classroom dialogue. Many important educational questions are treated as an afterthought and/or issues that can be readily resolved by teachers. The science, while technically sophisticated, can often be quite crude and impractical with respect to accounts of classroom practice, certainly as compared to the sophistication and concreteness of teachers' educational expertise and experience. What is needed are accounts that inform educational thinking and problems with powerful evidence from cognitive science, exploring educational theory and practice and cognitive science side by side.

Test-Enhanced Learning is a serious, honest and thought-provoking investigation into the interface between research and practice. It provides an evidence-informed and practical theory of the role of testing that connects the powerful idea of retrieval practice to a host of related concepts, including spaced practice (and successive relearning), interleaving feedback, metacognition, motivation, personalisation and much more. It also does important work to show the role of retrieval practice across stages of learning - to potentiate, encode and maintain learning. This moves us to a more nuanced, three-dimensional and powerful conception of testing as an educational practice. It is to his credit that Kristian has not shied away from the technical detail, complexity and uncertainty of the science. The research is often technical and hard to interpret. As a result, this book will challenge as well as inform. Equally, he has not strayed away from practical questions about what test-enhanced learning looks like in the classroom. Practice is uncertain, complex and messy. The 'takeaways' at the end of each chapter are hard-won conclusions from wrestling with the evidence, and the case studies are testament to the process that unfolds when principles and strategies from cognitive science are put into practice. Any account of what cognitive science looks like in the classroom that doesn't challenge you is offering an overly simplistic view of the science, of practice or both.

Perhaps one day we will be able to embed the lessons of cognitive science into educational resources and technology, or absorb them into the collective knowledge of the profession, in a way that makes them invisible and taken for granted - analogous to the way that the computer software and hardware I am using to write manages to render this text despite my complete ignorance of its inner workings. At present, though, I think there is some way to go and a value in intrepid teachers grappling with testing at the level of fundamentals. That is, teachers should be able to design their own teaching and learning with knowledge about how cognition, memory and testing work. The key contribution of cognitive science in support of this is to provide teachers with a powerful set of concepts and principles for learning that we can trust. *Test-Enhanced Learning* doesn't provide an oven-ready pedagogy or list of 'top tips' that you can put in place next Monday morning (but will have forgotten about by Wednesday). What it does is introduce, explain and explore what cognitive science reveals about testing and learning – equipping you to think scientifically and expertly about memory and learning.

The synthesis of educational and cognitive scientific knowledge is an incredibly challenging but important frontier for education. Equally, it is imperative that the profession develops a sophisticated conception of assessment *of*, *for* and *as* learning. Teachers becoming experts in testing should be as unremarkable as sculptors being handy with a chisel. Referring to learning as 'test-enhanced' would be as redundant as describing a television as being in colour. Kristian describes all that is test-enhanced learning and RememberMore as his 'edventure'. Personally, I am delighted that there are edventurous teachers out there who can push forward our thinking and practice about the myriad and powerful ways in which tests can enhance learning.

Dr Tom Perry
Associate Professor, Education Studies, University of Warwick

Acknowledgements

I will miss my 6:30am Friday morning calls with Pete Henshaw, a journalist and editor specialising in education and first editor of this book. Not only did the book benefit from his inquisitive questioning and editorial, I did too.

My thanks to Dr Tom Perry, Sarah Cottingham and Helen Webb for their conversation and critique: Tom for always cautioning me not to over-stretch the contribution of educational research, Sarah for sharing her expertise in educational neuroscience and advocacy, and Helen for always reminding me that teachers have to be able to apply this knowledge within the complexities of their own classroom. To the nine teachers who contributed a case study and much more in between – Helen Webb, Kirby Dowler, Dan Rosen, Helen Pipe, Andy Sammons, Kristian Shanks, Anoara Mughal, Ambra Carretta and Ben Windsor – thank you for sharing your insights and experiences from the chalkface. And, lastly, to the pupils in my classes, thank you for your honest critique and enthusiasm for test-enhanced learning. Is there a more powerful endorsement than pupils committing more of their discretionary time than they are asked for to keep a teacher motivated?

Contents

Introduction

It all began with Othello

In December 2021, in an article for secondary education magazine *SecEd*, I made the case that despite the 'wealth of evidence' (Agarwal et al., 2021: 1438) about the 'reliable advantage' (Yang et al., 2021: 299) of test-enhanced learning – more commonly referred to as the testing effect or retrieval practice – it is actually far more complicated than it is often presented as being and that 'retrieval practice alone is not enough' (Still, 2021). In that article, I argued that retrieval practice offered 'more than just improved memorisation skills and securing long-term learning', and encouraged teachers to exploit unsupervised, personalised spaced retrieval practice and to leverage the wider indirect benefits of testing. I argued towards adopting a set of learning principles or test-enhanced learning.

Feedback from that article led to a series of further articles in the same organ; the series then led to this book. In *Test-Enhanced Learning*, I will first explore the wealth of research, report the direct and indirect benefits of test-enhanced learning and review the ingredients of test-enhanced learning (i.e. cognition, repeated retrieval practice, spaced learning, interleaving, feedback and elaboration, successive relearning, metacognition and motivation), both inside and – just as importantly – outside the classroom. A review that ultimately points to the inherent inefficiencies of learning and the potential gains of personalisation. This review of the research (both laboratory and applied) is tied with my efforts to employ test-enhanced learning in my own classroom and with other teachers around the world.

Second, I outline my efforts to make personalised spaced retrieval practice available to teachers, educators and learners through RememberMore. This has three connected component parts. First, classroom.remembermore.app is an open and free web portal for creating bespoke classroom quizzes for teaching, retrieval and self-study in seconds (yes, seconds!). RememberMore.app is a digital flashcard system that boosts learning and reduces teacher workload. Importantly, it adopts confidence-based assessment to personalise spaced retrieval practice, thereby increasing retrieval gains. It also enables both teachers and learners to categorise and tag knowledge, providing a structure to organise knowledge and support interleaving. Finally, RememberMore includes a 'dashboard' that presents learner and flashcard insights via a graphical user interface to help inform teachers, teaching and learning. It is also the platform to quiz your understanding and the knowledge acquired in reading this book. Where would a book about test-enhanced learning be without a quiz about it?

Context is king

You may be expecting this introduction to start with an outline of what inspired me to dedicate most of my professional learning to investigating test-enhanced learning. However, my interest in this area of research started out with me simply trying to find a solution to what my pupils needed most at that time, which was being able to access knowledge to better understand the texts being taught in class. With clearly observable impact on pupil attainment and classroom culture, that interest led to reviewing the research more critically, connecting with researchers, while road-testing and iterating my own classroom practice. Finally, after three years' intensive work, I was asked to write this practical guide to improving academic outcomes for all pupils.

For context, I was returning to England from overseas after the new academic year had started. I was joining an oversubscribed, inclusive comprehensive secondary school with a pupil intake that reflects a wonderfully diverse and vibrant local community, in the third week of term as a full-time teacher of English (my second subject, having studied sports science (BSc) and kinesiology (MSEd)). I felt remarkably like I did when I started my teaching career. It was a school with a strong moral purpose, principled leadership, and defined and embedded school values: challenge, creativity, commitment, cooperation and courtesy.

Even with 20-plus years of teaching experience (eight years as a head teacher and senior leader), I knew that I would still need time to establish myself in a new school, and I didn't have all that much time to prepare – I was due to start teaching the following day.

Prior to meeting the classes, I put together a basic class profile (names, photos, prior attainment data and background), reviewed the long-term curriculum plan and schemes of work, and read the school's behaviour policy. The classes I would be teaching were predominantly low prior attaining, and a number of pupils had accumulated higher than average negative behaviour points. Just for good measure, I was (we were) nomadic – teaching in various classrooms throughout the school over the teaching week.

Following just a handful of lessons, the challenge was clear. The curriculum was rightly ambitious. I was new to the school and 'we' needed time to establish a positive classroom climate (made all the more difficult by often arriving to class at the same time as the pupils) and learning routines. In addition, it was evident that many of the pupils would benefit from experiencing success in lessons, as too many were more focused on what they couldn't do than what they could.

That first Friday evening, I was late home having made a lot of positive phone calls home and quite a few phone calls to introduce myself to parents/carers. A worthwhile investment, even with a busy weekend ahead of me.

With the unit outline already stuck in the front of the pupils' exercise books, I hurriedly built a basic knowledge organiser that defined and shared with pupils the substantive knowledge and explicit vocabulary from the scheme of learning that I expected them to learn. The process of building the knowledge organiser was as much for my professional learning as it was for the pupils, having not taught the assigned texts previously. I asked the pupils to add this to the back of their exercise books, as both a reference document and a tool for self-assessment.

I originally introduced a low-stakes retrieval practice (testing/quizzing) lesson starter routine (with self-assessed marking) as a practical solution to managing the chaotic arriving-at-the-same-time lesson starts – and to give me the opportunity to log in to the teacher's computer, take the register and set up the upcoming lesson. Equally, I was very aware of the wider benefits of test-enhanced learning – and the 'high utility' of both retrieval practice and spaced or distributed practice more specifically[1] – but this was as much about managing the learning as it was about leading it.

Early reflections

Was it easy? No. Did the pupils thrive on the low-stakes retrieval practice starters? Not at first. (We will discover that there is much more to test-enhanced learning than low-stakes retrieval practice starters.) What I can immediately share with you, however, is that pupils are more receptive to 'quiz' and 'quizzing' than they are to 'tests' and 'testing', that 'retrieval practice' doesn't mean all that much to them at all, and that pupils know little about how they learn or the difference between performance and learning, and would much prefer to adopt more familiar learning strategies or none at all.

The truth is that the pupils found it hard, effortful and, with only nominal reward in the opening half a dozen or so lessons, a little deflating. I would have to be honest and say that the pupils were not entirely convinced. I would later learn that I had not only missed a critical step, but I was also missing a lot of the knowledge and know-how that we will cover in this book. We will come back to this in detail later.

For now, I knew *why* we were investing in these high-utility, evidence-informed practices and the wider benefits of test-enhanced learning, but just the teacher knowing why is insufficient. Nor is it just the doing that matters, but *how well* you are doing it. *How you know how well* you are doing it is equally important. Still, as I will outline, there is more to consider beyond retrieval and distribution or, for that matter, the spacing of test-enhanced learning. The good news is that you will be much better informed than I was.

---

1   According to Dunlosky et al. (2013), 'high utility' refers to the generalisable benefits across learning conditions, pupil characteristics, materials and criterion tasks.

Coming up for air

By the end of the first term (12 weeks, or 60 or so lessons later), I had started to earn the pupils' trust and routines were more established (if arriving at the same time as the pupils ever gets much easier). Together, we had travelled through the 'valley of disappointment' (Clear, 2018: 20) – that is, the period of investment where teachers and pupils feel discouraged, having put in hours of effortful practice and experienced nominal results, preceding accelerated benefits. I had also gained some important practical pedagogical insights on the use of quizzing: on the benefits of every pupil having a directed focus and working independently through a routined lesson starter quiz, the style of questions or cues that were most effective, the breadth of questions to cover, how many questions to set, whether to report or not report scores, the use of timers, how to transition to teaching the lesson, the potency of relearning, and the importance of self-assessment and low-stakes routines generally.

Perhaps most importantly, the pupils could now reference tangible learning gains for themselves - directly in what they knew and could remember and in their improved end-of-unit assessment grade, and indirectly in how they felt about themselves as successful learners and how they approached their learning. (We will explore the direct and indirect benefits of test-enhanced learning throughout the book.) The end-of-term pupil feedback review responses were largely positive too. Pupils reported a growing confidence and 'security' in lessons, and on reflection, a wider group of pupils were now contributing to class and we were all benefiting from the routined start to lessons. We have to remember that these were particular pupils who were largely indifferent to their learning - or shall we say bruised by their experiences of English teaching, possibly of education generally.

Outside of class, I leant heavily of the knowledge and expertise of my department colleagues, and I continued to read research journals and the blogs of practising educators like Blake Harvard (@effortfuleduktr and theeffortfuleductor.com). I paid closer attention when guests on the Mr Barton Maths Podcast (www.mrbartonmaths.com/podcast) or Ollie Lovell's Education Research Reading Room Podcast (www.ollielovell.com/errr) mentioned memory, cognition or retrieval practice. The research clearly supported the performance gains of test-enhanced learning, of the testing effect and of retrieval practice, and it also signalled the benefits of spaced or distributed practice and interleaving (all covered in depth in later chapters of this book). What I rarely encountered was research connecting with metacognition, motivation and, given the speed of digital adoption at this time, personalisation (where learning is adapted to meet the needs of each learner).

The last point, personalisation, irked me. The fabulous work of Professor Graham Nuthall in *The Hidden Lives of Learners* (2007) (the only education book I have read three times) remained ever constant in my thoughts when reading the broader test-enhanced learning research.[2]

Our research has found that students already know, on average, about 50% of what a teacher intends his or her students to learn through a curriculum unit or topic. But that 50% is not evenly distributed. Different students will know different things, and all of them will know only about 15% of what the teacher wants them to know.

Nuthall (2007: 35)

I knew that, for all its benefits, the quizzing routines I was teaching were still being presented *to the entire class* – questions to many pupils and questions fishing for a correct response. Yet, what Nuthall kept on emphasising was that learning is highly individual and we need to ensure that new knowledge firmly connects to and integrates with previous knowledge, which is difficult, at best, when each pupil has unique prior knowledge. By the end of this book this will sound all too familiar. Was personalisation a potential solution to Nuthall's research observations 13 years later and to classroom questioning ineffectiveness and inefficiency?

In search of a personalised solution

In search of a more personalised (sometimes referred to as adaptive) quizzing or retrieval practice solution, I kissed quite a few frogs before settling on perhaps one of the most accessible flashcard platforms – AnkiApp (*Anki* is Japanese for memorisation). First, of course, as a digital solution, distributed or spaced practice came baked into the software. Second, it also meant pupils had access to the anywhere-anytime learning to which we have become accustomed. (Hold that thought!) My account showed that I had first used Anki in 2017, some three years previously. I also seemed to recall that Daisy Christodoulou – the author of *Seven Myths About Education*

---

2   For a short overview of Nuthall's work, see Jan Tishauser's (2019) *researchED* article or Tom Sherrington's (2020) helpful blog post.

(2013) and other education titles, former head of assessment at Ark Schools and now director of education at No More Marking – was an Anki fan, and used the app to try and prevent forgetting what she had read.[3] So started a mini research enquiry to investigate the suitability of Anki to support personalised spaced retrieval practice as a core component of my teaching.

With a full term under my belt, come January 2020 I would be faced with the additional challenge of teaching Shakespeare's *Othello*. This would be the teaching experience that became the driving *motivation* for the design and development of RememberMore, the digital flashcard system I mentioned back at the start.

Why knowledge is essential for learning

Having attended more than a handful of Professor Paul Kirschner's presentations, read his papers and books, and listened to him interviewed on various podcasts, it would be impossible not to be influenced by his eloquent expertise and infectious enthusiasm. Rarely does he fail to reference the work of American psychologist David Ausubel and that 'the most influential factor for learning new things is what the learner already knows'; prior knowledge to you and me. According to Ausubel, new things that we want or need to learn must be connected to what we already know. Kirschner (2022) hits the nail squarely and firmly on the head when he says: 'The more you know, the better you learn and the more you learn, the easier it gets!' If your pupils do not have the basic 'hooks', or relevant prior knowledge, to which to attach more complex information, they will very quickly find themselves adrift in the lesson.

Back to teaching and the introduction of *Othello*. Here was a multicultural, all-boy Year 8 class with very little to no prior knowledge of Shakespeare or Elizabethan England, or the issues encapsulated by the play, and even less motivation to study it. Although a good number of pupils see value in their learning and some may seek clarification or your help, some may do nothing, at ease with being adrift, while others may seek to derail the learning to mask their sense of vulnerability and avoid further academic bruising. Without some basic background knowledge of the play and Elizabethan England, much like the protagonist Othello himself, the class were going to be in for a tough learning experience.

---

3   'I love Anki! Planning to blog more about it soon …' (Christodoulou, 2022).

Take two – the spring term

I had the substantive knowledge prepped on a knowledge organiser and on hand within Anki, making knowledge available to pupils both in and out of the classroom. I may not have realised it back then, but it was unwise not to take account of both metacognition and motivation when teaching – and inconceivable when employing test-enhanced learning. That is why there are three chapters in this book dedicated to these important components of learning, too often passed by in general conversation around retrieval practice.

As before, the course outline was stuck in the front of the pupils' exercise books and the knowledge organiser in the back. In addition, we had a deck of flashcards available via Anki for quizzing in and out of class. We were now building on an emerging metacognitive belief that quizzing, test-enhanced learning and retrieval practice worked for these pupils, both directly and indirectly.

You see, when I set out on this 'edventure' (if Shakespeare can make up words, I would like to think we all can) with these academically bruised Year 8 pupils, I hadn't explicitly told the learners *why* or *how* quizzing worked, that retrieval practice was not the easy option and that the learning benefits are often deferred, if durable and demonstrable. Educating the pupils about cognition, and about test-enhanced learning, was the critical missed step I highlighted previously. (How to go about this will also be covered in more detail in the book via the work of McDaniel and Einstein (2020) and others invested in this process.) At least the second time around, in the spring term, I was better prepared and the pupils were more receptive based on their knowledge, informed beliefs, deepening commitment and personal successes. More pupils were starting to focus on what they could do and what they had done than what they couldn't.

So, every Friday after break, the pupils would wheel around the laptop trolley and we would invest in personalised spaced retrieval sessions as provided by the Anki platform.[4] The pupils were hugely positive about these Friday sessions, describing the learning as 'recapping lessons' and the lessons as 'quite relaxing'. The lessons were relaxed and calm yet purposeful – and why wouldn't they be, given the personalised nature of the learning? Remember, these were pupils who had accumulated higher than average negative behaviour points, turning up towards the end of break time to set

---

4   All documented at https://www.kristianstill.co.uk/wordpress/tag/anki.

up the laptops and leading their own personalised learning. Even the head teacher offered a slightly perplexed yet supportive glance after scanning our unlikely Shakespeare scholars hard at work while on one of his many tours of the school. The pupils' agency was palpable.

What's more, a good handful of the class downloaded AnkiApp onto their mobile devices, and some logged in to their web accounts at home and reviewed cards outside of class. Self-paced learning and then 'knowing stuff' in class appeared to be attractive to these boys. However, without them showing me, I had no way of knowing what flashcards they had quizzed and how successful they had been, as Anki lacked an administration dashboard and learner metrics.

Fast-forward to a second term (a further 12 weeks, or 60 or so lessons). Apart from the obvious tribulations of booking the laptop trolley, finding out who had the key last, wheeling it down the corridor during busy break times and racing to get 30 laptops packed away again, the class had become huge fans of Lucian Msamati's Iago (in the Royal Shakespeare Company's 2015 production), if not Shakespeare's writing.

They knew 'stuff' about the context of the play and about the character of Iago. They were rarely short of an opinion. But they now had access to knowledge and vocabulary to think with, to evidence and extend these opinions. They also had the confidence to engage with lessons. In this way, our four other lessons – and class climate – benefited immeasurably too.

In summarising Willingham's (2007) paper 'Critical thinking: why is it so hard to teach?', Mccrea (2019: 17) offers: 'As our knowledge becomes deeper and more comprehensive, our capacity for critical thinking, problem solving and creativity within that domain emerges.' Underpinning knowledge underpins thinking. This made me reflect on the commentary of world-renowned Canadian computer scientist Professor Yoshua Bengio. Known for his pioneering work in artificial intelligence and deep learning, Bengio speaks of 'productive thought' – that only once you have all the information, only after you have filled your mind with a problem, can you 'really start seeing through things and getting things to stand together, and solidly, and now you can you can extend science right now'.[5] The pupils were now able to 'think productively', and their writing had started to showcase it.

Towards the end of the term, one of these Year 8 boys told me: 'I found it easier to feel comfortable in class and not feel pressured or underprepared

---

5 See https://www.youtube.com/watch?v=d1qA8vvpZZk&t=4229s.

when a question is asked.' As in the previous term, I had noticed greater participation in lessons (particularly from some of the less likely class contributors), but perhaps these were the first hints that personalisation had a lot to offer pupil motivation, agency and self-efficacy, as well as knowing stuff. I just didn't recognise at that point that success precedes motivation, that test-enhanced learning could most certainly be designed to lower the failure rate and promote success, whereas self-directed personalisation almost completely removed the external threat of public class failure.

In addition to Shakespeare's *Othello*, pupils had opinions and feature requests for Anki too!

What next?

I would love to tell you that it was solely the pupils' end-of-unit assessment grades that convinced me to invest the next two years in developing a personalised spaced retrieval practice solution for teachers, educators and pupils. Of course, pupil outcomes are important. However, it was the climate shift in the classroom that accompanied the deployment of test-enhanced learning and personalised spaced retrieval practice (in and out of the classroom) that was most convincing: improved attention in class and pupil confidence, fewer distractions, better note-taking, far more robust class discussions and improved punctuality. I would even go as far as testifying to a deepened commitment to learning.

There are gains for the teacher, too, many highlighted by the teachers who have contributed case studies to this book, not least that building a deck of retrieval flashcards *is* professional learning, and organises and consolidates your own understanding of the content. Access to pre-planned and tagged questions at any point in the lesson is super-helpful, and the lesson-by-lesson benefits of routined and direct (with a little 'd') instruction make a teacher's life more manageable and more enjoyable. Experiencing a very busy end of term, including two parents' evenings, year group data captures and college applications for his Year 11 tutor group, teacher Ben Windsor reflected:

I must say, having a 5-lesson day and parents' evening, RememberMore as my DIN [do it now] has helped massively to pace myself and claw back some cognitive space.

Yet, Anki was not going to be the long-term solution, with its lack of an administration dashboard and learner metrics, and the numerous pupil feature requests. The search was back on.

Far more complicated

I continued to read and apply the research when, in early 2020, I stumbled upon Dr Katherine Rawson's earlier research on successive relearning. Add that to the perpetual Nuthall itch, the issue of personalisation (being able to pose the right question to the right pupil at the right time), my own and shared teaching experiences and a growing interest in test-enhanced learning research (which is a significant body of work), and I started to realise that there was more to test-enhanced learning than retrieval practice alone. That, at times, as educators, we oversimplify things to make them more accessible.

My interest in test-enhanced learning has always been about all learners having access to more knowledge, so they can engage and explore lessons more broadly and deeply and achieve better academic outcomes, but it has become so much more. It became an iterative investigation on how to create a successful and secure classroom climate, to seek teaching effectiveness and learning efficiency at the same time as reducing teacher workload.

Together with Alex Warren, a full-time senior software developer, I embarked on a project to design, build and iterate a digital flashcard system to boost learning and reduce teacher workload. A system that supported quizzing in classrooms and offered personalised spaced retrieval practice. A system that reported usable learner metrics and teaching insights with which to inform teaching. A system co-designed with pupils and with the support of a host of teachers, school leaders, applied cognitive psychologists and data scientists. We launched the RememberMore app in September 2021, making personalised, spaced, interleaved retrieval practice available to any teacher who wants to leverage the benefits of test-enhanced learning for their pupils.

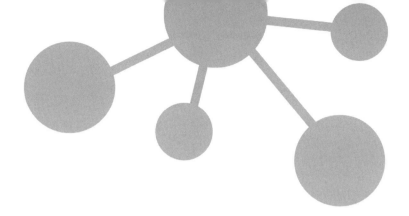

Chapter 1

Memory, learning, encoding and retrieval

Let's make some memories – stick

The subtitle of Dr John Sweller's presentation at researchED Melbourne in 2017 left a mark: 'Without an understanding of human cognitive architecture, instruction is blind'. In it, Sweller presents what teachers really need to understand about cognitive load theory.[1] Cue that frequently cited Wiliam quote (from a 2017 tweet): 'Sweller's Cognitive Load Theory is the single most important thing for teachers to know.'

So, why is an understanding of human cognitive architecture – memory to you and me – so important? Well, before I review the importance of Sweller's research, I would like to introduce Willingham's simple model of memory.

---

1   It is available at https://www.youtube.com/watch?v=gOLPfi9Ls-w.

Memory is as thinking does

'Memory is as thinking does' is a famous quote from Daniel Willingham (2003), who is a professor of psychology at the University of Virginia and the author of *Why Don't Students Like School?* (2009). Here's another: 'Teachers need what might be called a mental model of the learner: knowledge of children's cognitive, emotional, and motivational make-up' (Willingham, 2017: 166).

While this book focuses on the many ingredients of test-enhanced learning, we absolutely must begin with an understanding of memory. This is the lens through which we need to view the many ingredients of test-enhanced learning and therefore our teaching decisions. Acknowledging that we do not have space to cover everything, this chapter reviews memory, the underpinning of test-enhanced learning, and later chapters will focus on the inter-related components of retrieval, spacing, interleaving and feedback, plus two additional – but often dislocated (though not by Willingham) – areas of research: metacognition and motivation.

So, memory is as thinking does. When it comes to cognition – to thinking – theory is unavoidable; therefore, a model is almost always inevitable. Moreover, a model generative of pedagogical strategies helps us to understand the mechanics or processes of teaching, learning and test-enhanced learning. For the purpose of a shared understanding, let's go with Willingham's simple model of memory (Figures 1.1 and 1.2); other models are available, with Oliver Caviglioli's figure a personal and pupil favourite.

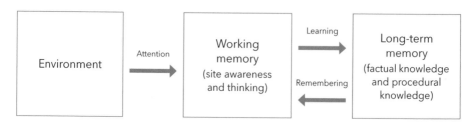

Figure 1.1. Willingham's simple model of memory (adapted from Willingham, 2009: 55)

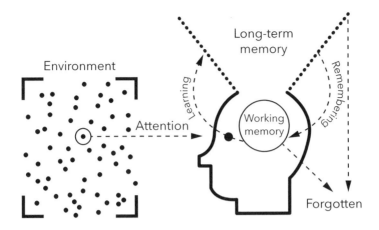

Figure 1.2. Willingham's simple model of memory as interpreted by Oliver Caviglioli (reproduced with kind permission from @olicav)

In both models, we have the environment on the left, which is all the things we see, hear, feel and so on. What we attend to or give our attention to – what we selectively concentrate on – is moved to our working memory on the right. (I should add that attention is a cognitive process that is very hard to pin down.)

Working memory, with its limited capacity, attempts to hold all the things we are thinking about: our reflections at this moment, thoughts about the last lesson, those dark clouds on the horizon. And, of course, you can also be aware of things that are not currently 'in' the environment – the smell of food from the school canteen earlier in the day or how you expect the next lesson to unfold.

The key component of working memory (beyond short-term memory, although these terms are too often used interchangeably) is the additional connotation that information is maintained *and manipulated* in some way in working memory – our conscious thought. Interconnected with working memory are 'learning' and 'remembering', which we will return to in a moment.

Long-term memory is the 'big mental warehouse' (Clark et al., 2012: 8) in which we maintain our knowledge of the world. Importantly, long-term memory resides outside of our awareness until called upon, and then these thoughts enter our working memory and so become conscious.

Thinking occurs when we combine information from the environment and from long-term memory in new ways. That combination happens in working memory as either learning (encoding) or remembering (relearning). A learner's prior knowledge (long-term memory) will, therefore, always be a key consideration for all teachers. In fact, it can often determine what our pupils attend to in the first place – as it was when introducing *Othello* to my Year 8 class. What pupils already know affects their learning; sometimes what they know prepares them and sometimes what they know interferes, is erroneous and needs to be challenged and corrected.

Hence, the maintenance of knowledge is assumed to reflect two distinct phases: an encoding (learning) phase and a maintenance (remembering/relearning) phase, where knowledge is periodically accessed, remembered or relearned. This distinction between encoding and maintenance is meaningful in relation to the intervals between successive exposures during learning and the intervals between retrieval attempts during the maintenance phase. If the access interval is too long, much of the acquired information becomes inaccessible: it is forgotten and must be relearned later in order to become a part of semi-permanent knowledge. This is expertly summed up by Bahrick (1979: 297–298):

One can, therefore, conceive of the total acquisition process as a cycle of acquisition, loss, and reacquisition of information, with diminishing amounts of information lost during the intervals between exposures until the information becomes part of permanent knowledge retrievable without further relearning.

More recently, researchers have investigated the impact of potentiating learning or 'pre-testing' the forward effects of retrieval practice (Latimier et al., 2019; Pan et al., 2020) – that is, the facilitative effect of retrieval practice on subsequent encoding or learning (testing ahead of teaching) – with some rather unexpected results. We will come back to the benefits of pre-testing later in Chapter 5.

Another helpful diagram is the three-store model of memory. The Education Endowment Foundation's very useful and accessible evidence review *Cognitive Science Approaches in the Classroom* (see Figure 1.3) reminds us that working memory has a 'limited capacity' and can be overloaded. In fact, many of the pedagogical strategies employed by teachers aim to focus specifically on the 'crucial interactions' between working memory and long-term memory (Perry et al., 2021: 10).

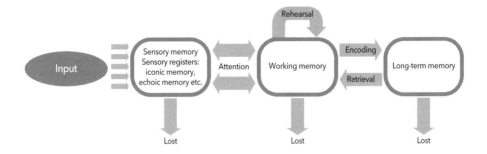

Figure 1.3. The three elements of memory: sensory, working and long term (Holt and Lewis, 2015: 33)

Let's add a little meat to the bones. Working memory is the memory system where the conscious processing of sensory information occurs (for an extra layer of detail, see Baddeley, 2003). Sensory and working memory are needed even for the simplest activities. (If you cannot remember the beginning of this sentence, you cannot understand its ending.) They are where small amounts of information are stored for a very short duration – what Clark et al. (2012: 8) call 'the limited mental "space" in which we think'.

As Professor Alan Baddeley (2022) explains: 'Working memory is a system for holding things in mind while you are working on them. It involves both a capacity to store information and also the capacity to manipulate it and relate it to other kinds of memory.'[2]

Again, working memory is extremely limited in both capacity and duration. Almost all information stored in working memory, not consciously processed or rehearsed, is lost within 30 seconds (Peterson and Peterson, 1959). Just take a moment to pause here to consider that information in the context of *learning* a completely new task and *teaching* a completely new task to your pupils. An average person can only hold a few chunks of information in their working memory at one time. Go ahead and forget Miller's (1956) now infamous prediction about storage capacity limits – that we can hold seven plus or minus two unique concepts, or five to nine items, in our working memory, as it is very likely to be a generous overestimate. Cowan (2001) suggests the figure to be as low as four.

Two interesting, short asides: firstly, there is evidence to indicate that there are differences in working memory capacity between individuals and that working memory capacity increases gradually until the teenage years (Swanson, 1999).

2   See video link at Baddeley (2022).

Secondly, Agarwal et al. (2017) report that retrieval practice with feedback yields a greater benefit for pupils with lower working memory capacity, although the wider literature shows a mixed set of results.

Of equal importance, Ericsson and Kintsch (1995) and Baddeley (2001) distinguish between the capacity of working memory when it is processing new information and new relationships (encoding – learning) compared with processing prior knowledge from long-term memory (remembering/relearning – maintenance) – a fundamental point in the design of classroom quizzes. This again emphasises the importance of prior knowledge, and the distinction between encoding and maintenance, recurring points throughout the book.

Long-term memory is where large amounts of information are stored 'semi-permanently', be that explicit vocabulary, people's names and faces, chess moves or sports skills. Long-term memory holds a virtually unlimited amount of knowledge and yet remains severely impeded by working memory. And for good reason: protecting us from catastrophic interference (McClelland, 2013) – that is, when newly learned information suddenly and completely erases information that was previously learned.

While we can access countless autobiographical events in vivid detail and sing along to hundreds of songs, it is impossible for most of us to keep more than a couple of digits in working memory at the same time. Making the most of human memory requires us to understand the 'important peculiarities' of the storage and retrieval processes (Bjork and Bjork, 1992: 36), to be aware of its weaknesses and exploit its strengths. As Sweller et al. (1998: 252) observe: 'The implications of working memory limitations on instructional design can hardly be overestimated … Anything beyond the simplest cognitive activities appear to overwhelm working memory. Prima facie, any instructional design that flouts or merely ignores working memory limitations inevitably is deficient.' Strong words indeed. You can see why Sweller's presentation may have left a mark and influenced both my instructional design and teaching.

Cognitive load theory

Cognitive load theory is based on a number of widely accepted theories about how human brains process and store information.

As with Willingham's simple model of memory, these assumptions include: that human memory can be divided into working memory and long-term memory; that information is stored in long-term memory in the form of schemas; and that processing new information results in cognitive load on working memory, which can affect learning outcomes.

Let's pause a moment on 'information is stored in long-term memory in the form of schemas'. Schemas are an interconnected network of related memories; they are most often domain specific, and we use them to make sense of our worlds. A schema provides a unique system for organising and storing knowledge according to how it will be used,[3] with skilled performance developed through building ever greater numbers of increasingly complex schemas and by combining elements of lower-level schemas into higher-level schemas. Consolidating knowledge as schemas takes time and often requires re-exposure or deliberate practice, and sleep. What we learn, therefore, is heavily dependent on what we already know (correct and erroneous). What we already know actually governs what we notice and focus on in the first place.

Renowned cognitive scientists Logan Fiorella and Richard Mayer emphasise that pupils make meaning when they select, organise and integrate information (Mayer, 2014). What you have stored in long-term memory dictates what you naturally pick up and focus on. Our brains are trying to update what we know. What we already have actually governs what we notice.

Crucially for cognitive load theory, schemas reduce working memory load or, in effect, bypass the limits of working memory; they enable working memory to be reallocated by allowing information to be accessed automatically from long-term memory. Alternatively, cognitive overload may occur when too much new information is presented at once, when too many elements interact or when information is transient. However, as expertise grows (knowledge in long-term memory and schemas), cognitive overload is less of a concern and therefore optimal teaching changes. More simply, if working memory is overloaded, there is a greater risk that what is being taught will not be understood by the learner or will be misinterpreted or confused, and will not be effectively encoded and transferred to long-term memory. As a result, learning will be slowed down or not occur at all.

Cognitive load research (Sweller et al., 1998; Sweller, 2017) demonstrates that instructional methods are most effective when they are designed to fit within the known limits of working memory, and therefore strongly supports

3   This is why RememberMore uses categories and tags to organise knowledge.

guided models of instruction, especially for teaching novice learners in 'technical' subjects such as mathematics, science and technology. It equally applies to modelling a sentence, a paragraph, an essay and, of course, an entire exam paper, as in the 'walking talking mocks' intervention where teachers model answering a full exam paper to a pupil audience that follows along live.

However, cognitive load theory does not consider, for example, factors such as pupils' motivation and metacognitive beliefs about how their own ability might influence the effectiveness of their learning. Nor do cognitive load theorists advocate using all aspects of explicit instruction all of the time. Put simply, Sweller's human cognitive architecture, with which we began this chapter, describes the necessary and sufficient conditions for learning. When designing learning, educators need to be cognisant of the possibilities and limitations of our human cognitive architecture and the interactions within it.

What's more, far too many of us assume that providing learners with additional or peripheral information is beneficial or at worst harmless. Additional information or redundancy is anything but harmless, as Sweller (2016: 8) himself has said: 'Providing unnecessary information can be a major reason for instructional failure.' Therefore, teach essential knowledge. Check what has been understood and retained. Respond accordingly. At a later point in time, revisit or reteach it to allow your pupils to remember or relearn it. It is the relearning that is sometimes overlooked. Once the load placed on working memory is reduced, due to practice and/or prior knowledge, relearning is highly efficient and, what is more, we can attempt more complex tasks at a lower cost to working memory.

Making memories

'Learning is the residue of thought.' Yes, we are back to Willingham (2009: 41). He also said: 'your memory is not a product of what you want to remember or what you try to remember; it's a product of what you think about' (Willingham, 2021).

The popular three-store model, whereby human memory is conceptualised as occurring in three stages – encoding (the process by which information moves from short-term to long-term memory), storage (securing newly acquired information into memory and maintaining it) and retrieval (accessing learned information held in long-term memory) – dates back at least to work by Köhler (1947) and Melton (1963).[4]

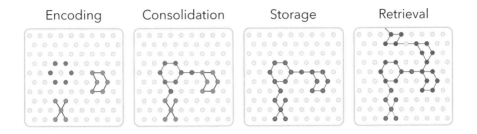

Figure 1.4. What encoding, consolidation, storage and retrieval might look like (adapted and used with kind permission from Efrat Furst, 2018)

The three-store framework holds that after we acquire new information, some of it undergoes storage into long-term memory, and then after a while some of this previously encoded information can be retrieved. The stages are considered logically and temporally separate. Memory is therefore discussed as having two strength dimensions (Bjork and Bjork, 1992):

1   Storage strength: how deep-rooted/interconnected memories are.

- Storage strength cannot decrease; rather, it is presumed only to accumulate.
- Storage strength cannot be directly measured, only inferred.

2   Retrieval strength: how accessible memories are.

- Retrieval strength of a given item can be high or low and can fluctuate between these values.
- Retrieval strength is measured by current performance (whether pupils can answer a given question in class or on a test).

Retrieval also helps people to create coherent and integrated mental representations of complex concepts, the kind of deep learning necessary to solve new problems and draw new inferences – think 'productive thought'. As Bjork regularly summarises, 'using our memory shapes our memories' (the things we recall, access, produce or reproduce become more accessible, durable and recallable), whereas 'the things in competition with the retrieved information become less accessible' (Bjork, 2011: 4). In that sense,

---

4   A four-stage model also includes consolidation, thus: encoding, consolidation, storage and retrieval (see Figure 1.4).

memory is dynamic – reconstructive rather than objective. As neuroscience expert Sarah Cottingham commented to me, memory is more an 'ecosystem than a library system'.

Sensory memory and attention

Incoming sensory information from the environment that is attended to (i.e. that makes it through the attention bottleneck) moves to our working memory. Neurons are activated and are either encoded or after a brief period of time are lost. Attention is the primary gatekeeper of learning and relearning and the ultimate commodity of our classrooms. The ability to direct, maintain and selectively focus on specifics is a learning advantage, as is minimising mind wandering and managing distractions. It is our responsibility as teachers to first select what knowledge is prioritised, then harness and direct attention, and minimise all other distractions or competition for it. Attention is *the* choke point, with 'mental effort or concentration a limited resource' and our narrow focus 'vulnerable to distraction' (Chew, 2021: 423).

Thereafter, what we are thinking about while encoding is stabilised. What we think about and what we attend to is what we learn about. Returning to prior knowledge, connections are formed within the information presented and potentially with prior knowledge. It is one possible reason why pupils with greater prior knowledge learn more and often learn faster. After consolidation, the memory traces are considered stabilised and stored. Learning is said to occur when information from working memory is transferred to long-term memory through conscious processing – linking new knowledge to what is already in our memory, or prior knowledge. When retrieving that information, an associative chain reaction of activating neural representations modifies that memory, promotes consolidation (storage) and slows forgetting.

And, yet, much of everyday, real-world learning is iterative: pupils encounter cross-curricular themes, discuss lessons between themselves, bring knowledge with them from home, are set targeted homework, watch television programmes, read books, play games, prepare for tests in various ways, and sit tests and exams. The classroom is not a laboratory. The proposition that there are discrete encoding and retrieval phases does not describe education well at all, and nor does this viewpoint capture the interactive nature of encoding and retrieval, learning, remembering and relearning, whereby retrieval can actually be considered a (re)encoding event.

Furthermore, our memories (what we think about and what we attend to) are encoded (consolidated or stored to be retrieved) or decay and are forgotten. As we will see throughout this book, knowledge of forgetting is very much a part of test-enhanced learning and spaced retrieval practice – as much as knowledge of remembering. Without the ability to forget or inhibit information, our world would become increasingly confusing. Forgetting is not the opposite of remembering; rather, we have to forget some things in order to remember others. And, as it turns out, we 'need' to forget in order to learn and relearn. Possibly, the most succinct explanation of the relationship between memory and the importance of forgetting comes from Henry Roediger: 'Remembering an event that is repeated is greatly aided if the first presentation is forgotten to some extent before the repetition occurs' (Roediger and Karpicke, 2011: 23). This is what Bjork and Bjork (2019: 114) refers to as 'forgetting as a friend of learning'.

This is why educators would be well advised to promote and forewarn pupils about an upcoming test. In this way, we can prompt pupils into attending to our teaching in the first place, using testing and a range of test-enhanced strategies (e.g. repeated retrieval, spacing, interleaving, successive relearning, metacognitive monitoring), thereby aiding consolidation and storage of that teaching in long-term memory. Or, more simply, building storage strength and retrieval strength for when that knowledge or memory is next required.

Remember, performance during learning is a poor predictor of future performance because it reflects the momentary accessibility of knowledge rather than how well it has been stored in memory (Bjork and Bjork, 1992).

Learning, remembering and relearning, then, is a process, not a product. We can only infer that it has occurred from pupils' performances over time and where we have evidence of their capabilities. Learning involves a relatively permanent change in long-term memory – in that sense, understanding is remembering in disguise. This change unfolds over time; it is not fleeting but rather has a lasting impact on how pupils think and act, on their beliefs and commitment, and on their motivations. Learning is not something done to pupils, but rather something pupils themselves do. It is the result of how they interpret and respond to their experiences – conscious and unconscious, past and present. If we anticipate that pupils will forget much of what we teach them, then the requirement to reteach is obvious. Testing is therefore extremely valuable mnemonically and metacognitively, signposting what to reteach and to whom.

Of course, even if we do all this, as teachers we still need to know what pupils value and understand their emotional and motivational foundations, by which I mean that understanding the cognitive science behind these approaches is essential. We also need to understand what engages and motivates our pupils, so we can ensure that they can realise the benefits of test-enhanced learning – but then you knew that anyway.

As Dr Tom Perry, who led the Education Endowment Foundation's *Cognitive Science Approaches in the Classroom* review (Perry et al., 2021), summarised in a recent conversation, 'We know a huge amount about learning, memory, cognition, attention, and it's creating some really powerful and practical principles that we can trust.'[5] But now it's over to the educators, he said, 'to really work out what good looks like in their own contexts'.

Takeaways

- A mental model of memory helps teachers understand the mechanics or processes of teaching, learning and test-enhanced learning.
- Thinking occurs when we combine information from the environment and long-term memory in new ways.
- When designing test-enhanced learning, a learner's prior knowledge (long-term memory) is a key consideration for teachers.
- The maintenance of knowledge is assumed to reflect two distinct phases: an encoding (learning) phase and a maintenance (remembering/relearning) phase.
- Memory is discussed as having two strength dimensions: storage strength and retrieval strength.
- Consolidating knowledge as schemas often requires re-exposure, or deliberate practice, and sleep.
- Attention is the primary gatekeeper of learning and relearning. Attention is a choke point. (Explicitly manage distractions.)
- Using our memory shapes our memory. It also makes our knowledge more accessible, durable and recallable.
- Working memory (where conscious processing occurs) is severely limited in duration and capacity.
- Learning is a relatively semi-permanent change in long-term memory.

---

5   T. Perry, interview with author (June 2022).

- Memory is reconstructive rather than objective.
- Test-enhanced learning includes potentiation, encoding and maintenance phases (retrieval and relearning) and much more.
- Long-term memory is virtually unlimited and yet severely impeded by working memory.
- Test-enhanced learning also includes potentiation or pre-testing, adding to encoding (learning) and maintenance phases (remembering/relearning) and much more.
- When using test-enhanced learning, consider encoding (or learning) and maintenance as two distinct phases.
- Knowledge of forgetting is very much part of spaced retrieval practice – just as much as knowledge of remembering.
- A pupil's performance during encoding/learning is a poor predictor of future performance.
- Memory and motivation are inextricably intertwined.
- If you only have time to read one paper on this topic: D. T. Willingham, Ask the cognitive scientist: What will improve a student's memory? *American Educator* (winter 2008): 17-25.
- Watching Robert Bjork's 'Using our memory shapes our memory' video comes a very close second: https://www.youtube.com/watch?v=69VPjsgm-E0.

Case study: Orchard Mead Academy

Helen Webb is a lead practitioner and experienced science and biology teacher at Orchard Mead Academy in Leicester. She also works as a professional coach, supporting teachers, leaders and support staff with well-being and career, professional and leadership development. She has an interest in how cognitive science and evidence-based practice can inform our classroom pedagogy.

The challenge

How do you create a whole-school teaching and learning model that draws on concepts and theories from cognitive science, which is practical, usable and enables students both to learn more and remember more?

At Orchard Mead Academy, our teaching and learning model is designed around Barak Rosenshine's (2012) principles of instruction. These 10 research-based principles, drawn from cognitive science, provide suggestions on how we might overcome the limitations of our working memory when learning new material, outline practices employed by master teachers and convert research into effective instructional procedures for learning complex tasks. We also refer to educational psychologist Paul Kirschner, who said 'Learning is a change in long-term memory' (Kirschner et al., 2006: 75), to Daniel Willingham's simple model of memory (2009) and John Sweller's cognitive load theory (1988).

Having a strong whole-school teaching and learning model has a multitude of benefits. It helps students to learn and remember more, which improves outcomes. The principles are structured into a template lesson plan or sequence of learning, which not only reduces planning time but also provides staff with a clear mental model of what a 'good' lesson includes. It also provides staff with a common vocabulary while easing quality-assurance processes.

What do students need to know?

We currently have two major focuses at Orchard Mead. Teachers need to be clear on:

1 The key facts, concepts, vocabulary, equations, units and so on that students need to know (and remember) for success and fluency in their subject and/or lesson.

2 How that information is explained and presented to students so they can learn (and remember) that information more easily.

At the heart of this is: what do students need to know or know how to do? To reduce cognitive load in a lesson, it helps to be explicit about what it is you want students to know (declarative knowledge) or know how to do (procedural knowledge). When you are in front of a class, it is easy to get sidetracked with 'hinterland' knowledge - entertaining students with interesting but potentially distracting anecdotes or other unnecessary facts - or you may simply just get lost in the waffle of overly lengthy explanations. You may also be guilty of sharing excessively busy PowerPoint presentations packed with an overwhelming volume of text or the inclusion of irrelevant images, icons or animations.

Exam board specifications provide a comprehensive guide to what students need to know and be able to do, and they are the starting point to most good schemes of learning. These specification points are then chunked down into lessons, and most of us are fairly well versed in presenting these as lesson objectives and learning outcomes. However, at Orchard Mead Academy, we are moving towards a 'what, why and how' approach to introduce to students to 'what we are learning today'. Teachers can chunk this information further into a bank of 'must-know' questions (the declarative knowledge for a subject), either for the lesson or for the entire sequence of learning/topic.

Avoiding cognitive overload

Having a bank of questions and answers has a multitude of benefits: it serves as an aide-memoire for teachers that reiterates the key teaching points of the lesson or topic and, as such, what information needs to be paid attention to. This reduces the cognitive load for the teacher and consequently reduces planning time and workload. It also provides a series of questions that a teacher can use for cold-calling, to form hinge questions, for independent practice and for retrieval quizzes. It is this bank of questions and answers that forms the bespoke flashcard decks for the retrieval platform RememberMore, which directly supports student fluency in lessons.

But, how do you explain new information so that students understand it more easily? At Orchard Mead, teachers employ a direct instruction approach to teaching new material, using the three phases: 'I do', 'We do' and 'You do'.

During the 'I do' phase, the teacher presents new learning in small steps so as not to overload students' working memory. This may include (but is not limited to) an explanation, elaboration (describing ideas in many details and making connections between what they are trying to learn and their own experiences, memories and day-to-day life), a demonstration or modelling activity, and concrete examples and non-examples.

Presentations may be used in lessons to support the encoding of information (the process by which information moves from short-term to long-term memory). Dual-coding theory suggests that providing both verbal and pictorial representations of the same information enhances learning and memory. However, to prevent cognitive overload and avoid distraction, any extraneous information, images or animations should be omitted.

Consideration is also given to the 'best' way that information is presented to students, so that it can be more effectively encoded and later recalled (e.g. bulleted list, comparison table, labelled diagram, flow diagram, timeline). Encoding strategies such as chunking, mnemonics or self-referencing (relating the information to yourself or 'real life' or encouraging students to prepare the information so they could teach it or explain it to another student) also support the initial learning phase.

During the 'We do' phase, the teacher guides student practice using prompts and retrieval cues, via further modelling or by providing worked examples, gradually phasing out scaffolding to increase the challenge. This rehearsal stage of teaching may also include techniques that promote automaticity (e.g. rote repetition, reading aloud as a class, note-taking, text mark-up).

During each stage of 'I do' and 'We do', the teacher asks many questions to check for understanding and for error correction using either cold-calling techniques or hinge questions with the support of mini whiteboards. This provides the teacher with the necessary information to decide their next step – reteach, provide another worked example/practice task or move on.

During the 'You do' phase, students carry out independent practice. These tasks may be differentiated to enable them to achieve a high success rate, but all have a focus on the 'must-know' questions of the lesson. To facilitate responsive teaching and assessment for learning, the teacher circulates, monitors, supports and continues to question students. The teacher may encourage students to explain or reflect on their learning or may employ live-marking techniques, where appropriate. This practice informs the teacher's next steps: error correction, feedback, planning or homework.

Moving information into long-term memory

Repeated retrieval practice (bringing information to mind) enhances learning and long-term memory. All lessons at Orchard Mead Academy start with a short review of previous learning. This comprises five 'Do now' questions that recap knowledge from previous lessons or topics but also relate to and activate learning for that lesson. This review phase, which provides an opportunity for spaced practice (see Chapter 3) may also include a recap explanation of previous material, a review of previous classwork or feedback on homework. Our weekly and monthly assessment model also provides students with repeated retrieval practice and an opportunity to reinforce their knowledge of the 'must-know' questions and answers.

This declarative (and procedural) knowledge is also applied and assessed in subject-specific ways. RememberMore's classroom platform provides teachers with a simple and usable resource to generate bespoke daily, weekly and monthly quizzes in seconds, which can be displayed at the touch of a button on an electronic whiteboard or printed as a paper copy for students to complete.

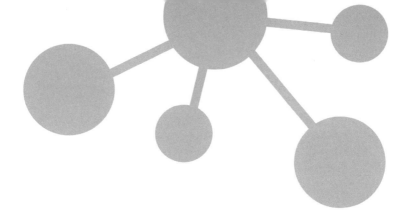

Chapter 2

Test-enhanced learning and repeated (repeated) retrieval practice

---

One idea is that retrieval of information from memory leads to elaboration of the memory trace and/or the creation of additional retrieval routes, which makes it more likely that the information will be successfully retrieved again in the future.

Roediger and Butler (2011: 25)

If retrieval is such a powerful tool in enhancing long-term retention, why would you wait until the end of your teaching unit to gain this benefit?

According to Yang et al. (2021: 399), 'testing is not only an assessment of learning but also an assessment *for* learning'. What does this mean in practice? Simply that answering a question yields a higher probability of retrieving the correct answer to that question on a later test than does simply restudying the answer, particularly if correct answer feedback is provided. (This applies equally to most teaching resources and worksheet-style activities.) This is variously known as test-enhanced learning, the testing effect or the retrieval practice effect. (Note: Be warned of the negative connotations of the use of 'test' or 'testing' with pupils.)

'Practice testing' is just one of two teaching techniques that received a high utility rating in Dunlosky et al.'s (2013) seminal paper. It is reported to 'benefit learners of different ages and abilities and has been shown to boost students' performance across many criterion tasks and even in educational contexts' (Dunlosky et al., 2013: 4), research conclusions which were reaffirmed by Donoghue and Hattie (2021).

Retrieving information from memory causes learning, both directly and indirectly. The direct effects of retrieval practice on learning (and relearning) refer to the fact that practising retrieval produces superior long-term retention, durability, accessibility and transfer of that knowledge. We learn more, we retain it for longer and we have access to this knowledge to support our wider learning. Critically, these direct effects (improved storage strength and retrieval strength, fluency and automation) are due to the act of retrieval itself and occur even in the absence of feedback (Karpicke and Roediger, 2008). Indirectly, retrieving information from memory helps to organise practised materials, inform current learning, potentiate future learning, increase transfer of knowledge to new contexts, reduce test anxiety, improve attendance (higher education), mitigate the impact of stress and inform study approaches.

Retrieval has even been shown to improve retention of non-tested but related material, or retrieval-induced facilitation (Chan et al., 2006; Chan, 2009) – that is, initially non-tested material can benefit from prior testing of related material. Retrieval, it would appear, serves more than to simply reinforce memory of a tested fact. A recent trend has been to explore the extent to which retrieval practice produces learning that can be transferred to new or different contexts and under what conditions transfer occurs (Roediger and Butler, 2011; Carpenter et al., 2012; Pan and Rickard, 2018). Without going into great detail, retrieval practice improves pupils' general test-taking abilities and helps on those occasions where pupils are required to problem-solve, make inferences or diagnoses.

Then there is potentiating learning or pre-testing (Latimier et al., 2019; Pan et al., 2020). Pre-testing might look like a quiz on the timeline of events, introducing key vocabulary, naming faces or categorising an item set, not only priming learning but also linking to prior knowledge. (We will take a closer look at pre-testing in Chapter 7.)

Suffice to say that given 'the strong evidence for its memorial benefits, many cognitive and educational psychologists now classify testing as among the most effective educational techniques discovered to date' (Pan and Rickard, 2018: 711). With that baseline established, how does retrieval practice relate to your teaching and to your pupils' learning and relearning, in and beyond the classroom? Retrieval practice may even open up a discussion on the role of testing, or quizzing or assessment, in your school or what responsive teaching looks like, as well as questions of teacher autonomy and the pace and direction through learning that teachers feel they are able to take. Critically, too often, the narrative of testing or quizzing 'as learning' is not a focused part of the conversation, with the benefits of metacognition and motivation bypassed.

In and out of the classroom

Even those simple terms – test-enhanced learning, the testing effect and the retrieval practice effect – hide a multitude of modulators:

1 **Subject or learner characteristics.** Age (both young and older populations); level of education and setting; ability; prior knowledge; atypical learners (impaired visual attention or memory capacity); prior knowledge; and metamemory abilities (judgements made about memory).

2 **Encoding activities.** Context (why test-enhanced learning is being employed – diagnostic tool, planned test, surprise test, for learning and rehearsal?); setting; instructions; the time between the learning, retrieval and final assessment; the use or not of feedback (corrective or elaborative – asking 'how' and 'why' questions); the learning activities; and the number of exposures to learning.[1]

3 **Retrieval format (the way retention is measured).** The format of retrieval practice (free recall from memory, cued or recognition recall); aural or visual; the response format (covert or overt – I will explain these terms shortly); the framing (paced or self-paced); and the 'stakes' of the test (most commonly referred to as low-level (not reporting performance or scores) or high-level).

4 **Materials and modality.** Basically, the types of materials or modes used – most commonly words (e.g. paired associate learning or completion of word fragments), sentences and general knowledge; landscape pictures, locations, regions on maps, abstract symbols or visual images (presumably not verbalisable) and even three-dimensional virtual reality displays, where subjects must learn the positions of objects in space or

---

1 In order not to overcomplicate an already complex topic, I have not covered post-testing and pre-testing.

navigate through a virtual building; the difficulty or complexity of materials and element interactivity (the connectedness of the information or the number of elements that must be simultaneously processed in working memory); collaborative or independent tasks; and digital modalities (websites and apps rather than pen and paper).

These four categories, as identified by Jenkins (1979) in his tetrahedral memory model (see Figure 2.1), all have an influence on the effectiveness of test-enhanced learning and retrieval practice. It just goes to show how complex encoding, retrieval and relearning is. As Roediger (2008: 229-230) is keen to point out, in reference to Jenkins (1979), the findings in any experiment about memory are 'context sensitive'. That is, it is far more complex than mere retrieval practice alone. He adds that the 'memory phenomena' we see are contingent on the subjects we study, the acquisition conditions we provide, the materials we work with and the measurement criteria we use. This experimental complexity is not unlike our own classrooms.

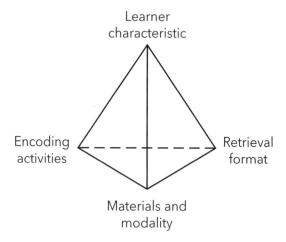

Figure 2.1. The tetrahedral model of memory experiments (adapted from Jenkins, 1979: 431)

It is worth pointing out that most teachers enter the test-enhanced learning arena at 'retrieval practice' – the way retention is measured. But this is at the point of assessing what has been learned and risks us not taking into consideration factors from points 1 and 2. Indeed, this form of post-testing has been the main course of test-enhanced learning research for the past 20 years, and the diet of teachers keen to adopt retrieval practice in their classrooms for their pupils.

This focus on post-testing is potentially misleading, if not damaging. As assistant head teacher Kristian Shanks, one of the case study contributors, queried in one of our many conversations: 'Is test-enhanced learning maybe a better umbrella term? I had an initial thesis that perhaps the term retrieval practice has unintentionally narrowed teachers' conceptions of what that type of work/activity could involve, both in terms of what it looks like and when it happens.'

Exactly that – and what's more, we shouldn't discount the other modulators at play. Let's take a closer look at the four categories above.

1. Learner characteristic

Roediger and Karpicke's (2006: 181) seminal paper suggested that 'frequent testing in the classroom may boost educational achievement at all levels of education'. What followed was a flurry of research papers and meta-analyses. First, Rowland's (2014: 1432) meta-analysis affirmed the 'robust nature of the testing effect', then Schwieren et al. (2017: 1) reported that 'The testing effect is a robust empirical finding in the research on learning and instruction'; and Adesope et al. (2017: 676) confirmed: 'Results show that testing effects do not vary with study settings.' In fact, the use of practice tests by secondary school pupils seems to have a bigger impact than with post-secondary students. Moreira et al. (2019) reported that reliable testing effects were yielded for all experimental conditions in 19 of the 23 reviewed studies.

More recently, Agarwal et al. (2021), Bertilsson et al. (2021) and Yang et al. (2021) have concluded that retrieval practice seems to be a learning technique that is not moderated by individual differences or working memory capacity, thus is possibly beneficial for all pupils. Anecdotally, we have heard from a number of teachers teaching with RememberMore who have highlighted the impact of test-enhanced learning for pupils who may have found learning challenging previously:

I think it [RememberMore/test-enhanced learning] definitely helps because the vocab we've selected occurs a lot in the extracts we're asking them to unpick. I'll tell you what's been really nice: of the two top scorers in the class, one is very bright and their success is to be expected; the other is SEND [special educational needs and disability] and low attaining in other English-style assessments. Just shows that when the knowledge is separated, he can do it. He just can't manage tasks that require multiple skills to be spun like plates. Lovely to see him the class champ to beat!

Year 8 English teacher

Improved attitudes towards chemistry, not necessarily all down to RememberMore, have helped to build relationships (setting prep which is fun/useful). Engaging with the topics through classroom.remember-more.app is effective and beneficial. EAL [English as an additional language] student exam attainment was a real success.

Year 11 chemistry teacher

Notably, retrieval practice during learning, when accompanied by feedback, may serve to level the playing field for pupils with lower working memory capacities (Agarwal et al., 2017). Most recently, researchers have reported consistent benefits of retrieval practice (about 10% or one letter grade higher) over restudy and that these benefits were similar for 'all levels of prior content mastery' or learners with low and high prior knowledge (Buchin and Mullian, 2022; Gupta et al., 2022).

A word of caution: retrieval practice appears to have a general declining impact as pupils get younger, with some studies finding little or even negative testing effects for elementary pupils (Leahy et al., 2015). Of course, with researchers increasingly urging educators to apply retrieval practice in the classroom (Nunes and Karpicke, 2015; Karpicke et al., 2016; Agarwal and Bain, 2019; Dunlosky and Rawson, 2019; Fazio and Marsh, 2019), educators are increasingly implementing and inventing their own retrieval practice approaches.

2. Encoding activities

There are no end of encoding (learning) activities (where incoming information from the environment is processed) – that is, the initial learning phase of teaching. However, as you might expect, researchers are a little more conservative, with most learning research categorised as either intentional (when subjects are asked to remember events) or incidental (when the impact of prior experience is assessed through transfer or priming). Both intentional and incidental retrieval is then compared most commonly to restudy or 'business as usual' – the initial learning phase or encoding activities. And, as you may be reflecting, that is not how classrooms typically operate.

But there are other factors too, such as whether the subsequent test pupils take is a surprise or not and the use of corrective or elaborative feedback (or none at all). There are also many overlaps with other categories. As Roediger (2008: 230) says: 'For example, "instructions" is listed under encoding, but of course, the effect of the instructions will depend on the type of subjects receiving them and the knowledge the instructions activate.'

For those whose interest is piqued, Roediger's paper offers a discussion of different formats and how these might link to later retrieval success. He asks a number of questions, not least: 'Does deeper, more meaningful processing during encoding enhance retention relative to less meaningful, superficial analyses?' (Roediger, 2008: 228). Sadly, the conclusion - as is so often the case with research into memory - is: it depends. It depends on many other conditions, not least the learners themselves. But, again, that is teaching.

3. Retrieval format (the way retention is measured)

There are innumerable retrieval formats: Q&A, A&Q (the answer prompts the knowledge recall), multiple-choice, true/false, matching exercises, timelines, grids to fill in, gaps to fill in or cloze questions, mind-mapping, image recognition, recitation, dumps (write down everything you can remember), relay races (write down everything you can remember and then pass to a peer), labelling, listing, organising, ordering, summarising, categorising, decoding, flashcards and plenty more. All have their strengths, although researchers prefer control, with most studies focusing on overt recall (see below) and categorising the possible approaches as either free, cued or recognition recall:

- **Free recall tests**. For example, pupils study a word list and then recall the words from the initial presentation; short-answer questions also fall into this category.

- **Cued recall tests**. For example, pupils study word pairs or paired associates (e.g. flower–daisy). During retrieval, they only get the cue (flower–?). Other examples include cloze questions or fill-in-the-blank exercises. For cued recall, there is a positive testing effect in 96% of published experiments (Rickard and Pan, 2018).

■ **Recognition recall tests.** For example, the presentation of a familiar cue that has been encountered before, such as in multiple-choice questions or other 'matching' exercises.

All of these retrieval formats have strengths and applications, and some have limitations, but Yang et al. (2021) predict larger learning gains for difficult, free recall tests when compared to easier recognition tests. Having to retrieve the answer from long-term memory is more effortful than spotting the correct answer from distractors in multiple-choice questions. That said, you will find plenty of support for multiple-choice tests – 'a cornerstone of assessment' that produces 'significant enhancements' (Yang et al., 2021: 404). There is good reason that multiple-choice formats are so popular, not least the question of reliability and ease of marking/auto-marking. Moreover, you may be seeking the lower challenge of recognition recall during the encoding phase of learning, using precise feedback to underwrite learning. (Two quick tips while we are here: always make all questions required (even generating errors helps future encoding), and provide feedback on correct as well as incorrect answers (so pupils know why they are correct and that errors do not persist).)

Assessment format

The format of the final assessment matters too. This relates to transfer-appropriate processing – the principle that performance will be highest when the characteristics of the encoding activities are similar to those of the retrieval assessment procedure. Having said that, some studies have explored how the testing effect is influenced by how cognitively demanding the retrieval processes are during the practice test. Kang et al. (2007) report that pupils who took a short-answer practice test outperformed (on the final test) those who took a multiple-choice practice test, regardless of the format of the final test. Either way, tests that imitate the mental processes to be performed during the actual examination are powerful preparation tools.

And, hence, we find ourselves going full circle and back to retrieval format.

So, why is this important? First, a large body of research highlights that the benefits of retrieval are more pronounced because levels of processing during retrieval are more demanding (effortful) - a desirable difficulty. However, while we say that difficulty is key, there is a fine line between difficulty and pupil motivation. This is our first signpost to the importance of motivation (see Chapter 9).

We might consider difficulty in multiple ways – for example, how hard the actual initial encoding phase is, the challenge introduced by spacing between tests (how long we wait until we test/retest), the weight of content sampled, how many questions are posed, the complexity of the answer itself, and the chronology (how far back/how long ago the information was last accessed) or sequencing and time constraints of the assessment.

What does this mean in practice?

Practically, when teaching, you may want to consider the purpose of the retrieval activity: is it to manage entry to the classroom and direct attention? Is it to promote self-confidence (ensure a low failure rate)? Is it to activate or connect with prior learning or connect already rehearsed knowledge? Is it for consolidation (low/medium failure rate)? Is it to potentiate learning? Is it to provoke curiosity (likely to have a high failure rate)? Is the routine embedded and secure? As teacher Helen Webb commented to me: 'Consider the structure of quizzes – start easy and ramp up the difficulty.' Of course, recognising the varying success rates is a second signpost to the importance and interconnectedness of motivation. We explore how teachers might employ hints in Chapter 5.

The cognitive demand of the quiz, test or retrieval format may be more relevant, particularly for retention – that is, how hard pupils are made to think or to dig for an answer. The importance of thinking hard has been upheld by Rowland (2014), Adesope et al. (2017) and Yang et al. (2021). More recently, Endres et al. (2020: 699) report that free recall tasks helped learners to 'remember a broader spectrum of information' and that 'free recall tasks increased self-efficacy and situational interest'. We might say that free recall tasks spark learners' interest for knowing whether or not they have answered correctly; not until the answer is shown do they know for sure.

I will leave the final word to Perry et al. (2021: 21): 'Planning test difficulty is particularly important – pupils should be able to retrieve at least some of the content they are tested on.'

Oh, and if you do find yourself teaching and utilising covert retrieval (see below), you might be interested in the production effect, whereby saying a word aloud during learning can enhance memory (compared to reading it silently). It plays to the intuitive notion that 'when an event or an element of an event stands out from its surrounding context, we remember it better' (MacLeod, 2011: 1198). For example:

Teacher: Repeat after me. [pause] Pal·pa·ble – palpable [i.e. modelled].

Pupils: Pal·pa·ble – palpable.

The use of syllabification, modelling pronunciation and leveraging production effects can be readily adopted as part of any whole-school literacy strategy. Hence, presenting new vocabulary, together with syllabification, can encourage its adoption and reuse. A reasonable explanation of this effect is that the creation of a verbal cue (which is not present when only reading the word) facilitates future retrieval (MacLeod et al., 2010).

If oracy is the focus, or more simply when checking for understanding, insist that pupils reply with the correct terminology and not simply 'Answer A'. Demand the full sentence or correct vocabulary: 'Try again, and this time frame your answer with …' or 'Great start. Can you give me your answer again using [WORD] in your response?'

Covert vs overt retrieval formats

A lesser-researched modulator of retrieval format is the distinction between covert and overt retrieval – that is, pupils retrieving information and mentally answering (covert) or writing/typing their responses (overt). Combining both covert and overt would see a learner mentally answer before speaking their answers out loud. Pupils' effortful thinking and processing is of equal importance in both modalities.

Why is this distinction significant? It is simply a question of efficiency: not having to write a response allows for many more retrieval attempts. However, covert retrieval is very difficult to research (how do you prove the participants are thinking?), therefore only a very few papers have discussed its benefits, and the findings are mixed. In two experiments, Tauber et al. (2018) asked students to study key terms and the corresponding definition for each using cued and matched formats. The students then restudied the key terms and definitions or tested themselves, responding overtly (typing their response) or covertly (mentally recalling the definition). The students' final recall was 'moderately' greater after overt retrieval practice than covert retrieval practice or restudy.

Previous research suggests that overt and covert retrieval have similar effects, particularly on learning simple facts or paired associates (Putnam and Roediger, 2013; Smith et al., 2013). Of course, teachers adopt different retrieval formats for different contexts, materials, modalities and complexity – cue the mini whiteboard debate.

As for the scheduling of retrieval questions or cues, there appears to be a Goldilocks principle at work, which has a knock-on effect when considering retrieval framing. De Jonge et al. (2012) reported that a presentation schedule which was either too fast (1 second) or too slow (16 seconds) resulted in suboptimal learning and poor immediate and delayed recall when compared with an intermediate presentation schedule (4 seconds). The 4-second presentation schedule condition resulted in less proportional forgetting than the 1-second and 16-second conditions.

We might be inclined to think that this insight offers a prescriptive recipe, but it should not. We know that 'think time' is important; however, don't leave the retrieval wheels spinning for too long when you could offer another cue, give this time over to the correct answer or feedback (interrogating that dissonance) or, alternatively, further retrieval opportunities.

4. Materials and modality

One of the challenges of this research is the interchangeability of terms. For the benefit of clarity and later understanding, let's start with the terms 'materials' and 'modality'.

The information, content or knowledge being studied and later tested is referred to as the materials. The overwhelming researcher's favourite material is Swahili–English paired associates, and their favourite modularity is flashcards. Think Swahili–English language flashcards. Why this material and mode selection? Swahili combats the effects of participants' prior knowledge, is pronounceable by native English speakers (e.g. mashua – boat, which is tested as mashua – ?) and flashcards are very familiar to most learners.

Modality refers to how the material is studied and tested. Paper-and-pen tests have largely been replaced with a growing number of digital solutions, apps and response systems, with ever deepening analytics and insights. Modality effects appear across numerous experiments, but there is little agreement about whether the experimental procedure and format impacts on the actual testing effect – that is, whether 'administration mode modulates the testing effect' (Yang et al., 2021: 407).

The testing effect is prolific and incontrovertible, with the benefits of retrieval replicated hundreds of times. It has been shown to enhance the learning of a wide variety of materials in the laboratory and, to a lesser extent, the classroom. However, we still don't have a good grasp of exactly what kinds of material can and cannot be retrieved or, for that matter, how much and for how long. As to the question of the potential impact of item or question complexity or difficulty, leading researchers Karpicke (see Karpicke and Aue, 2015) and Sweller (see van Gog and Sweller, 2015) continue to offer opposing views.

Much of the interest around modality has focused on retrieval difficulty and on the work of Elizabeth Bjork and Robert Bjork, particularly their paper 'Making things hard on yourself, but in a good way: creating desirable difficulties to enhance learning' (Bjork and Bjork, 2011; see also Bjork et al., 2014). The concept of desirable difficulties cleverly captures the counterintuitive finding that learning strategies which slow or hinder encoding during learning often produce superior long-term retention and transfer. This centres on the idea that there is a level of difficulty that is optimal for learning and retention, and which is dependent on the learner's prior knowledge.

If only it was as simple as how material difficulty influences retrieval success

Difficulty is often measured with reference to the spacing of retrieval practice and the time it takes to recall something (reflecting the accessibility of the information). But difficulty for retrieval tasks has many contributory factors: it is reflective of the initial learning and retrieval format, the extent to which other information competes or interferes with what is being learned and then retrieved, the duration for which this information is required to be remembered and the weight of the information being retained, not to mention the subject or learner characteristics already discussed and the cognitive biases or beliefs that pupils bring with them. Even then, it has become increasingly clear that 'successfully disseminating knowledge about strategies that produce desirable difficulties is often not enough to produce changes in learning behaviours' (Zepeda et al., 2020: 468). We are back at the point of explaining the importance of 'why' and 'how'.

We need to say it again: test-enhanced learning needs to be led as well as taught. Pre-empt the pupils' resistance, explain why and know how. Currently, the research is placing greater emphasis on the importance of learner motivation (Bjork and Bjork, 2020; Finn, 2020), both at the micro-level (the difficulty of an activity) and at the macro-level (the structuring of learning over time). This encourages teachers to remember that, despite the pronounced benefits of retrieval, many learners choose not to use retrieval practice, spacing or interleaving, to disengage and even discount their value in favour of less effective strategies (like rereading and restudy), even when presented with evidence to the contrary and even when presented with their own improved results! We will be digging deeper into the growing interest in learner motivation and the illusions of competence in due course.

As teacher Helen Webb told me: 'This highlights the importance of explaining the "why" of what you are doing in the classroom to students. Pre-empt their resistance by explaining that retrieval is more difficult. Getting the desirable difficulty correct requires teamwork. If students don't engage, is the test too hard or too easy? Get buy-in by explaining that their participation informs the next steps (reteach or requiz with easier or harder questions).'

What is most important to teachers and learners is that testing is not something that comes only at the end of the line. As Pooja Agarwal tweeted in December 2021: 'I've said it before and I'll say it a million times more: the first time students retrieve shouldn't be on a … final exam.'

And we might also quote Paul (2015): 'Retrieval practice does not use testing as a tool of assessment. Rather it treats tests as occasions for learning, which makes sense only once we recognise and accept that we have misunderstood the nature of testing.'

The presence of feedback

Getting feedback right is tricky. Kluger and DeNisi's (1996) review showed that in 38% of the well-designed studies they analysed, feedback actually made things worse! The learners would have done better if they had received no feedback at all.

Take possibly two of the most common forms of feedback: grades and rankings. Neither tell the pupils how to improve, just that improvement may be required. Both are as likely to disappoint the learner as encourage.

However, the feedback challenge would appear no less tricky for retrieval practice. The critical mechanism in learning from retrieval is successful retrieval or exposure to the correct response. Providing feedback after a retrieval attempt, regardless of whether the attempt is successful or not, helps to ensure that retrieval will be successful in the future. Of course, there is more to it than that, so much so that we will come back to feedback in Chapter 5. Suffice to say that offering corrective feedback significantly increases learning gains (Rowland, 2014; Yang et al., 2021).

In their meta-analysis of 10 learning techniques, Donoghue and Hattie (2021) confirm the major findings from Dunlosky et al. (2013) but stress the important role of feedback: 'It is not the frequency of testing that matters, but the skill in using practice testing to learn and consolidate knowledge and ideas.' (Take this comment with a pinch of salt, as we are about to find out that in controlled research settings, frequency is important during both the encoding phase and retrieval mode.)

How often should learners retrieve?

Our first task here is to separate retrieval repetitions from spaced retrieval practice or relearning and the two most commonly investigated schedules, expanding and uniform (see Chapter 3 on spaced learning). It is clear that a greater number of test repetitions yields a larger learning enhancement (I could quote any number of papers to support this). But what can we do to help the learning stick?

First, Rawson et al. (2018) showed that the power of relearning is more than just a 'dosage effect', meaning that it is more than the result of multiple exposures. For example, correctly recalling items one time across three sessions versus three times in one session yielded a 262% increase in retention test performance.

Second, it is important to recognise that the optimal spaced retrieval practice or relearning schedule depends on the memory strength of that item after initial encoding/learning (Cepeda et al., 2009; Mozer et al., 2009). Can a fact be recalled, a face be recognised or an item categorised?

If the memory strength is relatively high, the interval between repetitions should be longer than if the memory strength is relatively low, in which case an immediate repetition is better (Latimier et al., 2021). (Hence, classroom. remembermore.app offers teachers the opportunity to reorder a set of card prompts. Keep reordering the prompts to the point of successful free recall (remembering that success does not mean the cards have been learned – yet). Try it. Even such a simple reordering action can require pupils to think hard.) Successful knowledge encoding is suggested to be more effective when prior learning is reactivated and congruent.

You may well be familiar with Rosenshine's (2012: 12) advice from his 'Principles of instruction': 'Begin a lesson with a short review of previous learning.' Retrieval practice offers a very obvious opportunity to activate prior knowledge that has a pre-existing association, with van Kesteren et al. (2018: 4) reporting that 'reactivation of prior knowledge during learning of new information indeed results in stronger association of new learned information'.

And we shouldn't forget the fabulous work of Professor Graham Nuthall, which also offers a clue. He concluded that a pupil 'understands, learns and remembers a concept if they have encountered all the underlying information three times' (Nuthall, 2007: 155). What stands out most in Nuthall's research is that this 'three times' rule has predictive value. You might think, 'Where do I find the time for three exposures?' But note that these were not consecutive and included deliberate questions, independent and group work across several cycles of learning. We might add to that pre-testing, teaching, quizzing, assessment and, of course, homework – thereby also taking advantage of spaced relearning. Lastly, we should add revision.

We will come back to Nuthall's work again when we consider successive relearning (Chapter 6). We will also review repeated test exposures/retrieval practice and spacing (Chapter 3) and interleaving (Chapter 4).

Low-stakes testing

Finally, let's consider a phrase I often hear when discussing classroom-based retrieval practice: low-stakes. This is the inference that when we are testing for learning, and not for assessment, the process should be non-threatening and the need to report scores unnecessary. In fact, if teachers utilise the metacognitive benefits of self-assessment, could the stakes be any lower?

However, if anything, I find that the pupils want to share or report their scores and the success they are experiencing. Perhaps the middle ground is for pupils to self-assess and keep track.

After numerous cycles of teaching with test-enhanced learning and the free web portal classroom.remembermore.app across Years 5 to 11, here is a road-tested model that works for my personal style of teaching and subject (English), with corroborative feedback from teachers spanning the curriculum, prior attainment profiles and across year groups (Years 4–13).

We quiz every lesson. We quiz X number of cards (questions), most often using a timer. As pupils' success rate increases and as they become more knowledgeable, retrieval latency times (thinking time) reduce, so we quiz more cards in the same amount of time. We may also sample from a progressively weightier deck of flashcards. Pupils' success is rewarded with more cards and more knowledge in the same time allocation. We expect every card to be recorded and answered. We do not take questions during the quiz. We expect pupils to be attentive, think hard and work independently. Those pupils who finish ahead of the timer are directed to look for connections between question cues, answers or flashcard tags.

We self-assess every quiz using a 2-1-0 marking scheme: 2 marks if the answer is correct and accurate (where correct refers to the meaning and accurate refers to what is displayed on the board), 1 mark if it is correct and no marks if it is wrong. For example:

- Palpable - Capable of being touched. (In this case, fog.)

  2 marks - correct meaning and accurate

- Palpable - The fog was really heavy.

  1 mark - correct meaning but not accurate

- Palpable - Beating fast.

  0 marks - wrong

New information or corrections are highlighted by the pupils. This reduces the need for 'answer' queries. When self-marking, where pupils persist in clarifying the marks to be awarded, and they often do when you are establishing the routines or during an encoding phase, they are likely to be met with a common response: 'Make a decision.' The effort required by the pupil to process the decision is possibly a more effortful learning task than answering the question in the first place. After all, you will often hear Professor Dylan Wiliam (2018) advocate that 'the best person to mark a test is the person who just took it'. Every response is corrected to be correct and accurate. We peer-mark and collect scores every X number of quizzes, normally once a week in English.

Agreed, stress inhibits retrieval processes. However worthy and well-intentioned the phrase 'low-stakes' may be, I can find little empirical evidence to support it other than Khanna (2015: 177), who reports that 'ungraded pop quizzes do lead to higher cumulative final exam performance than using graded pop quizzes or using no quizzes'. On the other hand, she also reports that graded quizzes influenced pupils to attend class more frequently! Sotola and Crede (2021) found that, across 52 independent classroom studies, students were 2.5 times more likely to pass a course if their instructor incorporated frequent low-stakes quizzing than if the instructor did not. Quizzes or quizzing raises the average performance and lowers failure rate, benefiting pupils who struggle in a class the most.

Helpfully, Yang et al. (2021) report that there is no significant difference in testing benefits between high- and low-stake quizzes.

Takeaways

- Testing is assessment of learning and for learning.
- Retrieving information from memory causes learning, both directly and indirectly.
- Jenkins' (1979) tetrahedral model helps to explore the complexities of retrieval research.
- Assessment performance is improved when retrieval format and assessment format align.
- Low-stakes tests or quizzes in various formats (although I would recommend free recall) can be a 'cheap, easy-to-implement way of recapping material that might strengthen pupils' long-term ability to remember key concepts or information' (Perry et al., 2021: 21).
- Know why. Know how. Teach and lead the learning and relearning.
- For the largest learning impact, consider free recall over recognition recall. Be aware of the increased cognitive demand.
- If using multiple-choice-style questions, make all the questions required and provide feedback for all questions, including the correct answer; it may have been answered correctly by chance.
- In the initial learning phase, consider three learning exposures combined with at least three spaced exposures.
- Where memory strength is relatively high, include longer intervals between repetitions. Where memory strength is relatively low, an immediate repetition is better.
- Reactivate prior congruent knowledge when introducing new knowledge.
- Delivery (wait time) of retrieval cues in the classroom benefits from being 'just right', but teachers know that already.
- There is a fine line between difficulty and motivation. Pupils should be able to retrieve at least some, if not most, of the content on which they are tested.

- 'Quizzing or low-stakes testing may also reveal misconceptions' (Perry et al., 2021: 21). Make sure that pupils are supported to overcome them.

- See the section on hints in Chapter 5.

- If you only have time to read one paper on this topic: C. Yang, L. Luo, M. A. Vadillo, R. Yu and D. R. Shanks, Testing (quizzing) boosts classroom learning: a systematic and meta-analytic review. *Psychological Bulletin*, 147(4) (2021): 399–435.

Case study: Retrieval in action

Kirby Dowler is head of design technology, specialist leader of education for design technology and has previously led the school-centred initial teacher training subject leader programme for design technology. She works in a large rural secondary school (1,600 students) and teaches across all disciplines of design technology. Like almost all heads of department, Kirby is perpetually looking for ways to improve her own teaching and the quality of teaching across her department. Already teaching with retrieval practice routines, she was looking to extend and share her personal and professional success with retrieval practice with her department more broadly.

The challenge

As part of our whole-school continuing professional development, we complete a 'direct enquiry' question. We get to choose an area of professional interest in which we can trial an intervention or approach to see whether or not it has a positive impact on student progress.

I have always had a passion for the power of retrieval practice, having used this technique both in school and personally with great success. It was an obvious strategy to share across the department. My direct enquiry was as much about the 'how', as I was already convinced of the 'why'.

Although retrieval practice was embedded into my lessons, I didn't actively plan to repeatedly expose students to the same knowledge over and over again. It was more a case of adding retrieval questions to the lesson starts ad hoc. As you will be aware, covering the content of the curriculum across a very pressured academic year and then building in – or investing in – retrieval is a fine balance. Even more so, when repeatedly retrieving the defined knowledge.

What we did

Our aim was to ensure that all students, in all classrooms, were exposed to repeated retrieval from a bank of questions that we had collated collaboratively and quality-assured ourselves. Staff had access to these questions throughout their lessons and could deliver them with minimal preparation.

It was really important to explain to the students the importance of repeated retrieval, spaced retrieval practice and relearning. I shared some of the evidence that Kristian had previously discussed with me, so they could see what the benefits were for themselves.

I shared with the students that, as a department, we had defined the knowledge and had written the questions. They really liked this as they could see that we were investing in their progress.

We introduced 'retrieval books' to our lessons in which we documented all the in-class retrieval activities. These books helped to show our students that they were making progress with retention and knowledge, especially after they began to see the same questions more often – and see that they were getting them correct more often.

The next step was to use classroom.remembermore.app. It took a little extra effort to 'convert' our questions to retrieval flashcards (question-answer (Q-A) prompts), but it also offered us a little more versatility: flashcard Q-As, cloze-style cards and finish-the-sentence cards. Having said that, we mainly use flashcard Q-As.

We used the uploaded flashcards initially as a 'Do now' task when the students entered the room. They were familiar with this process as it was already embedded into lessons.

Once we were familiar with the routine, we started to use the tags in novel and different ways before exploring the various modes available to us as teachers. I made it competitive too. 'Can you beat the teacher?' and 'Can you beat your score from last week?' are firm favourites with the students.

I did this for several weeks, repeating their exposure to 'old' cards, while adding in 'new' cards over that time – extending the coverage of the deck. It was easy to select tags from current topics or mix tags from the current topic and previous topics.

It was fantastic to hear students saying, 'Oh, we did this two weeks ago' or, 'I should remember this as that question came up last week' or even, 'I saw this question at home last night!' (It was then that I realised the students were investing their own time outside of the lesson too.) The students were really enthusiastic when they could see cards reappearing and, in time, that they were remembering them more and more easily.

For me, as a busy teacher, once I had created the cards, I then had them at hand, to use and reuse at any point in my lesson (I don't just use retrieval practice at the start of a lesson these days). This gave me more flexibility, at timely points in the lesson, to add new retrieval cards that addressed a particular knowledge gap without any major planning. I found myself increasing the 'dosage' (more flashcards in the same allotted time), and I even had the students 'self-medicating' outside of class! I also found that the students were more efficient in their relearning. Knowledge was becoming more accessible, retrieval strength was increasing, the students were referencing prior learning more regularly and their knowledge was more durable.

As the students became more engaged in the use of repeated retrieval practice in lessons, I then gave them access to the RememberMore app. I set learning tasks as homework (e.g. Learn '1.0. Micronutrients and fat-soluble vitamins'), and because I was able to track both usage and mastery on the dashboard, I could check that students were completing these assigned tasks.

The outcomes

The feedback was extremely positive. Making it competitive was a big win: how many minutes had they engaged for? How many cards had they seen? How many could they remember?

We spoke about this both in the classroom and in the corridors. This was fantastic because when we focused on whole-class revision of knowledge, the students were 'buzzing' (their words, not mine) when they had a card they had been looking at in their own time. The students were learning on the school bus in the morning and even in the corridors at break time.

The difference we noticed as a department was that the students were getting better at free recall. We noticed a really big improvement in this compared to, for example, when the students have used revision apps and websites with multiple-choice questions. As they were able to free recall, this meant we could spend time on developing their exam answers and written technique. They knew the content, so we could focus on how to get that content into a written response.

What's next?

After effective implementation of repeated retrieval practice, we decided that the end-of-unit assessments (which we complete after every unit of work) would include some of the cards as assessment questions and act as some of the short-answer question stems. This further embedded the power of repeated retrieval, as the students could see that the revision was relevant and, most importantly, that it would be tested in high-stakes assessments even if learned and relearned in a low-stakes way.

We had many success stories from the introduction of repeated retrieval in our department. Students who were disengaged with learning seemed to find their spark again. In their own words: 'It's a bit addictive, isn't it, Miss?' They would answer 10 questions and then want to answer 10 more, and before they knew it they had done 30 minutes of retrieval practice. Of course, having access to the app then added a spaced/interleaving practice element too.

Some of my students would credit RememberMore as the reason that they revised more for their design and technology exam. The repetitive nature kept them going back for more and the competitive element in the class meant they wanted to remember more answers. All of this, combined with the repeated use in lessons, ensured that some of the students who could have very easily been borderline excelled.

Next, for us as a department, is to finish writing the department retrieval flashcards, weave these into our interim and end-of-year assessments, and continue to embed repeated retrieval across all key stages, not just Key Stages 4 and 5.

Chapter 3

Spaced retrieval practice[1]

The spacing effect - that is, the fact that spacing learning events apart results in more long-term learning than massing them together - is a robust phenomenon that has been demonstrated in hundreds of experiments.

Kornell (2009: 1297)

Memory is dynamic, and it keeps changing. And retrieval helps it change.

Mark McDaniel (quoted in Freemark, 2014)

Spacing involves taking the given amount of time that is devoted to learning and arranging it into multiple sessions spread over time. In this way, the learning sessions are said to be 'spaced' or 'distributed'. This is in contrast to 'blocked' or 'massed' practice, where the learner does all their studying in one session. (I will spare you the Ebbinghaus reference and diagram.)

Spacing was the second teaching technique to receive a high utility rating in the landmark Dunlosky et al. (2013) study (practice testing was the other - see Chapter 2). And as Dr Tom Perry highlighted in the SecEd Podcast (2022): 'Repeatedly in research, we find that rather than doing a whole hour

---

1   This chapter would not have been possible without the author's conversations with educational neuroscience expert Sarah Cottingham and her musings at https://overpractised.wordpress.com.

at once, you are best off doing 15 minutes four times.' However, spacing makes things harder for the learner, which in itself can present challenges for the teacher to overcome (as we will discuss later in this chapter) – a third signpost towards the importance of motivation.

But, as Perry et al. (2021: 15) state:

While spaced practice is thought to make learning more challenging for pupils as it prohibits information being held in the working memory, it may be able to increase the likelihood of knowledge being embedded in pupils' long-term memory. In having pupils revisit key concepts, ideas, or skills over longer periods of time in which content is almost forgotten, teachers may be able to improve learning retention.

Indeed, there is a clear advantage in distributing retrieval attempts over time rather than massing repeated retrieval attempts together. Studies show that distributing a fixed amount of practice over multiple sessions can boost scores on a delayed test (Pyc and Rawson, 2012; Dunlosky et al., 2013; Kang, 2016a; Karpicke et al., 2016; Yan et al., 2016).

Cepeda et al. (2006) looked at 254 studies with 14,000 participants and found that students scored about 10% higher on tests after spaced study than after massed study. Sobel et al. (2011) reported that after a week of spaced vocabulary training for fifth graders (10-year-olds), the children recalled almost three times as many definitions, or a 177% improvement, as they did in the massed condition. Five weeks later, the children from the spaced condition also showed 'superior long-term retention compared to massed practice' (Sobel et al., 2011: 763). More recent classroom-based randomised studies have supported these findings (Nazari and Ebersbach, 2019; Lyle et al., 2020; Emeny et al., 2021).

Dr John Dunlosky told the *TES* Podcast (2021): 'Spacing one's activities, and repeating those activities, is the basis of all mastery. If students are going to master anything, you are going to have to repeat that content over and over again. There is no getting around it.' Bjork and Bjork (2020: 478) define it as 'one of the most reliable and extensively studied phenomenon in the field of learning'.

A commonly used classroom strategy is to start the lesson with a short retrieval quiz that not only strengthens pupils' prior learning but also activates the relevant knowledge pertinent to that lesson, and consequently reduces the cognitive load for the proceeding taught episode. Practically, as

Perry et al. (2021: 15) outline, spacing is most often applied 'across days and lessons' rather than within a lesson. However, it can be across weeks, terms or topics.

Emeny et al. (2021) report that spaced practice (generally) not only produces higher test scores than massed practice, but that pupils' predictions of their own test scores were relatively accurate after spaced practice yet grossly overconfident after massed practice. This suggests that spaced practice improves metacognitive monitoring or, alternatively, addresses our own illusions of competence – a theme we will come back to in Chapter 8.

There is a very obvious glitch here. Not only is spaced practice not the default study habit for most pupils (particularly those who are performing poorly), but the subjective sense of fluency engendered by massed practice misleads pupils into believing they have made large gains in learning (Finn and Tauber, 2015). And, dare I say it, colleagues, neatly spaced practice isn't the default model for teaching; it certainly isn't for most textbooks. It needs deliberate planning, sequencing and forethought (not afterthought), and remains hampered by various curriculum inequalities which are baked into the timetable.

Yet, introducing spacing techniques doesn't need to be overwhelming, as teacher Helen Webb told the SecEd Podcast (2022): 'What is the work that needs revisiting? I don't think we need to talk about resequencing your entire curriculum model … Just think more purposefully about what it is you are doing in the classroom and different ways to revisit previous learning.'

As odd as it may sound, forgetting is a friend of learning: certain conditions, such as spaced lessons across a pupil's timetable that impair access to some to-be-learned information, enhance the learning of that information when it is restudied (Bjork, 2015). As we saw in Chapter 1, forgetting is not the opposite of remembering. If we forget a little before we restudy information, it allows us to boost that storage strength when we re-encounter the information. The ability to forget also helps us to offload outdated information, to generalise past experiences into specific categories and to design appropriate responses to similar situations in the future; to prioritise and see the forest for the trees. Hence, spacing across days and lessons is more effective than spacing within lessons, although limited research into the latter is promising (Perry et al., 2021).

Embracing spacing

More studies have examined the impact of spacing content across days and lessons than within individual lessons. Regarding the former, the evidence suggests a small positive impact across pupil ages and subject areas.

Perry et al. (2021: 15)

So, what kind of learning gains are we talking about from spacing? Well, practising retrieval once doubles long-term retention relative to reading the text once (34% vs 15%) and engaging in repeated retrieval increases retention to 80% (Karpicke and Roediger, 2010). Introducing and relearning the names and identities of characters in Shakespeare's plays (34 is the average), or any play or text for that matter, ahead of lessons or repeatedly during the opening sequence of lessons, not only helps pupils to retain that knowledge but potentially reduces the cognitive load placed on the learners when called to think about them more deeply. Something as simple as knowing the characters' names and which family they belong to in *Romeo and Juliet* starts the process of pupils organising their knowledge and thinking.

Lyle et al. (2020: 277) found similar results: 'Within-semester retention benefited significantly from practicing more and from spacing out practice. Across-semester retention benefited exclusively from increasing spacing.' Students whose retrieval practice was spaced outperformed those students whose practice was massed on the final exam in the precalculus class and on exams in the calculus class. More recently, Latimier et al. (2021: 982) reported the benefits of both retrieval practice and spacing, suggesting that 'they are best used combined with each other', thus enhancing the durability and accessibility of knowledge. This really is the short-term pain of spacing in order to reap its long-term gain in learning and durable retention.

There is a warning, of course, as we saw in Chapter 2 when discussing the fine line between difficulty and motivation. As the lag between retrievals and an initial test increases, so the likelihood of forgetting and the difficulty of retrieving also increase. Thus, spaced retrieval practice is a prime example of how retrieval success and retrieval effort trade off and why balancing these two components is crucial for promoting learning (and, as I keep on saying, so is corrective feedback in response to the retrieval effort).

Sarah Cottingham explained it to me thus: 'The longer the spacing interval, the more forgetting sets in and therefore the more challenging it is to retrieve the information. Effort is important but so is successful retrieval. We have to use spacing in a way which delicately balances effort with success for pupils.'

Teachers can take different approaches depending on their aims – perhaps you would like lower failure rates (increased success) as an entry into learning, or perhaps you want to increase the challenge of retrieval tasks in order to strengthen storage in long-term memory. Table 3.1 will give you some quick solutions.

Table 3.1. Design for low failure rates

Increase success	Increase difficulty
Single-part answer.	Multi-part answer.
During encoding.	During retrieval.
Use recognition recall: matched pairs, multiple-choice-style questions, fill-in-the-blanks.	Use free recall or cued questions, or reverse the cue (e.g. Q&A and A&Q).
Retrieve more recent learning or deeply rooted learning rather than selecting new retrieval prompts; retrieve then reorder.	Extend the chronological reference. Retrieve learning from last term or even last year(s)! Misalign the retrieval tasks and set homeworks from the previous topic.
Shorten time intervals (Eglington and Pavlik, 2020).	Extend time intervals.
Reduce the breadth of knowledge being probed.	Extend the breadth or weight of knowledge being probed.
Cue the retrieval or extend the cue(s) using hints.	Remove cues – free recall.
Massed practised retrieval – selecting the same retrieval prompts repeatedly or reorder the prompts.	Spaced practice – select new retrieval prompts from the same topic or refresh the cards.

Increase success	Increase difficulty
Block retrieval – securing high success rates on a set of flashcards before progressing.	*Interleave retrieval and new prompts from across topics.*
Self-paced.	*Time-pressured.*

We developed RememberMore to enable teachers to apply the research shared in these chapters. All RememberMore retrieval cards are categorised and tagged, giving that information a framework, a structure and an artificial schema, which also enables targeted pre-testing, post-testing, and spaced and interleaved retrieval practice, with session flashcards available to be reordered and refreshed. Effective study skills require that 'the information being learned has a framework or structure that can be used to organize both the learning and the retrieval, [so] memory is often considerably improved' (Eysenck et al., 1994: 365).

Effort is vital, and we must warn pupils of this fact: 'Human memory is fragile. The initial acquisition of knowledge is slow and effortful. And once mastery is achieved, the knowledge must be exercised periodically to mitigate forgetting' (Mozer and Lindsey, 2017: 35).

Very simply, the more occasions knowledge is tested, the larger the learning gains. According to Yang et al. (2021), learning gains increase the more we test knowledge, but of note for teachers is that the extent of the returns diminishes: one retrieval quiz (an effect size of 0.44), two quizzes (0.60), three retrievals or more (0.64) and unlimited retrievals (0.76). Perhaps three is the magic number, or at least a good bet, but it is more than a 'dosage effect'. We will return to this in Chapter 6.

Effects of the type of spacing schedule

Two broad schedules have frequently been compared: expanding spacing versus uniform spacing. For example, across a total of 20 days, we could plan an expanding 0-1-5-9 compared to a uniform 5-5-5-5. We could test or return to the target information after one lesson, then after another five lessons and then after nine lessons (1-5-9), or we could return to the target information every five lessons (5-5-5). (Of course, teaching timetables rarely afford such luxury.) In the expanding schedule, intervals increase after every re-exposure, whereas in the uniform schedule intervals are kept constant.

There is a third way known as a contracting schedule; however, this is rarely referenced in research. The idea behind an expanding schedule is that early recalls would afford high success rates, while the retrievals grow increasingly more difficult (because of the increased spacing). The notion is intuitive, and for years it was recommended as the optimal way.

However, a wealth of research since Cepeda et al.'s (2006) meta-analysis has failed to demonstrate a consistent advantage of expanding over uniform schedules. (That said, I foresee most teachers pointing to content-heavy curriculums and default to expanding schedules as a result.) Latimier et al. (2021) challenged the widely held belief that spacing schedules should be progressively increased. Interestingly, they also pointed out that 'the more learners are tested, the more beneficial the expanding schedule is, compared with the uniform one' (Latimier et al., 2021: 959).

So, our final question is: what is the optimal retrieval practice interval? And the answer is, rather disappointingly: it depends.

- You need to know the memory strength of that item after initial encoding (Pavlik and Anderson, 2005, 2008; Cepeda et al., 2009; Mozer et al., 2009). If stronger, extend the spacing and, conversely, where it is weaker or incorrect, offer feedback and reduce the spacing.

- You need to know how well it was learned in the first place given that 'the level of initial training moderates the effects of distributing retrieval practice' (Toppino et al., 2018: 975).

- You need to know 'the time elapsed since the last review' (Tabibian et al., 2019: 3988).

- Lastly, and critically, 'You need to decide how long you wish to remember something' (Cepeda et al., 2008: 1101). If the knowledge is required for an extended period of time, reinforce both the storage and retrieval strength – that is, how deeply it is embedded and how easy it is to access that knowledge.

And still we are left with a cautionary note: that the critical role of retention and forgetting suggests that the effectiveness of a given spacing schedule may vary as a function of a variety of factors. These include those presented in Chapter 1 (i.e. learner characteristics, encoding activities, retrieval format, materials and modality) plus the degree of initial learning and the interfering potential of interpolated material and the amount of information to be learned. 'Thus, it would be a mistake to assume that a particular set of lags would produce the same effect in all circumstances' (Toppino et al., 2018: 977).

Most recently, reframing the spaced retrieval goal towards maximising learning that is more ecologically valid, Yan et al. (2020: 212) shared a very practical point: 'Determining optimal schedules should not only consider overall accuracy at final test, but also the time cost of achieving that accuracy.' This throws a spotlight on how to use feedback effectively and efficiently, and also hints at the potential of 'adjusting schedules in light of prior performance' (Yan et al., 2020: 213) and personalisation.

The practical conclusion is: if the goal is short-term retention, employ shorter spacing gaps; if the goal is long-term retention, spacing of several weeks or months may be best (Carpenter et al., 2012). Carpenter et al. (2012: 373) add: 'In general, the optimal spacing gap equalled 10%–20% of the test delay. In other words, the longer the test delay, the longer the optimal spacing gap.' The researchers believe that spacing works because the time delay between study sessions forces the learner to work harder to retrieve the information, and thus helps to consolidate the information in long-term memory.

Keep in mind that shorter delays between studying sometimes fool the learner into thinking they know the information well (for long-term retention) because the information is more easily retrievable, but, alas, information is quickly forgotten. Here is the good news: 'the cost of "overshooting" the right spacing is consistently found to be much smaller than the cost of having very short spacing' (Pashler et al., 2007: 5). The recommendation is to err on the side of a longer interval.

What if the retrieval practice spacing could be controlled by each individual knowledge item? Or by the learner? Or by the knowledge items and learner? Now there is a line of enquiry … We will return to personalised schedules in Chapter 8.

Not all retrieval is good retrieval: interference

An ironic feature of human memory is that while the act of remembering a target piece of information may strengthen the retrieved information itself, it can also cause forgetting or weakening of other related information stored in long-term memory. This phenomenon is known as 'retrieval-induced forgetting'. Instances of retrieval-induced forgetting are typically accounted for by either interference (the heightened accessibility of other accessible memories) or inhibition (the suppression of memories). However, as yet, the theoretical underpinnings of retrieval-induced forgetting has yet to be reached.

Interference theory assumes that forgetting is due to retrieval failure rather than a direct weakening, decay or loss of the stored information. As such, forgetting can be thought of as an inability to remember; that the target information is inaccessible, at a particular time, due to retrieval competition. Competition from other items thereby produces forgetting (Anderson and Neely, 1996). The related information is still there in long-term memory, but the interference is making it temporarily difficult to retrieve (without any impact on the stored information itself).

Interference from other information that may have been learned previously is known as 'proactive interference', whereas information learned after is known as 'retroactive interference'. Interference is therefore a function of integration (how similar or connected the information is) and delay (or spacing). For example, proactive interference encourages you to write last year's date in January or leaves you struggling to remember your new mobile phone number because you keep recalling your previous number. Retroactive interference means that when you are learning a new piece of music, you suddenly find it more difficult to play an older, previously learned piece of music.

In contrast, inhibition theory is simpler to explain. It suggests that forgetting can occur due to the direct weakening or suppression of information in the memory. What is perhaps most notable about research on retrieval-induced forgetting is that it points to the critical interplay of how our memories work and reinforces the point made previously that 'using our memories shapes our memories' (Bjork, 2011: 4).

Teachers will benefit from being aware of this phenomena when planning lessons. We should avoid pupils encountering similar information too soon after they encounter the target material: 'scheduling testing with expanding intervals can promote both successful recall of true information and prevent unwanted recall of false information' (Storm et al., 2010: 252). It may be why Perry et al. (2021) found little evidence for spacing within lessons, although it is a promising line of enquiry for new research. Regrettably, it is not possible to advise on how long that wait should be, whether within a lesson or in a subsequent lesson.

Sleep tight

We all know how vital sleep is. One of the key aspects of spacing is that it allows for sleep. While we can learn without sleeping between learning sessions, sleep is unquestionably advantageous for long-term retention. First, sleep improves concentration, or rather sleep deprivation impairs attention and working memory. Second, sleep aids the consolidation of newly acquired information. Not only that, it requires no cost and no additional effort.

Sleeping provides optimal conditions for processes that integrate newly encoded memories into long-term storage (sometimes referred to as consolidation). Sleep also enhances new learning (Diekelmann and Born, 2010). Memories are reactivated during sleep, so rather than new memories being prone to decay, they are instead transformed into more stable memories that are preserved long term (van Dongen et al., 2012).

Sleep not only helps to strengthen memories but it also helps us to actively forget irrelevant information, thus optimising memory for what is relevant. Sleep leads to a twofold advantage. Such transformations allow learners to re-encode information faster and save time during the relearning sessions.

The practical consequence reported by Mazza et al. (2016) was that sleep between learning sessions reduced the amount of practice needed to relearn 16 paired words by half and also ensured much better long-term retention. (This could also partly explain why within-lesson spacing is less effective than between-lesson spacing.) Their recommendation is that, 'Sleeping after learning is definitely a good strategy, but sleeping between two learning sessions is a better strategy' (Mazza et al., 2016: 46).

Meanwhile, Kroneisen and Kuepper-Tetzel (2021) add that if students study in the evening, they should test themselves immediately after learning. If they study during the day, the practice test should be delayed in order to reinforce memory and reduce forgetting of the material.

That is all well and good. However, sleep deprivation (a debt of two hours) becomes a more significant concern as pupils move towards their examination years: 16% of 11-year-olds are technically sleep deprived, increasing to 41% at age 15 (Leger et al., 2012). Interestingly, it was more of a concern for girls than boys.

Implications for the classroom

Despite more than a century of research demonstrating the benefits of the spacing effect, it does not appear to have widespread application in the classroom. Conventional instructional practice, which is organised in a modular way, typically favours and makes massed practice more convenient. Teachers deciding to incorporate spaced practice or spaced retrieval practice into their teaching need to be encouraged to break free from these conceptual constraints. Remember, when pupils are re-exposed to information they have learned but temporarily cannot recall, they relearn this information much faster than information that is being learned for the first time. What is more, spacing learning over several weeks, during which time new learning will be acquired, provides opportunities to integrate old and new learning, fostering a more cohesive schema of learning.

As Kang (2016a:12) concludes: 'Spaced review or practice enhances diverse forms of learning, including memory, problem solving, and generalization to new situations. Spaced practice is a feasible and cost-effective way to improve the effectiveness and efficiency of learning, and has tremendous potential to improve educational outcomes.'

In a nutshell, spacing reduces retrieval strength but boosts storage strength. Spacing reduces the negative effects of recency, familiarity and fluency (success experienced during blocked practice), and increases the effort required to retrieve information, making learning more durable. Furthermore, as well as directly consolidating that knowledge, learners (and their teachers) are able to diagnose what they know and identify gaps in their knowledge. We will come back to this in more detail in Chapter 6 when we look at successive relearning.

The last word should perhaps be from a teacher who has crossed the research divide. William Emeny, who teaches maths at Wyvern College in Hampshire and has co-authored a paper on spaced mathematics practice, says: 'the key point is that teachers should shift their mindset so that the practice of a skill or concept is seen not as material that should be squeezed into one or two consecutive class meetings but rather as material that can be distributed across many lessons' (Emeny et al., 2021: 1087).

Takeaways

- Prioritise spaced over massed practice (be it retrieval or not).
- Combine spacing with retrieval and consider the benefits and appropriateness of interleaved retrieval (see Chapter 4).
- Optimal spacing needs to consider the memory strength of initial encoding, the time elapsed since the last review and how long you wish to remember something (when is the exam!?).
- Spacing reduces retrieval strength but boosts storage strength.
- Overshooting the right spacing intervals is less harmful than having very short spacing.
- Spacing across days and lessons is more effective than within lessons (Perry et al., 2021).
- Consider encoding and relearning as separate and distinct retrieval opportunities.
- Integration and delay govern when retrieval induces forgetting (and when it induces facilitation).
- Carpenter et al. (2012) recommend that teachers incorporate into each lesson a brief review of concepts that were learned several weeks earlier, use homeworks to re-expose important information, and set exams and quizzes that are cumulative. (Assessment that samples previously taught content as well as the most recently taught content.)
- Determining optimal schedules should not only consider overall accuracy at the final test but also the time cost of achieving that accuracy.
- The timetable represents a spacing opportunity; however, the spacing is not always 'ideal'. It may be more feasible to classroom teachers to manage their own spacing schedules, possibly utilising homework. A point also highlighted by Perry et al. (2021: 15).
- Sleep is an important spacing opportunity. Sleep improves concentration, supports consolidation and aids in the forgetting of irrelevant information.
- Homework is also a spacing opportunity.
- If you only have time to read one paper on this topic: A. Latimier, H. Peyre and F. Ramus, A meta-analytic review of the benefit of spacing out retrieval practice episodes on retention. *Educational Psychology Review*, 33 (2021): 959–987.

Case study: Spaced out

Dr Dan Rosen is head of secondary at an international school in Germany and organiser of researchED events in Germany. Dan is interested in test-enhanced learning and retrieval practice, not just as a teacher but also as school leader. He is particularly interested in how he can create systems and structures that enable staff to develop their research-informed practice and then implement it effectively.

The challenge

I am going to focus on how spaced retrieval practice can help with essay writing in a new subject. I currently teach International Baccalaureate psychology, which is nearly always a new subject for students. While the content is largely scientific in nature, the assessment is mostly essay based, meaning the skill of writing in psychology is indeed unique.

The biggest challenge is that essay writing is difficult without knowledge of the entire unit. As a result, essay practice is often left until the end of a topic, sometimes even the end of the module and, in some extremely rare cases, until the end of the course.

There is some value in waiting until the end of the topic, as it makes it more likely that students will already know the content. But, it also means that learning and practice of the skill of essay writing is massed or blocked (and, after reading this book, you will be more than aware of the dangers of that!).

We wanted to take advantage of a distributed or spaced approach to both retrieving knowledge and essay writing, leveraging homework to ensure that students re-expose themselves to knowledge, in addition to quizzes, assessments and exams in class.

A second challenge focused on simple school logistics and timetabling. Psychology has three timetabled lessons per week but two are on the same day. This is tough for two main reasons: first, the lessons are fixed and, as such, are retrieval opportunities; second, there is, in effect, minimal spacing between two of our lessons (and, no, there isn't an opportunity for students to sleep between lessons!).

These kinds of constraints are familiar to almost all teachers, possibly even more so for foundation subject teachers.

What we did

How did this work? To start with, we mapped out the specific aspects of knowledge that are required in order to write an effective essay, especially under exam conditions. These are:

1 Content knowledge about psychological theory.

2 Content knowledge about psychology studies: aim, procedure, participants, findings and conclusions.

3 Evaluative knowledge about these studies: real-life implications for findings; issues with the design, procedure or sample; and supporting or contradictory studies/theories.

4 Structural knowledge of an essay: introduction, body, conclusions; structure of body paragraphs (e.g. PEEL – point, evidence, explanation, link); and how these differ with each command term.

5 Metacognitive strategies for essay-writing practice: creating essay plans and writing sample paragraphs.

We then devised quiz questions based on the above topics to which the answers are typically one sentence, meaning they are quick to answer but do require some thought.

Sections 1-3 are completely dependent on the studies and so new questions need to be generated with every new topic, However, sections 4 and 5 are used throughout the course and apply to any essay. This means that we front-end the learning of structure and metacognitive strategies in advance of writing an essay, thereby ensuring that these memories are the strongest as they are the most often retrieved and can be used well before a sentence is written under the constraints of exam conditions.

Test-enhanced learning

We used a variety of applications to build the quizzes. Even though the database of questions is largely the same across the platforms, we wanted to utilise a variety of different interfaces to keep the learning fresh and unpredictable.

We also wanted to use different recall options – free and cued. While the final assessment is technically free recall, we can train students to utilise the actual question to prompt their thinking and planning of answers, and from there employ cued recall. But that is for a different time!

So, how did the spaced retrieval practice work? At the start of the course, there is nothing spaced about it. There cannot be as we haven't learned enough material to go back over. We spend this time developing positive learning habits and building core knowledge. Remember, one of the key practical issues of spaced retrieval practice is that you must have space and accrued knowledge to retrieve.

We use starter quizzes in every lesson based on the previous lesson's material and we make notes for homework. We are certainly in an encoding phase of learning, but once we reach the end of the first month the set-up changes.

In class, there is no predictability with regard to the content of the quiz. Students should expect the starter quiz to be on anything we have learned so far. On this point, it would be very useful if we could define when content was taught – and this is an opportunity we plan to explore with RememberMore.

At the moment, some quizzes are more challenging than others, and this will vary across the students (if only we could take a more personalised approach, the spacing would be more strategic). We currently select questions from at least two or three weeks prior and combine these with material recently learned to give us a 5- or 10-minute quiz.

The flexibility of combining questions across topics (see Chapter 4) allows us to vary the difficulty of quizzes with ease, as well as focusing on areas that we know require more practice from our continuous assessment for learning. It also encourages students to review and revise material from previous topics and units, as they know they could be quizzed on it. Most notably, it forces students to practise retrieving information about topics that they would otherwise ignore and leave until much later when it is time to revise.

Beyond class, homework also includes practising revision techniques to learn the current content. Note-making is still required, but this is as a prerequisite to the actual homework of revision or pre-reading.

When we do larger summative assessments, we invest significantly in metacognitive monitoring. If students cannot recall the strategies they should use (and did use), then this will be their feedback focus above and beyond any syllabus-related issue.

All quizzes are low-stakes with no marks taken in, but there are opportunities for students to self-mark and peer-mark to ensure immediate feedback is provided. It is important that they get to see the correct answer. We can also use data from our apps to correlate with free recall summative and formative assessments.

As mentioned above, we also have the added challenge of two lessons on the same day, separated by two other lessons and a break. We have shied away from using the starter in the second lesson to recap what was learned in the first. Instead, we focus on using these particular starter quizzes for recalling previously learned material (rather than recently learned) in order to leverage the gains of spaced retrieval.

The outcomes

Students not only benefit from this spaced approach, but with direct reference to it they are becoming more aware themselves that they are benefiting. They are able to articulate why this strategy of spaced retrieval is working for them.

For some students, it is the incentive to review material consistently and constantly that drives their improvement. For others, it is the active process of being forced to retrieve something that they appreciate – as it is easier for teachers to ask the question in class than for them to practise alone at home with all their other homework piling up. Fortunately, this strategy is replicated in many of their other classes across the school, so the students now expect this to happen.

I know that many staff experience student kickback when implementing such approaches. However, our first topic is always memory, so the students literally learn the science and psychology behind it all. Even though the content they are learning informs them about the best way to learn and form memories, they still utilise strategies (at least at first) that are not effective. If this happens in a psychology classroom, it must be infinitely more challenging elsewhere. I would encourage you to (a) share the cognitive science with your students and (b) stick to what you know works in the long term.

Another challenge for me is keeping tabs on what has and has not been asked recently. It is fairly straightforward at the beginning, and if I ever do ask questions in quick succession, I can always smile and say, 'It's for unpredictability!' But, deep down, I know that I have wasted an opportunity for spaced retrieval, and it irks. This is why app algorithms are extremely useful, as they can ensure that the most appropriate question is asked at any given time, although I am loathe to use just one app, as I think the variety of approaches provides other benefits.

Takeaways

My three theoretical takeaways are:

1 Spaced retrieval practice can be used to drive out-of-class revision habits.

2 Spaced retrieval forces students to retrieve information they otherwise ignore until 'revision time'.

3 Apps can help to monitor which topics should be practised, but variety of recall also has its benefits.

My three practical takeaways are:

1 Be strong and don't default to rehearsal-type activities – that is, activities where students are merely going through the motions without having to think or retrieve. It can be tempting to avoid having two quizzes in a lesson – one for older topics and one for

current - but don't lose sight of the long-term gains of spaced retrieval.

2 Don't worry about collating huge swathes of data about how well the students have performed. This is practice, and keeping it low-stakes and unrecorded means students see it as a learning strategy rather than a test.

3 Build a database of questions somewhere centrally. In that way, you can feed them into different apps/programs when necessary; short-term time investment for long-term benefits.

What's next?

As a school leader, one of the most important next steps is to ensure that consistent spaced retrieval is combined with metacognitive strategies for our younger students. We have started this process, of course, but there is always more to be done. Given that these strategies are content-independent, the more students are able to monitor their learning and have confidence that the strategies they are employing are working, the greater the benefit will be to all subjects.

Chapter 4

Interleaving

If your learning aim is to learn about the character of Sherlock Holmes and the character of Dr Watson, then you should block practice. If your learning aim is to understand the differences in their characters, then interleave. The choice depends somewhat on how similar or different Holmes' and Watson's characters are, and also how consistent Holmes' and Watson's characters are across situations.

Philip Higham[1]

In this case, the characters of Holmes and Watson are suitably different, consistently so, and therefore suitable for interleaving.

I found this explanation from Dr Philip Higham of the University of Southampton so useful that I made him repeat it three times during our conversation to ensure I got the quote right in my notes. It is also worth dwelling on the following from Clare Sealy (2019): 'In almost all learning domains, all subjects, all age ranges, substantive knowledge is taught. The building blocks of various subjects. This "substance" is central to being able to think mathematically, or scientifically, or historically, or to communicate clearly.'

An intuitive approach is to focus on learning one topic at a time (e.g. AABB), which cognitive scientists refer to as blocked or massed practice. Its use is consistent with the common assumption that we learn most effectively when

1   P. Higham, interview with author (October 2021).

topics are introduced in isolation, in sequence, and that repeated practice fosters the development of expertise and fluency after each topic.

It is how many of us were taught and how many of us teach. Indeed, Dedrick et al. (2016) report that 78% of mathematics textbooks were organised for blocked practice and only 11% interleaved (the remainder were difficult to classify). However, researchers have started to investigate an alternative approach, known as interleaved practice or interleaving. Interleaving involves switching between topics (e.g. ABAB), with learners forced to select an appropriate strategy for each topic.

Perry et al. (2021: 19) state:

Interleaving involves sequencing tasks so that learning material is interspersed with slightly (but not completely) different content or activities, as opposed to undertaking tasks through a blocked and consecutive approach. While similar to spaced practice, interleaving involves sequencing tasks or learning content that share some likeness whereas a spaced practice approach uses intervals that are filled with unrelated activities.

Kornell and Bjork (2008) famously presented learners with impressionist landscape artwork in blocked or interleaved formats and then tested their ability to identify the artist who had painted novel example paintings. There were two key findings: first, interleaving was superior to blocking in this test; and, second, students' metacognitive awareness of their learning was faulty, as they tended to believe (incorrectly) that they had learned better via blocking. We will revisit this interesting finding in Chapter 8, which has since been replicated multiple times. Generally, the research shows that interleaved practice is superior to blocked practice.

More recently, researchers have been more assertive. Rohrer et al. (2019: 40) 'conducted a large randomised classroom study and found that a greater emphasis on interleaved practice dramatically improved test scores', as did Samani and Pan (2021), and 'at no (or very little) additional time cost' (Wiseheart et al., 2019: 572). Furthermore, 'It can boost both memory and transfer and applies across different subject domains' (Firth et al., 2021: 668). Interestingly, Firth et al. (2021: 668) offer two particular contexts for interleaving: 'contrasting similar items that would otherwise be confused' and 'objective rule-based principles'.

So, why is blocked practice so popular?

One reason for the prevalence of blocked practice could be that pupils, teachers and textbook authors are not aware of interleaved practice. Or it might be that they are swayed by the resulting recency, familiarity and fluency of blocked practice (Bjork et al., 2013; Kirk-Johnson et al., 2019), which encourages pupils and teachers to falsely believe that blocked practice enhances efficacy. We will revisit this cognitive bias later when we discuss the illusions of competence in Chapter 8.

Finally, and less provocatively, it might just be that blocked practice is more convenient, following each lesson with a group of problems devoted to that lesson. Compared to this, 'interleaving instruction can feel disorganised and chaotic, and may require a significant time investment to restructure curriculum' (Sana and Yan, 2022: 787).

Let's not forget, if your teaching materials are not categorised or tagged, then relearning (and reordering learning) will be more time-consuming (not to mention daunting).

What is the theory behind interleaving?

Several theoretical mechanisms may account for the observed benefits of interleaving. However, these are not necessarily mutually exclusive. It is part of the reason that this area of cognitive psychology is hard to pin down empirically.

Rohrer et al. (2019: 41) state: 'In addition to any benefits of mixture per se, the interleaving of practice problems in a course or text inherently incorporates the learning strategies of spacing and retrieval practice, each of which is an effective and robust learning strategy.'

Clearly, interleaving incorporates both spacing and repeated retrieval practice, and as we have already discussed, that is far from straightforward. However, both spacing and repeated retrieval practice enhance the durability and accessibility of knowledge. The most prevalent explanations reference two theories as to why this is:

1   Inductive learning, where learners discover rules or concepts by observation and examples (as opposed to deductive learning, where they are given rules that they then need to apply).

2　The discriminative-contrast hypothesis, which suggests that pupils learn to discriminate and contrast problems when those problems are presented in interleaved form.

With blocking, once you know what solution to execute, the hard part is over; the predictability of blocking removes any need for the pupil to engage in strategy selection. With interleaving, each practice attempt is unique, therefore rote responses are unreliable. Pupils are continuously searching for different solutions, and that process improves their ability to learn critical features, processes and concepts, which then better enables them to select and execute the correct response.

Interleaving may also strengthen memory associations. With blocking, a single strategy temporarily held in short-term memory is sufficient. That is not the case with interleaving, where the correct solution is constantly changing. As a result, greater attention is required, contextual cues need to be re-encoded and pupils are continually required to retrieve different responses, repeatedly bringing them into short-term memory. Repeating that process 'fosters more relational processing' (Samani and Pan, 2021: 6), reinforcing neural connections between different tasks and correct responses, which induce retrieval processes that enhance learning. Hopefully, you can now see why the summary of cognitive architecture in Chapter 1 is so important.

In both cases, the similarity of materials is an obvious modulator. Again, think about the 'element interactivity' (the connectedness of the information). As Chen et al. (2021: 1517) point out: 'Differences between interleaved and blocked practice can be more difficult to obtain depending on the discriminability of the interleaved materials.' This basically means that when interleaved topics are 'very obviously different' and 'immediately discriminable', then 'the interleaving effect is unlikely to be obtained' (Chen et al., 2021: 1516). Accordingly, teachers would be advised to present materials that are more difficult to discriminate between – that is, Perry et al.'s (2021: 19) 'slightly (but not completely) different content or activities' – in order to leverage an interleaving benefit (as the knowledge is consolidated if not yet secure).

Lastly, Chen et al. (2021) introduce the mechanism of 'rest-from-deliberate-learning'. There is a possibility that resting from cognitive activity can allow the working memory to recover, which would provide an explanation for the spacing effect, while the discriminative-contrast hypothesis provides an explanation for interleaving. An open debate between Dr Chen and Dr Sana (Sana et al., 2022) continues.

Spaced and interleaved practices have both been identified as effective, but they are sometimes conflated as a single strategy, which has led to the erroneous assumption that both effects have the same cause. To be clear, spaced learning, with rest from deliberate practice, generally results in more improved outcomes than massed practice without rest from deliberate practice. Interleaved practice also consists of spaced learning, but topics are interleaved rather than involving rest from deliberate practice.

Finally, it is not merely the principle of interleaving that we need to take into consideration but also our learning aims. I refer you again to Philip Higham's quote at the start of this chapter.

Interleaving like medicine

Without doubt, my favourite interleaving reference is from Rohrer (2012: 365): 'Interleaving is like bad-tasting cough syrup'.

In a similar vein, I also refer you to the research of Birnbaum et al. (2013), who report that the great majority of the participants judged that they had learned more effectively with blocked than with interleaved study. Likewise, Samani and Pan (2021) conclude:

> *Despite benefiting more from interleaved practice, students tended to rate the technique as more difficult and incorrectly believed that they learned less from it. Thus, in a domain that entails considerable amounts of problem-solving, replacing conventionally arranged with interleaved homework can (despite perceptions to the contrary) foster longer lasting and more generalizable learning.*

Exploring the extended effects of interleaving on factual knowledge and problem-solving ability, Samani and Pan (2021) replaced the conventionally blocked homework with interleaved homework, concluding with an in-class surprise test. With respect to overall performance, students correctly solved more blocked than interleaved homework problems, confirming their metacognitive judgements.

However, 'belying the patterns observed on the homework assignments', they found that students who had completed interleaved homework 'well outperformed' those who had completed blocked homework on the surprise criterial test (with median improvements of 50% and 125% on the two exams, respectively). Interleaving improved their ability to correctly 'recall and use prior knowledge' in an attempt to generate solutions to novel problems. Importantly, as the weight of content increased as students progressed through the course, the effect size of the interleaving advantage was larger still.

Samani and Pan (2021) were also able to show the effects of interleaving on two distinct sub-measures of test performance: (a) whether students were able to correctly recall necessary formulas - or recall memory - and (b) whether students were able to devise and execute a multi-step problem-solving strategy - or problem-solving accuracy.

Pupils will find that using and applying a given equation in blocked practice is much easier than in interleaved practice, when they will have to work out which equation to use for the posed problem, then recall and apply it. For this reason, I tend to teach using blocked practice, and then revisit and do further practice using interleaved practice. Now, both spacing and interleaving have been shown to lead to slower and more error-prone learning in the short-term. However, they boost memory retention when implemented over a longer time period, with interleaved learning proving particularly durable, providing 'near immunity against forgetting' (Rohrer et al., 2015: 906).

Yet, in spite of being told their test scores, students still report that they prefer massed practice and rereading-style revision strategies. There is more to revisit when we discuss illusions of competence in Chapter 8, but, for now, signpost for pupils that 'we are using interleaved practice' and 'easy learning is easy forgetting'.

What about interleaved retrieval practice?

Sana and Yan (2022) posed an interesting question: can interleaved retrieval practice enhance learning in classrooms? Across a four-week period, 155 pupils took a 10- to 12-minute weekly quiz in their science courses, testing half of the concepts taught that week. Questions on each quiz were either blocked by concept or interleaved with different concepts.

A month after the final quiz, the pupils were tested on the concepts covered. They performed better on concepts that had been block quizzed (54%) than not quizzed (47%), as we would expect. However, the interleaved quizzes led to even greater benefits (63%).

To interleave or not?

To be able to interleave questions successfully, pupils need a relatively secure and consolidated understanding of the concepts, processes, procedures or meaning of the knowledge being quizzed or tested. Therefore, interleaving is more retrieval and discrimination (requiring greater attention) than it is encoding and learning.

When teaching, I use interleaving as part of my deliberate practice phase, interleaving questions from the current topic and recent and related topics. When it comes to revision lessons, which is essentially relearning, this is most definitely an opportunity to get your interleaved quizzing going, but it is not the only time.

Dr Veronica Yan, a cognitive scientist with a professional interest in interleaving, told me:

Exam season is the perfect example of how interleaving and retrieval practice go hand in hand. By interleaving practice questions, you are not only strengthening recall of individual concepts (through practising retrieval), but you are also strengthening your knowledge network (through interleaving the practice) - strengthening understanding of how concepts are similar and different from each other, how they are interconnected, how to recognise when one concept is more relevant in a particular situation than another, and so on.[2]

Furthermore, Yan and Sana (2021) shared the valid point that students rarely study only one course at a time. So, how should the study of unrelated courses be sequenced: blocked by course to avoid unproductive juxtapositions, or interleaved across different courses because it inherently involves spaced practice?

We know that interleaving completely different things (like science concepts with foreign language vocabulary) or across completely different courses is not terribly helpful (Hausman and Kornell, 2014), so carefully select the learning material and the category structure.

Yan's conclusions may prove useful for pupils studying multiple subjects. She told me that the optimal schedule involves interleaving 'at either the

2   V. Yan, interview with author (April 2022).

concept or the domain level, but not both, nor neither'. That is, interleave related topics to highlight the similarities and differences – for example, mitosis and meiosis in science (different types of cell division) or active transport and osmosis (different types of transport in cells).

Interleaving is clearly effective for the inductive learning of material with high similarity between categories of knowledge but not *within* categories of knowledge. Understanding the differences between characters in a text? Interleave. Understanding the different steps or processes in solving a problem? Interleave. For example, we might interleave *Romeo and Juliet* with *Othello*, but we should generally avoid interleaving two similar Shakespeare plays. Or, in a geography lesson, we could interleave tectonic hazards and urbanising, or tropical rain forests and energy consumption, but avoid interleaving coastal and river landscapes, or tropical rainforests and boreal forests (which are too similar).

A final note from Dr Higham

Of course, interleaving is more nuanced than the opening quotation, which I captured during one of my informal conversations with Dr Higham. Now that you are armed with a more comprehensive schema for interleaving, his more recent and extended summary from one of our many email exchanges will be of interest:

Generally, interleaving produces better inductive learning than blocking. After all, interleaving usually means that practice is spaced, which nearly always produces superior learning to massed practice. However, this depends somewhat on how similar the category exemplars are to each other, both within the same category and between categories.

If the categories are similar and confusable (i.e. exemplars from one category are similar to each other and also similar to exemplars in the second category, which are also similar to each other), then interleaving encourages discriminative contrast, which promotes learning. In other words, interleaving meets the challenge of identifying differences between the categories. However, if the exemplars are very different from each other, then the challenge is to find commonalities among exemplars belonging to the same category. Under these circumstances, blocking is better.

Takeaways

- 'The rationale for interleaving is that it may support learners to discriminate between two similar concepts or methods. Teachers may be able to increase the level of challenge presented through interleaved tasks by introducing more similar items of learning' (Perry et al., 2021: 19).

- When pupils must learn to distinguish between concepts, interleave rather than block.

- Break up longer assessments into more frequent shorter quizzes; similar topics can then also be interleaved.

- When building decks for RememberMore, carefully select the learning material, category and tag structure.

- Consider the sequence in which knowledge is assigned, relearned and revisited. When you revisit the topics, rearrange the order in which you restudy them.

- Both spacing and interleaving lead to slower and more error-prone learning in the short term and boost memory retention in the long term.

- Perhaps even more so for interleaving than for retrieval and spacing, teachers are competing against the pupils' own ill-informed metacognitive beliefs that interleaving is less effective than other study modes.

- Homework and lesson starters are often targeted for short spaced retrieval practice. Consider interleaving the retrieval items; this is easily achieved with classroom.remembermore.app.

- Interleaving and spaced retrieval practice go hand in hand during exam season when knowledge is relatively secure and consolidated.

- Interleave at either the concept or the domain level, but not both.

- If you only have time to read one paper on this topic: J. Samani and S. C. Pan, Interleaved practice enhances memory and problem-solving ability in undergraduate physics. *npj Science of Learning*, 6 (2021), article 32.

Case study: Interleaving topics

Helen Pipe is head of geography at an 11–16 secondary school, the trust subject lead and an early career teacher mentor. The curriculum ethos of the trust in which she works is one that is knowledge-rich, sequenced and draws on a strong evidence base to ensure efficacy. As part of the online geography community, Helen had already contributed to various geography flashcard decks for RememberMore before wanting to explore how she could promote a deep understanding of the numerous geography case studies her pupils studied by applying the principles of interleaving.

The challenge

- The GCSE geography specification is overflowing with core knowledge, whether this is the definitions of key terms, concepts or the details of contrasting case studies.

- There are more than 130 Tier 3 key terms that pupils are expected to recall, understand and apply.

- In exams, pupils are required to demonstrate their use of specific case study facts in order to gain a Level 2+ in their long-answer levelled questions.

- Pupils are revising for approximately 10 subjects with multiple exam papers and lack the awareness of how to revise effectively.

- On top of this, pupils and teachers are faced with the knowledge gaps that have arisen as a result of the COVID-19 pandemic.

What we did

Effective teaching and learning is delivered through a five-year curriculum plan. Pupils in Year 7 start with the foundation knowledge of the physical landscape of the earth, applying this knowledge to a continent, which leads into diverse human landscapes.

This foundation prior knowledge is built on in Year 8 when we explore human landscapes. In Year 9, there is a focus on the impact of humans on the physical landscape with an investigation of environmental issues – for example, management of physical landscapes and decisions related to the exploitation of forest biomes. This provides pupils with a secure base of mastered knowledge to deepen and expand on at GCSE.

With nine topics to revise for three exam papers, the main strategy for supporting pupils with their knowledge recall in order to 'make it stick' was the use of interleaving and learning through discerning the differences and similarities between papers, topics and key questions, including in-depth case studies and located examples.

Through geography curriculum planning for Years 10 and 11, alongside the implementation of the whole-school Year 11 strategy planning, a revision programme is communicated to pupils and parents detailing what retrieval activities are to be completed and when.

Pupils are encouraged to use the successive relearning of key terms, core knowledge and specific case study facts. Geography teachers have established how interleaving can be used, demonstrating this by using the RememberMore app.

I have made recommendations to staff and pupils about where interleaving would be most effective using examples and non-examples. For example, it would not be appropriate for pupils to revise using both the Haiti 2010 earthquake and Japan 2011 earthquake case studies simultaneously due to the high possibility of interference. This might make it difficult for pupils to recall the correct knowledge at a later date, such as confusing the number of deaths, the cost of the damage or the number of people affected. It is also inadvisable for pupils to revise both coastal landscapes and river landscapes together, as the knowledge is similar and, again, they may confuse landforms and management strategies.

Instead, pupils are recommended to interleave physical and human topics – for example, revising tectonic hazards and urbanisation in a megacity, or coastal landscapes and opportunities in a UK city. Pupils interleave when making Cornell Notes or self-quizzing using

RememberMore, thus minimising the potential for retroactive interference.

Pupils reactivate and consolidate the knowledge in their long-term memory via low-stakes testing at the start of lessons. This 'Do now' retrieval activity replicates tasks they may have completed independently at home – in itself a spaced learning approach.

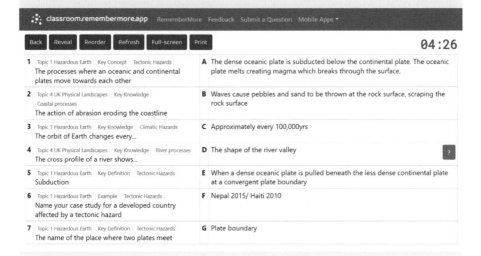

Figure 4.1. Interleaving topics (tagged flashcards) in classroom.remembermore.app

Interleaving is based heavily on the discrimination of differences, so it is important that geography teachers carefully select topics to interleave and pupils are also aware of this when revising geography case studies (as shown in Figure 4.1). I have found this particularly relevant for natural hazard case studies (e.g. tectonic hazards and tropical cyclones), where we need to ensure that pupils do not confuse causes, impacts and responses, and whether the example is in a developed or developing country.

The outcomes

Feedback from pupils has been positive. They appreciate the bespoke deck of cards; that the knowledge in the revision deck aligns with the case studies, subject-specific vocabulary and definitions delivered in class; and that topics can be selected individually or interleaved for quizzing.

Year 11 class analysis demonstrates that pupils are making good progress from their starting points (Year 10 pre-public examinations (PPEs)), which can be attributed in part to using interleaving and access to personalised learning via RememberMore beyond lessons. Other positive outcomes include:

- Low-stakes quiz scores have increased and, as a result, the confidence of pupils has risen.
- Pupils' have improved their application of knowledge to exam questions.
- Pupils have improved their ability to articulate when asked questions in class, such as for the 'Do now' retrieval tasks or through questioning when checking understanding.
- Pupils are developing resilience and independence.

What's next?

We want the strategy of interleaving to become embedded and routine practice for pupils when they are revising. This is a core part of the Year 11 curriculum planning for the spring and summer term. Pupils have had throwback lessons to previous topics in preparation for their internal examinations, to ensure that core knowledge is interleaved and there is discrimination between case studies to avoid interference in knowledge recall.

The next stage is to include identified knowledge gaps and interleave them into a sequence of further throwback sessions across all three papers. The learning will be personalised, giving pupils opportunities to address their knowledge gaps (based on their low-stakes quiz scores and PPE feedback) with relearning opportunities.

My takeaways

- Explicitly teach, plan and use consistent language. (The definitions that appear in RememberMore are also used in 'Do now' retrieval tasks and reflect exam marking schemes.)
- Ensure that the questions set for self-quizzing and 'Do now' retrieval tasks demonstrate interleaving.
- Provide pupils with examples and non-examples of interleaving.
- Model interleaving when delivering intervention/revision sessions.

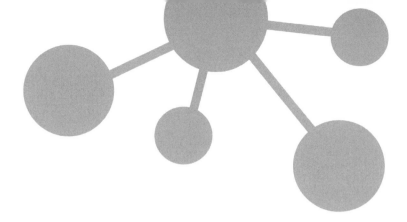

Chapter 5

The importance of feedback, the power of hints and the art of elaboration

Feedback is a goliath of educational pedagogy research. It is a critical component of any learning process because it allows learners to reduce the discrepancy between actual and desired knowledge (Black and Wiliam, 1998). Of course, it is not only learners who benefit; testing insights are equally valuable to teachers. Remember the American psychologist D__ A__, who stated that the most influential factor for learning new things is ____?[1]

Let's not forget that part of test-enhanced learning is the testing practice itself, and there are many books dedicated to the craft of assessment and questioning. However, the fact of the matter is that we cannot discuss the pedagogy of test-enhanced learning (repeated retrieval practice, spacing or interleaving) without stopping off to focus on feedback and the potential gains of elaboration.

---

1 Answer: David Ausubel: 'the most influential factor for learning new things is what the learner already knows' (see p. 7). Desirable difficulty: had you heard of David Ausubel before reading the book? How many times did you review (encode/learn) that information when reading the introduction? What was the spacing between reading the introduction and reading Chapter 5? Did the D and A cue help? Was the cued question easier than the free recall question?

A broad view of feedback

Generally, feedback is reported to make learning more transparent, by addressing knowledge gaps (Son and Kornell, 2008) and enhancing the experience of competence.

A meta-analysis of 435 studies by Wisniewski et al. (2020) revealed a huge variability in the effectiveness of feedback, but also showed a medium positive effect size of feedback (d = 0.48). The authors concluded that feedback was 'a complex and differentiated construct that includes many different forms with, at times, quite different effects on student learning' (Wisniewski et al., 2020).

However, as we touched on briefly in Chapter 2, feedback can also be detrimental to learning. Kluger and DeNisi's (1996) review showed that in 38% of the well-designed studies they analysed, feedback actually made things worse; that is to say that the learners would have done better if they had received no feedback at all.

And we cannot discuss feedback without mentioning the research summaries within the Education Endowment Foundation's Teaching and Learning Toolkit, which continues to rank feedback as second only to metacognition and self-regulation when it comes to boosting learning progress for students:

Feedback is information given to the learner about the learner's performance relative to learning goals or outcomes. It should aim to (and be capable of producing) improvement in students' learning.

Feedback redirects or refocuses the learner's actions to achieve a goal, by aligning effort and activity with an outcome. It can be about the output or outcome of the task, the process of the task, the student's management of their learning or self-regulation, or about them as individuals (which tends to be the least effective).

This feedback can be verbal or written, or can be given through tests or via digital technology. It can come from a teacher or someone taking a teaching role, or from peers.[2]

---

2   See https://educationendowmentfoundation.org.uk/education-evidence/
    teaching-learning-toolkit/feedback.

Feedback and retrieval practice

The first point to address is an issue of metacognitive belief and control (we will discuss these issues further when reviewing metacognition in Chapter 7). Most pupils (90%) use retrieval practice terminally to assess their knowledge at the end of a phase of study – what has been referred to as post-testing; 64% report not revisiting material once they feel they have mastered it; and only 36% report that they restudy or test themselves later on that information (Kornell and Bjork, 2007; Hartwig and Dunlosky, 2012).

Pupils often overlook the benefits of testing (retrieval practice, spacing and interleaving) for encoding and consolidation, despite the powerful learning and metacognitive benefits on offer (Rivers, 2021). Hence, the benefits of feedback from retrieval practice all too often don't even get a look-in before it is too late – the end of the unit or course.

But there is some good news. Hui et al. (2021: 1853) report that individual feedback about retrieval practice performance led to enhanced use of retrieval practice in the long term: 'We found such individual feedback to significantly impact students' retrieval practice decisions in both the short and long term.'

In their study, after receiving feedback on actual learning outcomes following retrieval practice and restudy, 'students who had experienced the testing effect chose retrieval practice more often than those who had not benefited from retrieval practice' (Hui et al., 2021: 1845). The individual feedback may have opened students' eyes to the fact that their actual learning did not match their perceived learning (Dobson and Linderhold, 2015). It would appear that a spoonful of feedback helps the cough syrup go down. These are much like Carpenter's (2017) conclusions.

Securing buy-in for retrieval practice or quizzing is hard enough, as I observed in the introduction. Teachers using RememberMore consistently report that the second term is much more successful than the first, and that only once the pupils have experienced the benefits do they see value in their effortful investment – their future success. Success precedes motivation. That is the fourth signpost to the importance of motivation. But, beware: changing pupils' beliefs is not easy, even in light of the quizzing and assessment evidence. We will explore this more fully in Chapters 7 and 8.

The second point is that there is a need to draw a distinction between supervised and unsupervised conditions, by which I mean retrieval practice for encoding, learning and relearning in the classroom and directed by the teacher, and self-regulated retrieval practice as either preparation for learning or consolidation of learning, mainly though homework or revision.

Third, and finally, where there is feedback, there is emotion. Feedback, metacognitive beliefs, monitoring, control and commitment decisions, and motivation are possibly inseparable.

A complex and differentiated construct

Feedback is equally complex and no less differentiated (Wisniewski et al., 2020) when considered with reference to test-enhanced learning, retrieval practice, spaced retrieval practice and interleaving. Hence, providing feedback after an attempt to retrieve information from memory is critical because it helps to correct memory errors (Pashler et al., 2005) and maintain correct responses (Butler et al., 2008), and in the case of multiple-choice question tests, corrective feedback protects pupils from 'learning' from selecting incorrect answers – that is, from errors.

In Chapter 2, we explored the numerous modulators a teacher must consider (subject or learner characteristics, encoding activities, retrieval format, materials and modality), and there are equally important modulators to consider for feedback itself. Is feedback required only during encoding or the initial learning phase? Or only during the retrieval, consolidation and relearning phase? What type of feedback is required for each format? For each material? Should hints be available? When should feedback be offered? Immediately? After a delay? At the item or question level? Or summatively? Should that feedback be with reference to previous performance? Is how long you study for considered informative feedback? What learning metrics should be considered as feedback? How does feedback work for covert retrieval? I think we should pause there …

Most studies report successful testing effects independently of whether feedback was provided or not. Previously, Rowland (2014) found that corrective feedback doubles the benefits of testing, but Adesope et al. (2017) observed that corrective feedback does not add any additional value. These inconsistent findings have made it 'problematic theoretically as well as confusing' (Yang et al., 2021: 403) for teachers to know when, if at all, to use feedback with retrieval practice.

With a substantially larger dataset (48,478 students' data extracted from 222 independent studies with 573 effects), strictly focusing on classroom research, Yang et al.'s (2021) conclusions were more elucidatory. According to whether corrective feedback was offered or not, the effects were assigned to one of three categories – yes (feedback provided), no (feedback not provided) and unknown (not reported). A total of 262 of the effects provided information on feedback.

Consistent with Rowland (2014), Yang et al. (2021) report that offering corrective feedback following class quizzes significantly increases learning gains as compared to not providing feedback at all, including inducing greater re-exposure and larger learning gains. No significant difference in effectiveness was detected between recall and recognition tests, regardless of whether feedback was provided.

How do we use feedback?

Arguably, the critical mechanism in learning from testing is successful retrieval. Hence, if pupils do not retrieve the correct response and have no recourse to learn it, then the benefits of testing are sometimes limited or absent altogether. Therefore, providing feedback after a retrieval attempt, regardless of whether the attempt is successful or unsuccessful, helps to ensure that retrieval will be successful in the future. Or, to put it another way, feedback helps to make up for a lower level of initial performance.

If we are looking for a summary, Rowland's (2014) meta-analysis demonstrates that the largest testing effect (relative to restudying) is seen when the initial test performance is greater than 75% and no feedback is given. Intermediate benefit is seen when the initial test performance is 51–75%. No reliable advantage appears when the initial test performance is less than 50%.

What you might be surprised to learn is that delaying feedback often produces better retention over time (Mullet et al., 2014). This led to the researchers wittily stating: 'When you take a few extra days to grade student work, feel free to tell them it is for their own good' (Mullet et al., 2014: 228).

Now, I am one of those teachers who will often cite that 'feedback is like sushi, best when it's fresh'. However, the point being made here is that delayed feedback acts as another form of spaced learning. It is important to note that if full processing of the delayed feedback cannot be guaranteed, then giving immediate feedback is probably the better choice. Equally, it appears that correct answer feedback is critical if graded quizzes are unavailable to pupils when they restudy (McDaniel et al., 2021).

The amount of time spent processing the feedback should be given careful consideration. The practical conclusion put forward by Vaughn et al.'s (2017) work is that spending a few extra seconds processing the correct answer seems to be a worthwhile time investment. Where learners fail to retrieve the answer after a few seconds, they should terminate their search and spend more time processing the correct answer. In other words: 'Spinning your wheels while trying to retrieve does about as much good for learning as spinning your wheels when your car is stuck in the mud' (Vaughn et al., 2017: 313). Affirming Dunlosky et al.'s (2013) research, Donoghue and Hattie (2021: 7) stress the important role of feedback: 'It is not the frequency of testing that matters, but the skill in using practice testing to learn and consolidate knowledge and ideas.' These are efficiencies that are hard to ignore, and which we will explore further when reviewing successive relearning (Chapter 6) and the benefits of personalisation (Chapter 8).

According to Helen Webb (SecEd, 2022), there is 'no need to wait for everyone to finish a quiz/activity before answers are shared. Once the majority of the class have completed the test (or have simply lost focus as they can't do the next bit), review answers to keep pace of the lesson.'

Swinging back around to the power of hints

Saying you should test yourself without making it fun is like saying you should eat your spinach without making it taste good.

Vaughn and Kornell (2019: 12)

When you don't know the answer, would a hint help? If we are to increase test-taking, how do we make taking tests more desirable? How do we create a situation where our pupils prefer tests to restudying, and are motivated to quiz and test as learning? The route explored by Vaughn and Kornell (2019) was to allow participants to decide the difficulty of the test trials.

In Experiment 1, participants were able to choose from a pure test trial (idea: __), a two-letter hint (idea: s__r), a four-letter hint (idea: se__er) or a pure study trial (idea: seeker). They also had the option to take tests with hints. Participants opted to test themselves on the majority of the trials.

This preference was reversed in Experiment 2 when the researchers removed the hint options. The most popular hint was the four-letter model (54%). No one selected the zero-letter trial for any of the questions. All retrieval trial type models yielded significantly better recall performance compared to the restudy trial control type.

Experiment 3, meanwhile, demonstrated that hints do not decrease learning outcomes – but only if they are not too easy. When the target is too easy, the hints make testing less effective. For example, without knowing anything about the area of study, you know the answer to: king-q__en. Such a hint could potentially impair learning, it seems.

When offered two options, either restudy or taking a test, Vaughn and Kornell's participants chose the less effective restudying on the majority of trials, but when allowed to request hints during test trials they preferred testing over restudying by a sizeable margin. So, hints encourage self-testing, making self-regulated, self-testing study more enjoyable and effective. But, as we know, desirable difficulties are not always desirable to pupils because they typically, but incorrectly, assume that poor short-term performance is equivalent to poor learning (Bjork et al., 2013; Soderstrom and Bjork, 2015). Importantly, hints do not decrease learning if the target is unguessable, but a lack of hints leads pupils to avoid self-testing altogether. Do you get the hint?

Hints are particularly important when pupils would otherwise fail to answer most of the test questions without them. Hints may be more effective when encoding/learning new material than when relearning, or if the material is difficult (not necessarily complex) or procedural. In this case, reflecting on Vaughn and Kornell (2019), hints make the spinach (the testing) taste good.

Agency is powerful. It is also fickle. The Year 8 class studying *Othello* wanted more personalised learning, and they committed to it. Pupils wanting to quiz, rather than being told to quiz, has two advantages. First, metacognitive beliefs do not always lead to better metacognitive control action. In other words, changing a pupil's beliefs about the benefits of testing does not always change how they choose to study. Pupils often think that testing is good for them. However, Vaughn and Kornell (2019) hypothesise that the reason they choose restudying instead of testing is not because they think testing is bad. Rather, it is because they are trying to avoid failure. So, lower the failure rate (especially during encoding). Even better, show them the preferred answer and let them decide how right they were. Second, as this belief extends to commitment, and that commitment often extends beyond the four walls of the classroom, testing as unsupervised study can only be a good thing.

The interplay of retrieval difficulty, retrieval success and feedback

One final point on item difficulty, successful retrieval and feedback: there are competing forces at play. The conundrum is how to create conditions that increase initial retrieval success without short-circuiting the benefits of initial retrieval effort.

We first introduced the concept of 'desirable difficulties' back in Chapter 2 and the common thread that 'challenging and effortful' learning impedes initial performance but enhances long-term learning (Bjork, 1994; Bjork and Bjork, 2011). This is directly relevant to retrieval practice and the role of feedback. More retrieval effort is helpful, but if the test is so hard that retrieval attempts are often unsuccessful, such increased effort is less beneficial for later memory (at least in the absence of correct answer feedback). It is less beneficial for motivation too. As a teacher, I am not wholly convinced that corrective feedback mitigates for high failure rates, at least not for all learner characteristics or all pupils.

Having said that, easier retrieval is not necessarily more effective. Retrieval practice remains more effective when the learning conditions promote effortful retrieval – reaching the correct answer. However, we then add the human factor: pupils (and teachers) are prone to actively seek strategies that safeguard retrieval success, or at least to avoid strategies that might stimulate retrieval failure. Know that these adjustments are often misguided. Effortful retrieval is a very effective way to learn, relearn and revise.

One important caveat: these retrieval practice recommendations are insensitive to the time costs of feedback, as they often are insensitive to difficulty and an individual pupil's prior knowledge. What if there was no need for feedback? We will come back to estimates of optimal difficulty when we consider personalisation in Chapter 8.

The danger that consistent retrieval failure will undermine pupils' motivation is real and should not be taken lightly, but ideally pupils should learn to accept struggle as part of learning. Instead of worrying about retrieval success, pupils and teachers should embrace errors as a path to knowledge. Feedback will at least get pupils to the correct answer. Teachers may be thinking, 'Yes, in an ideal world. However, we work in an outcome-driven exams system.' Process over outcome, always. Keeping the curriculum narrow, over-practising, employing self-assessment, learning and relearning, and success will feed motivation. And when knowledge surfaces in lessons, notice it, harvest it and celebrate it; claim it to be the fruits of retrieval's labour.

This issue is discussed by Karpicke (2017), who suggests that the benefit of initial tests (without feedback) can only be seen when the learner is reasonably successful on the initial test (see again Rowland's (2014) meta-analysis as mentioned above). Giving feedback on the initial test boosts its effects on later memorability, overcoming issues with poor immediate performance.

And this is not forgetting the metacognitive benefits of feedback: reducing the discrepancy between perceived learning and actual performance, correcting previous errors, relearning correct answers, informing restudy activity and subsequent studying (McDaniel and Little, 2019). In fact, these indirect metacognition benefits could be more significant than the direct retention gains associated with retrieval practice. Hence, pre-testing or potentiation effects is such an intriguing area of research. Lastly, I ask you to reflect on the time costs of feedback and, in light of Nuthall's (2007) research, exactly which pupils are benefiting.

Feedback from potentiation or pre-testing effects

One potential way of offering effective feedback and supporting metacognition is via the use of potentiation or pre-testing: 'Studies have shown that pre-questions – asking students questions before they learn something – benefit memory retention' (Carpenter et al., 2018: 34). They can inform what pupils know and do not know yet, as well as priming that knowledge to be learned and sparking a sense of curiosity.

Even unsuccessful retrieval attempts promote later learning. As peculiar as it sounds, attempting to retrieve a memory enhances subsequent learning even if the attempt is unsuccessful (Kornell et al., 2015).

What we do know is that 'extra time processing the answer after a retrieval attempt is more beneficial than spending more time in retrieval mode' (Vaughn et al., 2017: 313). We also know that feedback can often puncture the general overconfidence of pupils, which we explore in more detail in Chapter 8.

What might this look like in classrooms? Ahead of teaching the content, a quiz on the timeline of events, introducing key vocabulary, naming faces, categorising materials or sharing five key questions that they will be able to (and have to) answer by the end of the lesson. Not only priming or potentiating learning but activating prior knowledge too.

The art of elaborative interrogation

What is elaborative interrogation, and how does it relate to feedback? Right/wrong feedback is straightforward enough: corrective feedback indicates the correct answer and elaborative feedback offers an explanation as to why the answer was correct.

The concept of elaborative interrogation among cognitive psychologists is broad and can mean a lot of different things. However, most definitions in an education context tell us that elaborative interrogation is essentially prompting learners to offer an explanation for an explicitly stated fact (their answer); the teacher asking 'how' and 'why' questions, to you and me.

To elaborate further, asking (and attempting to answer) 'how' and 'why' questions on the correct answer in the feedback can be important for the later application of that knowledge (Butler et al., 2013). This involves supporting the integration of new information with existing prior knowledge, explicitly or implicitly inviting learners to process both the similarities and differences between related concepts, and encouraging the organisation of knowledge or the connecting and integrating of knowledge with new ideas.

Enders et al. (2021: 102) showed that 'elaborate feedback provides an additional and effective learning gain beyond the potential benefits that testing knowledge and corrective feedback produces', with students profiting more from elaborate feedback on incorrect answers than correct answers. As a practical recommendation, the researchers suggest that self-administered formative tests with closed-question formats should at least provide explanations as to why students' answers are incorrect.

Dunlosky et al. (2013), in their review of effective learning techniques, rated elaborative interrogation practice as having moderate utility.

The purpose of elaborative interrogation is primarily to improve our memory of the new information. An additional benefit is that it begins to organise our knowledge in a more coherent way. One further step may be to construct meaning from the subject matter by explaining, elaborating, making inferences, and connecting new facts and ideas to prior knowledge – the food and drink of many an expert practitioner.

In one of the largest and most comprehensive meta-analyses of undergraduate science, technology, engineering and mathematics education, Freeman et al. (2014) report that average examination scores improved by 6% in 'active learning sections' (elaboration) and failure rates reduced from 34% to 22% where elaboration was established practice. Butler et al. (2013) state that elaborating on the correct answer in the feedback can be important for the later application of that knowledge.

Finally, not all elaborative techniques are equal. Elaborative interrogation tends to increase performance when it helps to specify the relevance of target information. In this situation, retrieval practice that is 'cued' or 'tagged' in some way immediately highlights knowledge as interconnected. These interconnections then provide excellent openings for teachers to probe and interrogate.

Giving pupils the opportunity to elaborate encourages them to infer missing information, synthesise the presented information and process their thinking. We know that learners who are encouraged to self-explain experienced 'improved the accuracy' in their reading and improved relative meta-comprehension accuracy (Griffin et al., 2008: 93).

In fact, RememberMore has a space dedicated to further information or elaboration, with 'Notes' adding a pop-up opportunity on flashcards to share, probe or prompt, or simply ask 'how' and 'why' questions.

Takeaways

- Feedback as a part of test-enhanced learning is far from simple.

- Feedback makes learning more transparent by addressing knowledge gaps and enhancing the experience of competence.

- Where there is feedback, there is emotion. Feedback, item difficulty and motivation are interconnected and inseparable.

- Feedback protects against pupils learning incorrect knowledge or multiple-choice distractors. At the very least, provide explanations as to why answers are incorrect.

- Feedback punctures general overconfidence (see Chapter 8).

- Feedback timing is an interesting area of research; delayed feedback has its advantages.

- Hints make testing more attractive and do not decrease learning outcomes.

- A successful retrieval presents a fertile opportunity for elaborative interrogation.

- Studying correct answers matters more than spending more time in retrieval mode.

- Over-practising and employing self-assessment success will feed motivation.

- Potentiation informs pupils of what they know and need to learn as well as sparking a sense of curiosity.

- 'How' and 'why' questions following a correct answer promote the later application of that knowledge.

- If you only have time to read one paper on this topic: A. C. Butler, J. D. Karpicke and H. L. Roediger III, Correcting a metacognitive error: feedback increases retention of low-confidence correct responses. *Journal of Experimental Psychology: Learning, Memory, and Cognition*, 34(4) (2008): 918-928.

- And if you're lucky enough to have the time to read two papers, then consider: L. Hui, A. B. H. de Bruin, J. Donkers and J. J. G. van Merriënboer, Does individual performance feedback increase the use of retrieval practice? *Educational Psychology Review*, 33 (2021): 1835-1857.

Case study: Feedback for both teachers and pupils

Andy Sammons is head of English at a large comprehensive school in Wakefield. His school generally performs above the national average and has a solid core of consistent practitioners. Since leading the English team, Andy has overseen a steady improvement in the quality of the English curriculum in terms of the relevance for pupils as well as the academic rigour with which they approach the subject. Andy is clear on his reasons for adopting retrieval practice.

My interest in retrieval practice is, above all, one that is linked to social mobility; English is a subject that lends itself to discussion, flair and originality, but I do think it needs to take the opportunity to ground itself in the fundamentals in terms of declarative knowledge: what the pupils know and remember. Flair and originality are not stand-alone pursuits: they must be rooted in accurate and incisive understanding of the content being studied.

The challenge

Given the size of our year groups – and, indeed, the size of the department – home learning is not something that has been an area of strength for us. As the vast majority of educators reading this will appreciate, homework completion is problematic, often raising more questions than answers, such as:

- Which pupils will actually complete it?
- How can we ensure consistency of quality?
- Will all pupils benefit in equal amounts?
- Does each pupil have an equal opportunity in terms of space and time to complete it?
- Will it serve only to isolate and give another reason for some pupils to push back against the subject?

My understanding – from trusted colleagues via social media and personal experience – is that the effect size of home learning is somewhat questionable. Setting homework relevant to the content being covered in lessons makes homework substantially more impactful.

Considering the amount of detailed knowledge that pupils must be able to access and recall, it is important that we operate firmly with a 'high challenge, low threat' mentality; RememberMore offered us a key pathway for this. For me, the most attractive element of RememberMore was the fact that it provided us with the opportunity to take true ownership over the content that we wanted the pupils to learn, enabling them to direct feedback on the content of the texts that we determined to be the essential knowledge.

Don't get me wrong, software packages and external products have their place, but I was extremely excited by the prospect of codifying the core knowledge that we wanted the pupils to successively relearn.

The solution

I made the decision to use RememberMore within the department in Years 10 and 11 in order to promote knowledge acquisition and recall. Home learning would be 30 minutes on the RememberMore app per week, supplemented by daily use from a pool of questions (sometimes targeted and notifying pupils in advance, sometimes not). This would allow us to respond to a number of the traditional problematic questions listed above.

The plan

Above all, this was a plan that had feedback at its heart. We wanted gentle and supportive feedback which would enable the pupils to understand how successful they were becoming at retaining information in their long-term memory. However, we also wanted feedback for our teachers in order for us to understand how confident the pupils were feeling as they moved towards their exams.

As a leader of English, in particular, I feel that it is disingenuous to expect pupils to revise without clearly articulating how they can be successful in improving their knowledge and understanding. As a department, we designed questions linked to the texts that we study within the following frameworks: plot and structure, characters, key quotes, and context and symbolism.

Each week, staff would be encouraged, rather than compelled, to use RememberMore to begin lessons, but we would instruct pupils to use the app beyond the lessons and then sanction for those not completing 30 minutes of recall. We would then triangulate the minutes used against outcomes achieved in our externally marked mock exams. The key was that, in one sense, pupils were generating their own feedback and continually reflecting on what they did and did not know, but not in a way that they felt overly negative about for not knowing because the cards were cropping up more regularly when they felt less confident in them.

RememberMore directs attention and promotes retrieval in two main ways:

1 To target specific aspects of knowledge in anticipation of a lesson. An example of this would be to relay to a class that we would be covering Stave 2 of *A Christmas Carol* the following week, and therefore they would be expected to have spent a minimum of 15 minutes quizzing on this aspect of the text. When the time came, we were able to ask the pupils not only to answer the questions but also to predict how many out of 10 they would score. Both the scores and the predictions were of interest because they provided a very tangible platform to connect preparation and performance.

2 To use the dashboard in order to understand pupil confidence regarding particular aspects of texts, as well as the effectiveness of our own teaching. We have an interleaved curriculum, and therefore when we revisit different texts, we are able to deliberately reteach areas where pupils were lacking in confidence.

A combination of the above enabled us – with varying degrees of success – to build a culture of recall and accountability within classes. Undoubtedly, this was because we used RememberMore initially in order to clearly articulate the knowledge of the texts that we wanted the pupils to retain in their long-term memory.

The outcomes

The results were remarkable, particularly for those of middle to lower prior attainment. Having fed back and discussed with colleagues, we were able to deduce the following: consistent app usage correlated with approximately an entire grade increase, and the correlation between app usage and grade improvement grew considerably stronger when also used in lessons. In both cases, this correlation strengthened for pupils that were in receipt of pupil premium funding.

When it comes to educational outcomes, there is an age-old assertion that those pupils who are most compliant are those who are most likely to achieve positively, irrespective of the intervention. For this reason, the results of our study are perhaps most interesting when we compare classes of pupils with similar ability. While usage of the app was similar in terms of home learning, where classroom. remembermore.app was consistently used in class the effect was approximately 0.7 of a grade per pupil.

I acknowledge that there can be no magic bullet, and certainly there is no substitution for hard work (and nor should there be). All we can hope for are reliable indices of success, and RememberMore gave us that. This is a strength because – at the risk of becoming overly philosophical – life is not just about getting it right. Life is about the mistakes, the learning and the reflection. When a pupil scored poorly in their short quizzes, the discussion could still be supportive and nurturing. When a teacher's class scored poorly in a quiz, their reflection could be private or public – whatever they felt they needed to drive the learning. When a question caused significant issues for pupils, the learning for us could be about question design or teaching.

After-action review

Although it is difficult to prove the effect size of interventions in the classroom unequivocally, the results of our study are consistent enough to have confidence that the use of RememberMore as a home learning tool was a successful initiative. Learning is messy – unavoidably and deliciously so! RememberMore's beautiful simplicity allowed us to shine a light on some of the connections, gave us a sense of understanding about how effective we were and, more importantly, gave the pupils an insight into the connection between hard work, strategy and outcomes – not least, feedback on what they knew and could remember.

We have also learned that we need to ensure that classroom teachers are using the same content more consistently in order to help pupils understand the gains they are making. I stand by my feedback to Kristian Still and the RememberMore team: 'Simplicity and speed remains key. Having access to the insights from RememberMore, having eyes on the pupils' commitment via the insights and having the ability to reward pupils ahead of deadlines was a positive. I'm sending texts each Friday saying "Amazing work – get your 30 mins in before Monday."'

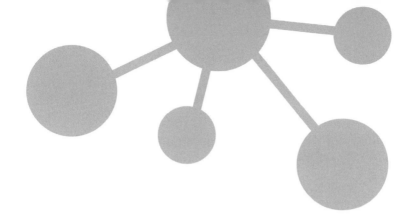

Chapter 6

Successive relearning

Practice tests and spaced study are both highly potent for enhancing learning and memory. Combining these two methods under the conditions in which they are most effective (i.e., practice tests that invoke successful retrieval from long-term memory and spacing study across days) yields a promising learning technique referred to as successive relearning.

Rawson et al. (2013: 523)

When you want to learn something that's going to remain with you, that you can retain for the long term, you know one exposure ... one encounter with the information is probably going to be insufficient.

Dr John Dunlosky (TES, 2021)

Like most educators, I first encountered post-testing retrieval practice, then moved on to spacing and interleaving, before my investigations led me to the work of Dr Katherine Rawson and successive relearning – specifically Rawson et al. (2013). It took a little longer to find because the search phrase 'retrieval practice' does not appear in the paper's title, abstract or key words.

Conducted in an 'authentic educational context', psychology college students learned 64 course concepts using a computerised flashcard computer program under the following three conditions:

1 Successive relearning: students engaged in retrieval practice spaced throughout the semester and they had to retrieve information correctly three times.

2 Spaced restudy: students engaged in restudying spaced throughout the semester (without retrieval) – arguably the most common approach.

3 Baseline: students engaged in 'business as usual' without using the flashcard program.

In two experiments, the successive relearning condition increased students' course exam performance by a letter grade (from C to B) compared to the baseline conditions. This was consistent for both higher- and lower-performing students.

The terminology was familiar (retrieval, spacing) and the modality of retrieval practice was familiar (flashcards), and I was a teacher who simply wanted that same learning benefit for my own pupils, as I am sure you do too. What I would later recognise was that this paper introduced a number of important pedagogical conditions or considerations:

- At what point something is considered learned or mastered.

- The huge potential of successive relearning, as the authors termed it, and the notion of relearning.

- The role of self-regulation (or, more to the point, the potential pitfalls of pupils' self-regulation – see Chapter 7).

- The notion of low- and high-fidelity conditions – classrooms or laboratories.

- The potential contribution of metacognitive monitoring to retention.

Rawson et al. (2013) was the third paper in a series focused on combining the two high-utility techniques of practice testing and spacing. Outcomes from the previous two papers (Rawson and Dunlosky, 2011, and Rawson and Dunlosky, 2012) were encouraging. In both studies, undergraduates who successively relearned key concept definitions showed relatively high levels of retention on cued recall tests administered one and four months after relearning (up to 68% and 49%, respectively, depending on the schedule of relearning, as compared with around 11% in the baseline control condition).

Here, we have a series of papers that discuss how we might achieve a level of mastery learning over multiple spaced retrieval sessions – much like Ebbinghaus (1885) reported more than 135 years ago when he discussed memory decay and introduced his 'forgetting curve'. Successive relearning seemed to be a particularly promising technique under both supervised and unsupervised conditions, and Rawson (2014), a compelling public speaker, reminds us that, 'If at first you do succeed, try, try again.'

At this point, I had not connected Rawson's findings with Graham Nuthall's now infamous work, *The Hidden Lives of Learners* (2007: 155): 'Learning is rarely a one-shot affair. Single, isolated experiences seldom give birth to learning. What creates or shapes learning is a sequence of events or experiences, each building on the effects of the previous one.'

How is successive relearning different from spaced retrieval practice?

Successive relearning involves alternating retrieval practice with restudy opportunities during initial learning until each item is recalled correctly, followed by additional retrieval practice with restudy on one or more subsequent days until each item is again successfully recalled. Thus, successive relearning involves precisely those conditions in which testing and spacing are most effective.

Rawson et al. (2013: 524)

[Successive relearning involves] repeated retrieval practice of the same information (with feedback) over multiple, spaced sessions.

Higham et al. (2021: 928)

Track back through the successive relearning research literature and all paths lead to the work of Harry Bahrick – in particular, his work on successive relearning (Bahrick, 1979). This describes multiple successful retrievals that are distributed across sessions, alternating between retrieval and study attempts until a certain level of retrieval success has been met (e.g. a criterion of one successful retrieval), and then relearning that material (by again alternating between retrieval and study) to a certain level of retrieval success in subsequent sessions.

Nearly 30 years later, Cepeda et al. (2006: 370) commented: 'If the field of learning and memory is to inform educational practice, what is evidently needed is much less emphasis on convenient single-session studies.' (I couldn't help but sense that this successive relearning approach would add to our pupils' sense of achievement, in much the same way that the Anki sessions had when learning context and plotline knowledge about *Othello*.) To summarise Rawson's (2014) McMaster University symposium presentation, 'Just one relearning session triples your long-term retention.'

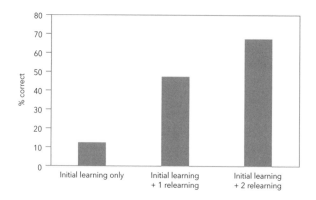

Figure 6.1. A simple example of the power of relearning (Rawson, 2014)

The paper on which the data informing Figure 6.1 is based was published two years later (Vaughn et al., 2016). The advice is as simple as it is plain to see: that 'using extra time to learn to a higher initial learning criterion is not efficient. Instead, students should devote their time to subsequent spaced relearning sessions, which produce substantial gains in recall performance' (Vaughn et al., 2016: 897). The potency is not in the learning but in the successive relearning; that although failed retrieval may show modest memorial benefits, multiple successful retrievals distributed across time is 'particularly efficacious for enhancing long-term retention' (Pyc and Rawson 2012: 976).

Successive relearning, therefore, combines repeated retrieval practice testing to success and spacing (Chapters 2 and 3) and feedback (Chapter 5), and could leverage the benefits of interleaving (Chapter 4) 'under conditions in which they are particularly effective' (Rawson et al., 2013: 540) – a finding that is perhaps understandable when you note that the second author of the three papers is Dunlosky.

To date, given the voluminous literature, only a handful of published studies have investigated the effects of successive relearning on long-term retention (Bahrick, 1979; Bahrick et al., 1993; Bahrick and Hall, 2005; Rawson and Dunlosky, 2011, 2012; Dunlosky et al., 2013; Rawson et al., 2013, 2018; Vaughn et al., 2016; Janes et al., 2020; Higham et al., 2021). For the most part, all involve verbal learning tasks and employ the same basic materials, modalities and methodology. Given this observation, it is very easy to conceive how this might look in a classroom.

Famous last words: research on successive relearning in authentic classroom contexts is limited; but, not to be deterred, laboratory studies demonstrate powerful, long-lasting and durable learning. And, yet, 'few students use this approach to obtain and maintain knowledge in formal educational settings' (Rawson and Dunlosky, 2022: 362).

To illustrate the potential of successive relearning, consider one noteworthy study: Bahrick et al. (1993). Over the course of nine years, the researchers investigated the retention of 300 foreign language translations across several conditions, exploring different combinations of relearning sessions and spacing. Each relearning session began with a paired-associate translation test – again, think flashcards. Participants were presented with one half of each pair and they had to respond with the matching half.

When an item (often single words) had been correctly retrieved, the card was dropped from practice for that session. When an item had been incorrectly retrieved, they reviewed the item on the back of the card and set it aside for another test trial later in that session. A relearning session was complete when each of the translations had been correctly retrieved. Final retention tests were administered one, two, three or five years following the last relearning session. Considering the length of these delays, levels of final retention were impressive. In one condition, in which relearning sessions were spaced at a 56-day interval, more than 75% of the items were recalled after a one-year delay and more than 60% of them were still retained after a five-year delay.

Other investigations of successive relearning have yielded similarly impressive and 'sizeable advantages' (Rawson et al., 2020: 853) over single-session learning (Bahrick et al., 1993; Vaughn et al., 2016; Rawson et al., 2018; Janes et al., 2020; Latimier et al., 2021; Yang et al., 2021). What's more, we know that there are strong intercorrelations among recall, tests to criterion and final-test performance – a case for efficient learning as a construct. In fact, learning efficiency scores from one day to the next are highly consistent over three years (Zerr et al., 2018).

Without question, it is the durability of successive relearning that will be of particular interest to teachers, especially those leading external examinations. This is even more impressive now we know that most retrieval practice research favours 'near learning', where tests are taken relatively soon after the intervention.

The more I read around the research, the more successive relearning felt aligned with the ebb and flow of traditional classrooms and traditional curriculums, and the more I was convinced that repeated and successive relearning were critical components. Indeed, Rawson and Dunlosky (2022) continue to try and shift research agendas away from single-session, fixed-time studies to multiple practice sessions where time is treated as an outcome variable of interest. Why is this important? In doing so, they aim to 'align the outcomes of cognitive-education research with real-world learning objectives' (Rawson and Dunlosky, 2022: 362) – that is, ensure research aligns more closely with classroom teaching.

How much successive relearning is enough?

Let's turn to Rawson and Dunlosky (2011). Across three experiments, 533 students learned conceptual material via retrieval practice with restudy. The items to be remembered were practised until they could be correctly recalled by the students between one and four times during an initial learning session. They were then practised until the students could correctly recall them across one to five subsequent relearning sessions. This was some study: across the experiments, more than 100,000 short-answer recall responses were collected and hand-scored. A consistent qualitative pattern emerged.

The authors found that the effects of the initial learning were strong prior to relearning but then diminished as relearning increased. It meant that 'relearning had pronounced effects on long-term retention but with a relatively minimal cost in terms of the additional practice trials required' (Rawson and Dunlosky, 2011: 283). On the basis of the overall patterns of durability and efficiency, the authors' 'prescriptive conclusion' (their words) is for students to practise recalling concepts in the initial learning session to three correct recalls and then to relearn them three times at widely spaced intervals.

Rawson et al. (2018) later reported that this relearning potency is much more than just a 'dosage effect'. Correctly recalling items one time in three sessions versus three times in one session yielded a 262% increase in retention test performance. (Just pause there for that research finding to sink in.) Again, the potency is in the relearning.

Successive relearning is super-efficient

Absolute levels of retention achieved by successive relearning range from 75% to 91% over intervals of two to seven days and 60% to 76% over intervals of three to four weeks (Rawson et al., 2018). Our decision as educators, then, is to decide whether that success rate is high enough. If not, fortunately, the rapid reacquisition or relearning that has been demonstrated (Vaughn et al., 2016; Rawson et al., 2018) provides some assurance that knowledge can be quickly and efficiently relearned or reactivated and maintained.

Previously, Vaughn et al. (2016) had demonstrated that successive relearning is extremely efficient, with just seven minutes being required to relearn 70 pre-learned word pairs. Rawson et al. (2018) reported 'pronounced effects' and 'minimal cost'. This is absolutely the case when teaching with classroom. remembermore.app. Relearning or activating prior knowledge takes barely minutes when relearning routines are secured.

For example, if revisiting is deployed, 15 plotline questions from the previous act, or Elizabethan English translations, or term-definition pairs, or chemical equations can be easily relearned in less than two minutes. If relearned covertly, reduce that to 30 seconds. It is all about selecting the right questions, the right breadth of questions and the right success rate. There is a lot to be gained from asking the same questions more than once! Or three times at widely spaced intervals.

This area of research - what we might refer to as the efficiencies of learning - has been explored by Yan et al. (2020) and Eglington and Pavlik (2020). They have found that:

- Easier items (or questions) are recalled faster, permitting for more trials (or questions), if perhaps providing less learning per question than when challenged.
- More practice leads to faster responding, which leads to even more trials.
- Harder items may provide more learning but take longer (especially if the pupil fails to remember), permitting fewer trials.
- Harder items are more likely to be answered incorrectly, which is frequently more time-consuming due to reviewing corrective feedback, permitting fewer trials.

Eglington and Pavlik's (2020: 1) conclusions highlight three key points. First, the optimal difficulty or desirable difficulty is less than typically thought: success rates of 80% led to '40% more items recalled' than the next best conventional schedule. Second, the optimal difficulty likely varies according to the type of content and how feedback is implemented. Third, existing recommendations, insensitive to the time costs of feedback, content difficulty and an individual pupil's prior knowledge are, at best, 'inherently suboptimal' or, at worst, flawed. Simply put, the learning gains and costs for correct and incorrect trials can be quite different, and quite time costly. Thus, content difficulty for each individual pupil is highly relevant to optimising practice scheduling, even more so when time is limited. As de Jonge (2014: 145) observes, 'when time to learn is limited, it matters a great deal how one puts to use the available amount of time'.

When I was in conversation with Dr Luke Eglington, he quipped, 'Students have limited time to study, and thus the total time cost is a vital consideration. In fact, we found that practising efficiently had an even larger effect on memory than spacing usually does!'[1]

The benefits of successive relearning cannot be overlooked by teachers. However, they also need to consider the differing status of retrievable and non-retrievable knowledge – factors such as item difficulty, complexity and the relative time expense of feedback.

What might that mean for teaching?

Now you are armed with knowledge of human cognitive architecture, retrieval practice, spacing and feedback, I hope successive relearning makes sense and is far more attractive than perhaps you first thought. It closely resembles authentic classroom cycles of teaching, learning and relearning, and offers a practice approach to using spaced retrieval practice as learning for maintenance, relearning and revision.

As teachers, we need to be conscious of revisiting taught knowledge within a lesson, across a sequence of lessons, within and across subjects, and even across academic years. We need to be deliberate in how we access knowledge stored in long-term memory and not forget the potential of self-directed opportunities outside of class. Meanwhile, Rawson and Dunlosky (2022: 362) call on researchers to 'shift research agendas away from single-session

---

1   L. Eglington, interview with author (May 2022).

studies in which time on task is fixed toward studies involving multiple practice sessions in which time on task is tailored for students and is treated as an outcome variable of interest'.

Perhaps as important as mnemonic benefits (i.e. more accessible, durable and recallable knowledge, potentially lowering cognitive load), Higham et al. (2021: 928) found that successive relearning was associated with improved metacognition, increased self-reported sense of mastery, increased attentional control and reduced anxiety. Crucially, Higham's participants found successive relearning to be both 'enjoyable' and 'valuable'. These wider benefits of test-enhanced learning are explored further in Chapter 7.

Lastly, let's not overlook that Rawson et al. (2013) reported that these gains were attained in both supervised and unsupervised conditions, the inference being that successive relearning could also be implemented outside the classroom without sacrificing class time. In fact, Dunlosky and O'Brien (2022: 234) reviewed the implementation of successive relearning using flashcard programs and concluded that it 'shows promise for helping students master a broad variety of content, from simple associates to complex definitions'. Vaughn et al. (2021) found that low-cost self-testing websites garnered widespread use among college students and that this was associated with increased exam performance. And, where pupils are unsupervised, which they increasingly are as they progress in their academic careers, what additional benefits might be achieved if spaced retrieval practice is personalised? (We review personalisation in Chapter 8.)

Here is a timely relearning reminder for teachers: 'One shot, one encounter with a set of materials isn't likely to promote long-term retention, so we know in order to retain something well it's probably the case that we need to re-encounter, revisit, review the information again and again' (Kang, 2016b).

Takeaways

- Successive relearning combines retrieval practice and spaced practice – that is, repeated retrieval practice of the same information (with feedback) over multiple spaced sessions.

- When encoding, we should repeatedly expose learners to retrieval or to an initial learning criterion. Reordering cues offers minimal additional difficulty.

- Don't forget the importance of feedback (although it has an expensive time cost) after retrieval attempts (see Chapter 5).

- Extra time learning to a higher initial learning criterion is not efficient. Three successful recalls is more than enough.

- Relearning is potent, durable and efficient. Relearning is an excellent lesson task to activate prior knowledge or homework task to consolidate knowledge (and not just lesson starter tasks).

- Successive relearning research is shifting research agendas away from single-session, fixed-time studies to multiple practice sessions where time is treated as an outcome variable of interest.

- When maintaining, consolidating or relearning, ensure learners have had time to forget what was initially taught.

- Learners should experience multiple relearning opportunities and repeat or revisit the knowledge. We can do this by reordering or refreshing the cues/flashcards (depending on success rates).

- Ensure that retrieval is successful – or, at least, that there are low failure rates (as low as 10-20%).

- Encourage learners to elaborate on or connect their thinking with what they already know.

- Test for and as learning – commonly known as low stakes. Results may or may not be recorded.

- Relearning is equally effective in supervised (classroom) and unsupervised (homework and independent study) conditions.

- Use self-assessment to leverage the benefits of metacognitive monitoring (see Chapter 7).

- If you only have time to read one paper on this topic: P. A. Higham, B. Zengel, L. K. Bartlett and J. A. Hadwin, The benefits of successive relearning on multiple learning outcomes. *Journal of Educational Psychology*, 114(5) (2021): 928-944.

- If you are lucky enough to have the time to read two papers, then the Rawson et al. (2013) study completely redirected my thinking when it came to retrieval practice: K. A. Rawson, J. Dunlosky and S. M. Sciartelli, The power of successive relearning: improving performance on course exams and long-term retention. *Educational Psychology Review*, 25(4) (2013): 523-548.

Case study: Tackling an increasing weight of knowledge

Kristian Shanks was formerly a curriculum leader for history in a North Yorkshire comprehensive. He has recently been promoted to the role of assistant head teacher for teaching and learning at a large secondary school. The backdrop to his interest in test-enhanced learning was the need to ensure that pupils could remember more of the curriculum content. Historically, pupils had performed at an extremely low level - nearly 1.5 grades below the expected level of attainment per pupil of schools in the top-performing 20% (according to Fischer Family Trust rankings). It was clear that there were significant gaps in learners' knowledge.

The challenge

The challenge of improving students' curriculum content knowledge was further compounded by the nature of the GCSE specification. The amount of content students need to know is vast. They study five separate topics and sit three exams over a grand total of over four hours. The exams feature a large number of compulsory questions, which assess a narrow sample of the content compared to what they are required to know. As a result, one of the biggest challenges faced by history teachers is to ensure that students are prepared for the various possible permutations of content that may be assessed in any given exam.

Specific topics present additional challenges. When learning the American West, for example, students have very limited prior knowledge to bring to bear (sadly, young people are far less likely to watch Western movies than they used to be!), meaning their schema is rather limited and making the knowledge less sticky. With the Weimar and Nazi Germany topic, a significant amount of political knowledge is required in the first section of the course (for example, around what a constitution is or the difference between left and right wing), which for many students can be quite intimidating. This is particularly the case for middle- and lower-attaining students – key groups who were struggling to cope with the vast quantity of content to learn. To illustrate the difficulty posed by this GCSE course, approximately only 40% of the marks are required to achieve a Grade 4 pass.

Part of the solution

I was familiar with the promise offered by retrieval practice from previous schools, but John Dunlosky's paper 'Strengthening the student toolbox' referenced the power of continued testing 'until they correctly recall each concept once from memory', as well as the importance of ' "get[ting] it right" on more than one occasion' (Dunlosky, 2013: 14) – in other words, successive relearning. The concept was developed further by Katherine Rawson, in collaboration with Dunlosky, in their study 'The power of successive relearning' (Rawson et al., 2013), which identified disproportionately greater benefits of this approach, where students needed to correctly recall the information three times over spaced intervals, as compared to other strategies. This seemed an ideal strategy to help us tackle our problem.

The plan

It was clear that we had to rethink our approach to teaching this history course. We needed to ensure that we homed in on the most challenging knowledge for students to know and remember, and that we reinforced remembering this knowledge on multiple occasions and in multiple ways. These included:

- Regular free recall quizzes at the start of lessons that targeted this tricky knowledge.

- The use of timeline activities in order to identify the key pivot points within a time period, so students could see how different events linked together.

- Multiple-choice homework quizzes via Google Classroom, introduced when the COVID-19 lockdowns required us to move towards significant online delivery.

■ Willingness to give over entire lessons, or significant chunks of lessons, to retrieval practice from time to time, to ensure that it was not seen as something merely for the start of a lesson.

From 2021, this was supplemented by the addition of RememberMore flashcards, which I had some input in designing. This has enabled more precise and systematic targeting of specific content using the tagged cards or questions and answers. This has been helpful when teaching the aforementioned American West topic. This unit is tagged into three chronological periods, with certain themes recurring across each period (for example, conflict between the US government and the Plains Indians). Being able to precisely target and revisit knowledge from the previous two time periods in a way that supports learning of the third period was very helpful.

For example, knowledge of the Second Fort Laramie Treaty (1868) is extremely important to support learning of the Black Hills War and the Battle of the Little Bighorn in 1876. Therefore, it has been helpful to reinforce this through retrieval activities via RememberMore where students are required to recall this information multiple times. In addition, giving students access to the app has enabled them to regularly reinforce the key concepts and knowledge needed for success in this and other units.

The outcomes

We have found that a larger number of students are able to deploy more knowledge on exam questions on this topic. The 2018 GCSE results indicated that the American West was our weakest topic; we are now seeing low-attaining learners able to attempt more of the questions rather than leaving swathes of the paper blank in their mocks. In 2022, I expect that performance in this topic will be at least comparable to other topics within a trend of general improvement.

For most students, this has been a slow-burn process over a period of time. In history, the nature of the subject and the volume of the content dictates that it takes a while to master. I don't think you should go in, at least in my subject, and expect miracle results in a short space of time. However, for some individual students the results were undoubtedly more rapid, and the boost to their confidence of being able to recall knowledge more effectively was considerable.

What's next?

Moving forward, I would like to ensure that our approach is more systematic - for example, building our homework programme around this approach - and that we do more work to burrow down further into our content to establish more of a hierarchy of knowledge. I think that distinguishing between the core foundational knowledge and the more peripheral - yet still important - knowledge might help us to go further in ensuring our lower-attaining students can navigate the vast scale of initially unfamiliar content they encounter in GCSE history.

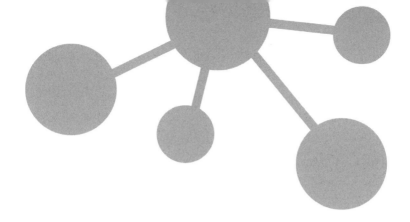

Chapter 7

Metacognition and testing

Those students who corrected their own tests improved dramatically.

Sadler (2006: 1)

The best person to mark a test is the person who just took it.

Wiliam (2018)

As we have discovered throughout this book, a clear and present danger with test-enhanced learning is that it seems harder to the pupils than massed or blocked practice, and so is often rejected as a learning strategy. This is why a consideration of metacognition is a crucial ingredient.

Metacognition refers to learners' understanding and regulation (and self-regulation) of their own learning process, including their beliefs and perceptions about learning, their monitoring of the state of their knowledge and controlling their learning activities (Dunlosky and Metcalfe, 2009).

Again, we look to the Education Endowment Foundation's Teaching and Learning Toolkit,[1] where metacognition – the most searched term on their website (Mould, 2022) – is presented as the interplay of knowledge of task, knowledge of strategies, knowledge of self and regulation of planning, monitoring and evaluation. Pupils' metacognition about what recency, processing fluency and familiarity signals about learning quality – their a priori

---

1 See https://educationendowmentfoundation.org.uk/education-evidence/
teaching-learning-toolkit/metacognition-and-self-regulation.

beliefs about which study methods are most effective – influences their willingness to implement them. What's more, their appreciation of how to apply these strategies influences whether their study strategy and schedules produce conditions that maximise learning (Bjork et al., 2013).

Metacognition, regulation and self-regulation approaches that encourage pupils to think about their own learning (often by teaching them specific strategies for planning, monitoring and evaluating their learning) have consistently high levels of impact. That seems like a very reasonable place to start. Of course, explaining metacognition to pupils is not easy. It has often been described as like fish trying to understand water.

Understanding metacognition and testing

Broadly speaking, metacognition consists of three primary components: beliefs (including knowledge and perceptions), monitoring and control (Flavell, 1979; Bjork et al., 2013; Rivers, 2021).

- Beliefs: why do some learners correctly endorse the effectiveness of retrieval practice, spacing and interleaving for learning whereas others do not?

- Monitoring: knowing how to assess and manage your own learning and react accordingly.

- Control: decisions about when, why and how to study.

According to Bjork and Bjork (2020: 476):

The fact that conditions of learning that make performance improve rapidly often fail to support long-term retention and transfer, whereas conditions that create challenges (i.e. difficulties) and slow the rate of apparent learning often optimize long-term retention and transfer, means that learners – and teachers – are vulnerable to mis-assessing whether learning has or has not occurred.

More simply, as cognitive psychologist Pooja Agarwal (2022) suggests: 'Easy learning is easy forgetting. Challenging learning strengthens our remembering, our learning, our memories.' Our role as teachers is to ensure that our pupils know and believe this (even if some of the newest research exploring learning efficiencies or optimisation is challenging this well-established view).

A learner's beliefs about effort and their subjective experiences of difficulty during encoding and retrieval influence their evaluation of the effectiveness of the methods and, as a result, their metacognitive and self-regulatory decisions. Most often, they seek strategies that over-value recency, familiarity and fluency and undervalue testing and self-testing.

As we have already highlighted in this book, the learning benefits of test-enhanced learning, retrieval practice, spacing and interleaving are all too often ignored by pupils when selecting study activities (Karpicke, 2009; Rivers, 2021). We know that learners have a 'tendency to conflate short-term performance with long-term learning when, in fact, there is overwhelming evidence that learning and performance are dissociable' (Soderstrom and Bjork, 2015: 182).

As we saw in Chapter 5 on feedback, while 90% of pupils reported using self-testing, most of them did so in order to identify gaps in their knowledge rather than because they believed that pre-testing, post-testing and self-testing conferred a direct learning benefit. Moreover, 64% of pupils reported not revisiting material once they felt they had mastered it, while only 36% of pupils reported that they would restudy or test themselves later on that information (Kornell and Bjork, 2007; Hartwig and Dunlosky, 2012). Think back to Dr Katherine Rawson's research and consider how misleading that notion is – and how little extra effort would be required to triple retention.

Let's meet Mariah

To help illustrate the three components of metacognition, let's consider Mariah, a Year 11 pupil preparing for end-of-term assessments in two of her classes. She has not been using spaced retrieval practice, successive relearning or interleaving as part of her learning. Almost impossibly, Mariah scored 60/100 on her end-of-Year 10 assessments and, as unbelievable as it sounds, the assessments were of the exact same difficulty. I know I am pushing it, but Mariah enjoys her subjects equally and invests her time and effort commensurately.

For science, she decides to prepare by rereading her textbook. For geography, she decides to create her own flashcards and quiz herself (a form of practice testing). She even adopts the Leitner system,[2] which she has seen on social media.

As Mariah approaches her assessments she feels like she is learning more of the material for science than for geography, which leads her to believe that rereading is the more effective strategy. Informed by her ongoing monitoring and beliefs, she decides to adopt rereading as her primary learning strategy for both science and geography. In contrast to her (misguided and misinformed) belief about which strategy would be more effective, she performs comparably better in geography than science. Will she revert back to using flashcards for her final exam revision? Keep an eye out for some shocking findings from Karpicke et al. (2009).

Judgements of learning (monitoring and beliefs)

Metacognitive monitoring concerns learners' ability to assess the progress of their learning. The accuracy of their metacognitive monitoring influences study choices and, consequently, how well information is learned and retained.

Learners like Mariah misinterpret momentary accessibility of knowledge as a marker of long-term storage strength. Swayed by illusions of recency, familiarity and fluency (Bjork et al., 2013; Kirk-Johnson et al., 2019), pupils prefer massed and blocked practice and restudy. Moreover, these beliefs and feelings can be difficult to overcome with pupils 'insensitive to their own performance' (Yan et al., 2016: 932), even when presented with contrary results and despite fairly extensive debasing attempts. Thus, identifying and understanding the conditions that promote accurate metacognition is critical for promoting efficient and effective learning.

Of course, spaced learning is inherently metacognitive. When I first began reading test-enhanced learning research, I would often encounter

---

2   The Leitner system is the widely used analogue, spaced practice method of efficiently using flashcards, which was proposed by the German science journalist Sebastian Leitner in his book, *So Lernt Man Lernen* (How to Learn to Learn) (1972). A 'learning box' is separated into three to five compartments into which flashcards are sorted depending on how well the learner knows the material on each card. All flashcards start in compartment 1. Correctly answered cards move to the next compartment. Compartment 1 is reviewed daily and compartment 2 every other day. Compartment 3 is reviewed every third day and so on, slowly extending the spacing for correctly retrieved cards.

references to judgements of learning (JOLs). JOLs are predictions (prospective) of how likely participants are to remember material that was learned with a particular strategy after the event. Regrettably, 'students' predictions were almost always higher than the grade they earned and this was particularly true for low-performing students' (Miller and Geraci, 2011: 303).

It is worthwhile knowing that learners both tend to be overconfident in predicting their own learning (Soderstrom and Bjork, 2015) and tend to terminate their encoding before materials are sufficiently committed to memory (Kornell and Bjork, 2008). The accuracy of JOLs can play a large role in determining how adaptive (or maladaptive) study decisions end up being (Kornell and Metcalfe, 2006). JOLs are inspired and formed by learning beliefs and learning experiences.

Belief-based cues refer to what we consciously believe about learning, about memory and about remembering, with learners having been shown to use the heuristic 'easily learned means easily remembered' (Koriat, 2008: 417), and all too often failing to recognise the mnemonic benefits that testing provides as a learning strategy (Karpicke and Roediger, 2008; Tullis et al., 2013).

It is important to remember, therefore, that learners are more sensitive to experience-based cues and not belief-based cues (Kornell et al., 2011). Experience-based cues include anything learners can directly experience, including monitoring and control metacognitions. It is also why your second cycle of test-enhanced learning will be considerably easier to lead, and more potent, than your first cycle. Once pupils experience success, feel a sense of confidence in lessons and secure better grades, they will not only expect to be tested, they will ask to be tested.

You will not be surprised to discover, then, that 'JOLs about restudied and tested material tend to be inaccurate – whereas learners recall more tested than restudied material, their predictions often do not reflect this recall difference' (Rivers, 2021: 237). That is, learners' experience is that they learn more effectively and efficiently (or perceive that they do) when restudying. This is a big problem.

Accurate calibration

Judgements of learning are predictions. Confidence-based judgements are 'postdictions' (retrospective). These are important because they can help learners to identify learning topics that need further clarification and thereby promote learning. They are effectively metacognitive monitoring decisions.

Confidence-based judgements have been used to assess the monitoring accuracy of learners across a wide range of tasks – comprehension of texts, performance on learning tasks and, crucially, predictions about future performance. Next, we need to compare these confidence-based judgements with actual performance to arrive at a measure of accuracy, or calibration.

Calibration is the process of matching the learner's perception of their performance with the actual level of performance. Although learners' JOLs (or predictions) are often dissociated from test performance, postdictions (made after a test) tend to more accurately reflect test performance (Siedlecka et al., 2016), as established across a variety of contexts. As a teacher, asking pupils to make confidence-based judgements is a very simple and efficient activity which demands that pupils think about what it is they know and do not know confidently. It improves monitoring accuracy and reduces overconfidence (Hacker and Bol, 2019).

Essentially, testing provides both an efficient metacognitive opportunity and diagnostic feedback to inform learners about the gap between their anticipated and actual learning level (Szpunar et al., 2014), which then motivates them to expend more effort to narrow the perceived gap.

Monitoring accuracy

In between prospective and retrospective judgements are real-time concurrent metacognitive judgements, predominantly measured using confidence-based ratings per item – for example, a single flashcard or exam paper question. (Although they are technically retrospective, they are taken immediately after each item in order to capture feelings of confidence, as opposed to beliefs formed before and after an exam.) In your classroom, you might ask pupils to forecast their level of performance or confidence on each exam question as they work through the paper, rather than their confidence or predicted grade on the whole paper before or after the exam.

Following the exam, you would compare their real-time (concurrent) rating with their actual performance.

Nietfeld et al. (2005) found that real-time confidence judgements were strongly associated with objective accuracy in a multiple-choice test. Couchman et al. (2016) reported that confidence ratings for each individual question accurately predicted performance and were a much better decisional guide than retrospective judgements. As such, they suggested that the best strategy for learning is to 'record confidence, as a decision is being made, and use that information when reviewing' (Couchman et al., 2016: 182).

Barenberg and Dutke (2019) examined the potential of retrieval practice during learning to improve the accuracy of learners' confidence judgements in future retrieval. In the final test, the proportion of correct answers and the proportion of confident answers were higher with retrieval practice than the control condition. They concluded that confidence judgements can 'stimulate the learners to reflect their understanding of learning topics and the quality of knowledge they acquired' (Barenberg and Dutke, 2019: 277). What's more, this reflection, as mentioned earlier, can help pupils to identify the learning topics that need further clarification and help them to improve the accuracy and lessen the bias of their confidence judgements.

Coutinho et al. (2020) report that confidence judgements were accurate indicators of performance and that those pupils who scored higher in monitoring accuracy (calibration) performed better on the exam than those who scored lower. Why? 'It prompted the students to engage in an analysis of knowledge' (Coutinho et al., 2020: 419).

Here is the good news: testing not only enhances pupils' memory performance but it also improves their metacognitive monitoring accuracy. As Tullis et al. (2013: 429) observe: 'Retrieval has enormous potential to enhance long-term retention, particularly if learners appreciate its benefits and utilise it properly during self-regulated learning.' Testing helps learners make more accurate predictions about future performances (Ariel and Karpicke, 2018).

There is good news for Mariah too: 'Building digital flashcards provides a potentially powerful authentic assessment task' (Colbran et al., 2015: 69), which is shown to yield medium to large effects on comprehension, recall and problem-solving (Song, 2016), as a result of deeper processing and reflection of the learning material.

And, while we are here, two meta-analyses (Graham et al., 2015, and Sanchez et al., 2017) demonstrated a positive association between self-assessment and learning. On average, 'students who engaged in self-grading performed better on subsequent tests than did students who did not' (Sanchez et al., 2017: 1049), as did students who peer-graded. Here is the kicker: on average, students do not grade themselves or peers 'significantly differently than teachers' (Sadler and Good, 2006: 16). In fact, the assessments showed a moderate correlation ($r = 0.68$) with teacher grades. So, why not tell your pupils this and develop both self- and peer-assessment routines for marking the quizzing activities in class and reduce your workload?

What's more, training how to assess leads to 'substantially larger' gains: knowing how to manage and assess our own learning is critical for becoming efficient and effective learners. Moreover, employing self-assessment brings with it a raft of positive affective benefits: friendlier and more cooperative classrooms, a greater sense of shared ownership for the learning and, of course, a more positive attitude towards tests as useful feedback (Sadler and Good, 2006; Andrade, 2019). It also makes good use of knowledge organisers too easily left forgotten in the back of exercise books.

I am confident that you will have plenty of ideas, such as marking in a different coloured pen (not for Ofsted), forecasting scores/performance, cold-calling for a series of answers before asking other pupils to judge the best answer (and explaining why) or cold-calling for answers before asking other pupils to offer elaborations. Lastly, following a quiz, ask pupils to record three items that need to be learned before the next quiz and generate flashcards to target this knowledge.

They have the power (control)

Directly linked with monitoring is control – decisions about what, when and how to study. When monitoring is inaccurate, decisions about studying can be suboptimal. Remember Mariah? Here we can again cite Kornell and Bjork's (2007) finding that 90% of students reported using self-testing but most only did so in order to identify gaps in knowledge rather than for the direct learning benefits (see also Hartwig and Dunlosky, 2012). You have plenty of evidence to challenge that now.

Karpicke et al. (2009) asked a large group of college students about their study approach: 57% said they would reread their notes or textbook and

21% said they would do something else. Only 18% said they would attempt to recall material after reading it. Even after students were shown their results, and the benefits of retrieval practice, little changed: 42% of students said they would practise retrieval and then reread, but 41% still said they would only reread (17% said they would do something else). In other words, 58% of students who knew better indicated that they would not practise active retrieval when they would have the opportunity to reread afterwards.

Little has changed in 10 years. Rivers (2021) reported that 58% of students adopted ineffective or low-utility learning techniques (rereading 43%, copying notes 11%, highlighting 4%). Endres et al. (2017) and Hui et al. (2021) are more optimistic. Both studies report that, after exposing students to the results, the proportion choosing retrieval practice increased significantly in the following review phase, and in the Hui et al. study in the long term also.

The solution? Hui et al. (2021: 1852) simply suggest that 'feedback about the perceived learning as well as the actual learning may make students realise the mismatching of the perceived learning and the actual learning'. Metacognition and self-regulation approaches that encourage learners to think about their own learning (often by teaching them specific strategies for planning, monitoring and evaluating their learning) have consistently high levels of impact with learners. However, as Rivers (2021: 823) states: 'Without support, learners lack metacognitive awareness of testing as a tool to enhance memory but do recognise that testing can be used as a monitoring tool.'

Cogliano et al. (2019) report that students who completed metacognitive retrieval practice training scored higher on the final exam, with improved metacognitive awareness, accuracy for well-learned and yet-to-be-learned topics, exam preparation, monitoring strategy, control strategy and practice test frequency all contributing to this improved success. What's more, trained students continued to repeatedly use practice tests more often than the control group. Similarly, Ariel and Karpicke (2018) found that students who had experienced a similar intervention also showed potential for long-term changes in their self-regulated learning, spontaneously using repeated retrieval practice one week later to learn new materials.

Bringing this together

Of course, metacognition and self-regulation is a much larger area of study than this chapter's restricted focus on the elements of test-enhanced learning. But, allow me to summarise for our purposes. Learners hold the belief that testing of knowledge is only useful under certain conditions: when retrieval is either easy or successful, or when preparing for an assessment (driven by the goal of identifying which information is well known or not rather than the goal of increasing retention).

Yet, testing is most effective when learners engage in multiple successful retrieval attempts and relearn at spaced opportunities. However, learners rarely engage in such a strategy, often because they don't know the value and efficiency of successive relearning and how memory works or, alternatively, due to overconfidence or a stability bias (the human tendency to act as though our memory will remain stable in the future).

Test-enhanced learning practices also improve metacognition processes, creating a virtuous learning cycle with higher calibration associated with higher overall achievement in test-takers (Bol and Hacker, 2001). Considering that as learners travel through their education careers more and more learning takes place without direct supervision, a failure to understand and monitor our own learning process and adopt some of the most powerful learning strategies would be short-sighted.

Pupils may also choose to avoid difficult learning strategies if they are focused on a short-term performance outcome (recency, familiarity and fluency), if their competence beliefs are low, or if their performance expectations are less ambitious or distinct from those of the instructor (see Ariel et al., 2009; Kirk-Johnson et al., 2019).

Metacognitive monitoring appears to be an independent skill that can be cultivated separately from test-enhanced learning and may have profound implications for education, for pupils' outcomes and for teachers' workload.

My final point is not in any way meant disparagingly: reviewing over 40 years of empirical research showed me that teachers' ability to estimate pupils' learning is rather mixed. Teachers overestimate pupil achievement and underestimate the difficulty of testing tasks (Urhahne and Wijnia, 2021). Nevertheless, it can be enriched by the learners' own ability to estimate their learning gains. Should we not expect more from our pupils? Deeply ingrained in my memory is Wiliam's (2015) stoic statement that 'Feedback should be more work for the recipient than the donor.' Why not almost all the work?

Takeaways

- Metacognition is a crucial ingredient of test-enhanced learning. Test-enhanced learning positively contributes to all aspects of metacognition (beliefs, monitoring and control).

- Metacognition and test-enhanced learning is complex. It is the interplay of knowledge of task, knowledge of strategies, knowledge of self and regulation of planning, monitoring and evaluation.

- Educating learners about metacognitive approaches has consistently high levels of impact.

- Know that the introduction or first cycle of spaced retrieval practice will be met with scepticism and complaints.

- Changing beliefs is very difficult; drawing on past experience is easier. But, without changing beliefs you are unlikely to impact on the controlling decisions.

- Forewarn pupils about the misleading metacognitive influence of recency, familiarity and fluency.

- Retrieval practice, metacognitive monitoring and self-assessment all help learners to make more accurate learning predictions, and more accurate learning predictions lead to better study (control) decisions and better outcomes.

- Concurrent metacognition may have potential applications in the classroom and can be used to provoke purposeful dialogue.

- Self-assessment offers logistical (time saving), pedagogical (reduced workload and spacing), metacognitive and affective benefits.

- Test-enhanced learning practices also improve metacognition processes, creating a virtuous learning cycle.

- Teachers often overestimate pupil achievement and underestimate the difficulty of testing tasks; is there an opportunity to expect more from pupils?

- If you only have time to read one paper on this topic: M. L. Rivers, Metacognition about practice testing: a review of learners' beliefs, monitoring, and control of test-enhanced learning. *Educational Psychology Review*, 33(3) (2021): 823–862.

Case study: How testing can improve learning outcomes for all pupils

Anoara Mughal is an experienced primary school teacher and senior leader. She is passionate about closing the advantage gap and has a keen interest in testing and retrieval practice as a way of deepening knowledge and improving retention. Anoara is the author of Think! Metacognition-Powered Primary Teaching (2021) and founder of inspiremetacognition.com.

The challenge

At primary school, pupils are largely dependent on teachers and parents to scaffold learning and are guided through their school journey to learn independently. There are some pupils at primary school stage who have well-developed metacognitive strategies in place; however, many do not and need support in developing self-regulation strategies. Even though metacognitive strategies can be seen in pupils as young as 3 or 4, unless these strategies are continued to be taught explicitly, they can be lost as pupils progress through Key Stage 1.

Knowing about the benefits of retrieval practice, we were keen to incorporate retrieval practice into the curriculum. Working out the frequency of spaced retrieval required to improve accuracy of judgement, memory, confidence, motivation and self-regulation was a challenge.

One of the misconceptions about spaced retrieval is that pupils will find it more difficult to recall knowledge if it is spread out over the curriculum and time, rather than if it is retrieved in massed or blocked practice, and so it is something that is often rejected as a learning strategy by teachers. However, it is this challenge that we need to address in order to develop the deep reflective skills of metacognition, which ultimately helps pupils to understand themselves as learners.

Retrieval is a bit like cough medicine: if something feels too difficult, pupils are normally turned off it. Tasks should be challenging enough to enable pupils to develop reflective skills, but at the same time they should not be so challenging that they become demotivated. This is called the Goldilocks effect.

There are two ways of conducting retrieval: either we tell them, show them and let them see the results; or we follow Dunlosky's 'Let them fail at first, before giving them the strategies to succeed' model, where we let them try and fail and then show them the result. As we were in the middle of a global pandemic, the pupils were well aware that they had missed some areas of learning in maths, and we had also noticed an overall decrease in pupil confidence in this area of learning. We carefully considered the right model to implement, so as not to exacerbate the issue further.

An impact of the limited use of spaced retrieval is that pupils are unable to accurately judge their own learning, as they have nothing to which to compare their current learning. Although most pupils had lost confidence in maths, there were a handful of novice learners who thought they were performing at a higher level than they actually were. This prevented them from evaluating and adapting new learning strategies.

Another challenge was that teacher workload was at an all-time high, partly due to the COVID-19 pandemic. We thought carefully about how we were going to implement spaced retrieval practice without creating extra work for teachers.

Since learning is not visible, part of the solution of using spaced retrieval practice was to make it conspicuous for pupils to enable them to develop metacognition and self-regulation. We needed to ensure that pupils could also see the gaps between their anticipated and actual learning in order to improve motivation and narrow the perceived gap.

The plan

We already had daily maths retrieval planned into lessons, so we decided to analyse where spaced retrieval occurred naturally within the curriculum. Our analysis showed us that in the medium-term planning, place value was taught four times and addition and subtraction were covered twice, with other maths topics being covered only once, including topics such as multiplication, division and fractions, which are cognitively more challenging. Although we were aware that having secure knowledge of place value is the foundation of successful maths learning, we were also aware that teaching it four times over an eight-week period was perhaps not the best use of curriculum time. In addition to this, place value is a less cognitively challenging topic than fractions, for example. We decided, therefore, that we would reduce the number of weeks we spent on place value to the first two weeks in the autumn term only. Then we would plan in spaced retrieval of place value questions in the form of regular low-stakes quizzes throughout the year.

Massing or blocking topics such as fractions to once a year doesn't allow for pupils to become secure in their understanding. In addition, by the end of Year 6, pupils should have knowledge and understanding of ratio, and fractions are the building blocks to understanding ratio. If fractions are taught only once during the year, and then spaced retrieval is used to recall that knowledge much later on (when they need to recall ratio, for example), it becomes harder for pupils to access the strategies of adding, subtracting, multiplying and dividing fractions. This is partly due to some of the strategies requiring them to remember multiple steps, which can be a huge challenge for some pupils. The recall of place value strategies is far easier, however, as there are fewer steps to remember.

We decided to adapt our medium-term planning to ensure that fractions were timetabled in twice: once in the autumn term and once in the spring term. This would give us an insight into what the pupils believed about effort and challenge during the retrieval process after having a gap in their learning of fractions. This would help them to evaluate the effectiveness of their learning and, as a result, their metacognitive and self-regulatory decisions.

Due to the fact that there is no agreed period of spacing that leads to success (see Chapter 3), we decided to leave it up to teachers to decide, depending on pupils' memory strength after first being taught the material. Where memory was strong, retrieval could be spaced out over a longer period of time; where it was weaker or incorrect, spacing would need to be reduced. We also made sure that after a session on spaced retrieval that time was allocated to analyse with pupils any gaps in knowledge, which would improve the accuracy of their judgement.

In addition to this, largely due to confidence levels dropping as a result of the pandemic, we decided to follow the model of telling, showing and letting pupils see the results. Furthermore, we decided to use a combination of classroom.remembermore.app (in the classroom) and RememberMore, five daily questions and paper-based testing, so teachers would have resources on hand to use, which would reduce their workload.

The outcomes

By adapting the curriculum to include regular spaced retrieval practice, pupils' neural pathways strengthened, which helped them to calibrate their judgements. As a result of this, the accuracy of their judgement improved. This really helped those pupils who had been overconfident in their maths ability.

Self-monitoring improved too, with pupils better able to accurately judge whether they needed to practise more spaced retrieval or not. It was also a way of providing diagnostic feedback to inform pupils about the gap between their anticipated and actual learning level. Spaced retrieval practice motivated them to expend more effort on narrowing their learning gap, and they started to ask for more paper-based tests and more RememberMore tests, and they became further engaged in analysing their own knowledge. Pupils started to identify their own learning gaps and set themselves new goals and targets.

In addition to this, pupils became more motivated to learn and, as a result, more engaged in the material being taught. We noticed a decrease in behavioural issues during lessons and increased self-regulation. For example, there was a child who as soon as maths lessons started would want to leave the classroom. However, when we started spaced retrieval practice, he could 'see' that he was learning, based on the improving results, and quickly became more engaged. After a few weeks, he never wanted to leave the classroom and his confidence increased.

As pupils' metacognitive skills and knowledge improved, resulting in them becoming more aware of themselves as learners, their test scores also improved and they began to test themselves at home when they felt the need to do so. Being able to participate in their learning independently and with increasing success was very empowering.

What's next?

Our after-action review revealed that it was a challenge to vary the spaced retrieval practice to match the individual needs of the learners exactly, as maths was taught in mixed-ability classes. This is something we will consider in the future. Our next step will be to review the whole curriculum and look at how to include regular spaced retrieval practice in all subjects.

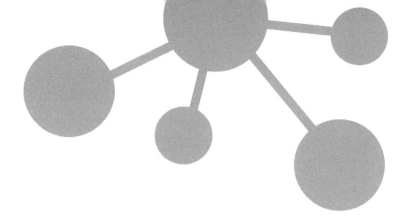

Chapter 8

Personalisation and overcoming illusions of competence

To be effective in assessing one's own learning requires being aware that we are subject to both hindsight and foresight biases in judging whether we will be able to produce to-be-learned information at some later time.

Bjork et al. (2013: 423)

Managing our ongoing learning effectively is not straightforward. Not least because conditions that enhance performance during learning can fail to support long-term retention and transfer, whereas conditions that appear to create difficulties and slow the acquisition process can enhance long-term retention and transfer. Despite 'overwhelming evidence that learning and performance are dissociable', there appears to be a lack of understanding on the part of instructors and learners alike that performance during acquisition is a highly imperfect index of long-term learning (Soderstrom and Bjork, 2015: 188). In other words, pupil performance when learning is a poor predictor of future performance. Real learning is counterintuitive and feels counterproductive. Ironically, pupils who practise repeated retrieval consistently predict lower performance than those who repeatedly study or engage in other activities (Roediger and Karpicke, 2006; Karpicke and Blunt, 2011), yet they score higher.

These misconceptions, faulty beliefs and inaccurate monitoring and study decisions – what Koriat and Bjork (2005: 959) refer to as 'illusions of competence' – often leave learners 'misassessing and mismanaging their own learning' (Bjork et al., 2013: 417). They also lead to ineffective or suboptimal learning, relearning and revision strategies. Even when provided with corrective feedback, learners overestimate their remembering and underestimate their forgetting (Kornell and Bjork, 2009).

The misinterpreted-effort hypothesis (Kirk-Johnson et al., 2019) maintains that learners' perceptions of greater mental effort lead them to feel that they are actually learning less, particularly concurrently and partially retrospectively. This leads Kirk-Johnson et al. (2019) to conclude: 'The more learners perceived a study strategy as mentally effortful, the less they judged it to be effective for learning.' Not only did perceptions predict whether or not learners chose to employ testing or retrieval practice, but that choice in turn predicted performance on a test of retention.

Hence, although test-enhanced learning strategies are highly robust, promote long-term retention, lead to more accessible and durable knowledge, and develop metacognitive accuracy, without acquiring knowledge about these strategies their practical usefulness in a classroom is maligned and further limited in self-regulated learning contexts. Put simply, test-enhanced learning suffers from an image problem, so until those experience-based cues kick in, teachers will have to lead the learning. Remember: 'Know why. Know how. Teach and lead the learning and relearning.'

As easy as KBCP?

McDaniel and Einstein (2020) argue that effective strategy training to promote self-regulated learning (and, to a lesser extent, classroom learning) involves four essential components. Their knowledge, belief, commitment and planning (KBCP) framework proposes:

1 Acquiring knowledge about strategies.

2 Belief that the strategy works.

3 Commitment to using the strategy.

4 Planning of strategy implementation.

Moreover, 'each component alone is not sufficient to promote sustained learning-strategy self-regulation' (McDaniel et al., 2021: 1363).

Knowledge

McDaniel et al. (2021) emphasise three knowledge components: (1) knowledge about the strategy, (2) evidence that the strategy is effective and (3) knowledge about how the strategy is implemented for authentic learning tasks. The 'why' and the 'how'. Their conclusions – which are very clear: 'sparse evidence' findings that 'do not necessarily inspire confidence' and a lack of 'sustained' adoption of test-enhanced learning strategies (McDaniel et al., 2021: 1367–1369) – suggest that teachers have not been very successful in their efforts to encourage their pupils to adopt test-enhanced learning (the experiences outlined at the start of this book). In summarising Biwer et al. (2020) and Endres et al. (2020), McDaniel et al. (2021: 13) conclude that imparting knowledge about specific learning strategies is 'valuable but not sufficient'. I certainly learned the hard way. Many schools adopting this approach will learn the hard way too. Forewarned is forearmed.

Belief

How do you instil a belief that this strategy will work for your pupils? The first challenge is to overcome pupils' 'eagerness to believe that one is unique as a learner' (Yan et al., 2016: 918). Hence, Einstein et al. (2012: 192) advocate the benefits of gaining first-hand experiences, on the basis that this has a pronounced impact on a pupil's belief in the effectiveness of the strategy and drives the self-regulated use of learning strategies thereafter. What's more, experiencing the effects of different strategies improved metacognitive accuracy. It stands to reason that pupils must believe in the effectiveness of a strategy to spontaneously adopt it, and there is a wealth of evidence that self-efficacy (the belief that you have the ability to attain a desired result) is positively associated with persistence of that behaviour change.

Second, and inextricably woven with pupils' motivation, design questions with a single focused answer. Repeat questions. Reorder questions. Offer hints. Let the pupils use knowledge organisers. Use self-assessment practices. Notice successes. Track or gather evidence to present later. See also Table 3.1 on tackling low failure rates.

Belief comes before commitment. With disaffected learners, success begets motivation. Oracy often greases the wheels of effort, and covert retrieval strategies are almost equally effective. Oracy also offers test-enhanced learning in open teaching environments (for example, the sports field in outdoor learning) and low-literacy environments.

Commitment

Pupils may have knowledge of an effective strategy, believe that it works for them and still fail to exert the effort required to implement it. Commitment, or motivation, is considered in association with increasing the perceived utility value of a task (Harackiewicz et al., 2016) – that is, the value pupils place on an activity. As Einstein et al. (2012) point out, encouraging pupils to reflect on the inherently positive outcomes associated with effective strategy use drives adoption. This in turn increases interest, motivation and persistence in activities related to that task (Hulleman et al., 2017); in other words, fostering a commitment to action and studying with these more difficult learning strategies for an extended period of time and explicitly demonstrating their impact. Hence, the second cycle (or term) of teaching with test-enhanced learning rides the wave of your own commitment and pupils' successes in the first cycle (or term).

As previously outlined, in my own classroom we quiz every day. When knowledge surfaces in lessons, we notice it, harvest it and celebrate it, and we claim it to be the fruits of test-enhanced learning's labour. But how we quiz is very much dependent on what phase of learning we are in.

Every Thursday, we quiz and I record the pupils' self- or peer-assessed scores; it is our weekly routine. Tracking, boxplotting and sharing the Thursday quiz scores imparts a collective academic responsibility to improve in a very powerful and visual way. We celebrate improvement, metacognitive accuracy and high attainment. The steady creep of improvement is evident every cycle, and so it should be. Yet, knowledge, belief and commitment are still not sufficient for pupils to effectively follow through on their intentions to employ these validated test-enhanced learning strategies. That intention needs to be planned.

Planning

Knowing that commitment is not sufficient for the effective follow-through of intentions, McDaniel et al. (2021) recommend supporting the formulation of an action plan for implementing effective strategies. Biwer et al. (2020) investigated the impact of an extensive three-part Study Smart intervention programme on undergraduate students' metacognitive knowledge and use of learning strategies across 12 weeks. The study took place over three years (2018–2020) and involved approximately 1,500 students and 50 teachers in five different faculties at a Dutch university. The intervention involved: (1) instruction about when and why particular learning strategies are effective, (2) reflection and discussion on strategy use, motivation and goal-setting, and (3) gaining experience with an ineffective strategy (highlighting) versus an effective strategy (practice testing).

Compared to a control group, those randomly assigned to receive the intervention gained more accurate declarative and conditional knowledge, rated practice testing as more effective and rereading as less effective, and reported an increased use of quizzing and practice testing after the intervention.

Did this translate to better student outcomes? Neither McDaniel et al. (2021) nor Biwer et al. (2020) directly report an answer to this question.

Now, I could not ignore this interesting anecdote shared by Dr John Dunlosky in the *TES* in 2021. He applies a rather interesting 'experiencing' (or 'try and fail and then show them the result') approach. Dunlosky explains that many of the students he encounters at Kent State University believe they know how to study. Rather than try to convince them there is a more effective or efficient approach, he gives them an early test. Why? Well, he figures that if a student does poorly in an exam, then 'that is pretty good evidence that you did not prepare properly for it'. Only after the test does he present his pitch for successive relearning: 'The students who don't do as well as they should might have a higher likelihood of embracing the new strategies I will be teaching them.'

McDaniel and Einstein's (2020) KBCP framework offers an excellent practical and theoretical roadmap to maximising pupils' learning potential and helping them to become effective lifelong learners, with preliminary and informal results described as 'encouraging' (McDaniel et al., 2021: 14). Perhaps the researchers' parting reflections will resonate with you: 'Armed with effective learning strategies and the commitment to use them, students who face inequities in instructional, environmental, or personal contexts – or those at lower cognitive ability levels – could plausibly show significant gains in achievement' (McDaniel et al., 2021: 15).

Personalisation

The data on personalisation was tantalising, but very limited.

Dr Tom Perry (SecEd, 2022)

Without question, the most efficient schedule is an adaptive one, accounting for the learner's rates of forgetting and prior knowledge.

Latimier et al. (2021: 980)

Confucius put forward the idea of teaching students according to their aptitude. David Ausubel (1968: vi) wrote: 'the most important single factor influencing learning is what the learner already knows'. Making pupils aware of effective learning strategies and desirable difficulties, stimulating reflection on the value of these learning strategies and supporting them to experience the actual learning versus the experienced learning are ways to motivate them to adopt effective learning strategies. We will come back to motivation in Chapter 9.

However, these are still largely one-size-fits-all. We should also not forget that 'successive relearning places greater demands on students for effective time management, organisation, and planning of practice sessions' (Rawson et al., 2020: 856), and that too many students resort to ineffective study strategies (e.g. cramming the night before the test) to compensate for their lack of proper time management (Taraban et al., 1999; McIntyre and Munson, 2008; Seo, 2012).

Another approach is to personalise the learning, to adapt the question sequence based on a performance variable (there are quite a few to choose from or combine). This requires us to balance two seemingly opposing goals: (1) maximising the time between repetitions of an item to get the biggest spacing effect, and (2) minimising the time between repetitions of an item to make sure it can still be retrieved from long-term memory.

In a series of papers, Heitmann et al. (2018, 2021, 2022) investigated various mechanisms to optimise practice quizzing when compared to note-taking, starting off in the laboratory and finishing with a field experiment with 155 undergraduate pre-service teachers at Bielefeld University. Two adaptive (personalisation) mechanisms were investigated in the laboratory: performance-based and cognitive demand-based, as well as learners' achievement motivations. In the performance-based approach, performance on quiz questions was used as an indicator of retrieval success (Heitmann et al., 2018). In the cognitive demand-based approach, 'perceived cognitive demand' when answering the quiz questions was used as an indicator of retrieval effort (Heitmann et al., 2022).

The conclusion is clear in the title of the 2018 paper: 'Testing is more desirable when it is adaptive and still desirable when compared to note-taking'. These benefits led to learners achieving higher testing performance and lower perceived cognitive demand during testing. The inference is that both adaptive quizzing and quizzing (retrieval practice) freed up capacity or thinking for processes that are beneficial for learning, gains applied when the real test, the exam, came along. Of the two approaches, cognitive demand-based adaptations 'substantially increased the quizzing effect' (Heitmann et al., 2018: 10) and were applied in the field study.

The field study results led Heitmann et al. (2021: 603) to conclude that the benefits of practice quizzing 'in authentic learning contexts are even greater when the quiz questions are adapted [personalised] to learners' state of knowledge'. In this field study, adaptation by simple cognitive demand ratings yielded learning outcomes superior to quizzing and note-taking. Interestingly, the study also provided further evidence for knowledge transfer (as highlighted in Chapter 2), suggesting that practice quizzing is a suitable tool to foster meaningful learning.

Dr Svenja Heitmann explained: 'What has been missing is informed teachers in classrooms teaching with adaptive quizzing, teachers with a broader audience who can make adaptive quizzing better known. Teachers need to know that it's a good idea to adapt questions' difficulty.'[1]

As for learner achievement motivations, quizzing benefits were moderated by 'hope of success' scores but not 'fear of failure' scores; although these findings were reported in the field experiment, they were not statistically significant.

As discussed in Sense et al. (2016), such personalised practice models have been 'developed and implemented with great success' (Lindsey et al., 2009)

---

1   S. Heitmann, interview with author (October 2022).

and have been shown to 'outperform the flashcard condition' (van Rijn et al., 2009: 6). Flashcard control conditions are considered useful because 'many students report using similar procedures to study for exams' (Sense et al., 2016: 307).

Meanwhile, Grimaldi and Karpicke (2014: 67) conclude that 'combining the powerful learning produced by retrieval practice with sophisticated scoring algorithms could prove to be a particularly potent way to enhance student learning'.

Van Rijn et al. (2009: 6) show that 'adapting the sequence to the characteristics of individual learners improves learning gains considerably, even if the learning session takes only 15 minutes'. The overall impression was that personalisation generally leads to 'less frustration during study sessions', 'improved students' and teachers' satisfaction' and 'higher test performance and improved long-term knowledge retention'.

Having contested that learning with a limited, pre-set number of presentations was not 'comparable to most real-world learning situations', Mettler et al. (2016: 907) chose to study adaptive spacing combining both accuracy and response time. Their results showed 'significantly greater learning' in both fixed and equal spaced conditions which persisted across delays (one week), having taken into account prior knowledge.

Equally important was the fact that adaptive response time-based sequencing (ARTS) was able to extract useful assessments of 'ongoing learning strength while in use by learners' (Mettler et al., 2016: 914). Even more interesting is the range of tasks to which the ARTS system has been applied, including complex tasks such as interpreting electrocardiogram (ECG) tracings. Add personalisation, determine mastery and focus learning where it is most needed, and Thai et al.'s (2015: 2354) model produced 'faster, more accurate, and more efficient learning'.). Meanwhile, Krasne et al. (2020) report improvements in both accuracy and fluency of ECG diagnosis but also durability one year later.

Lindsey et al. (2014) developed a method of using a personalised flashcard review system (item difficulty, student latent ability and study history), which combined statistical techniques for inferring individual differences. In the study, 179 students learned vocabulary words and short sentences in English and were required to type the Spanish translation, after which corrective feedback was provided. This took place across three 20–30-minute sessions during class time.

The first two sessions began with a study-to-proficiency (criterion) phase for the current chapter the students were studying and then proceeded to a review phase. Sound familiar? During the third session, these activities were preceded by a quiz on the current chapter, which counted towards the course grade. During the review phase, study items from all chapters were covered.

In a cumulative exam administered at the end of the semester, the researchers compared time-matched review strategies. Personalised review yielded a 16.5% boost in course retention over current educational practice (massed study) and a 10% improvement over a one-size-fits-all strategy for spaced study – that is, 16.5% for just '10% of the time students were engaged with the course' (Mozer and Lindsey, 2017: 23).

Mozer and Lindsey (2017: 23) observe: 'Our experiments go beyond showing that spaced practice is superior to massed practice: taken together the experiments provide strong evidence that personalization of review is superior to other forms of spaced practice.'

Lindsey et al. (2014) suggest there are two connected failings in most classrooms. First, a one-size-fits-all review is significantly less effective than personalised review. Second, traditional means of encouraging systematic review in classroom settings (cumulative exams and assignments) are unlikely to be ideal. They go on to explain that personalisation always requires an assessment of a pupil's memory strength for particular knowledge, and that: 'Educational failure at all levels often involves knowledge and skills that were once mastered but cease to be accessible due to lack of appropriately timed rehearsal.' However, this appropriately timed and individualised rehearsal is simply beyond what most schools can provide. They conclude: 'Our results suggest that a digital tool which solves this problem in a practical, time-efficient manner will yield major payoffs for formal education at all levels' (Lindsey et al., 2014: 644).

With the proliferation of handheld devices and technology use during the COVID-19 pandemic – indeed, with mobile phones at near saturation by the time pupils arrive at secondary school and with usage on the increase (ChildWise, 2020) – personalisation is ever more attractive.

In sum, personalisation offers an '"efficient housekeeping" function' to ensure that mastered knowledge remains accessible and at the core of pupils' competency (Lindsey et al., 2014: 24). It addresses cognitive bias and protects against illusions of competence, promoting time-efficient, high-utility learning as well as making the most of unsupervised study. Not least of all, it provides learner metrics that can be aggregated to offer teaching insights that can be used to refine and improve teaching in the first place. Tantalising, most definitely, and perhaps not so very limited?

Takeaways

- Illusions of competence are largely metacognitive – for example, misconceptions, faulty beliefs and inaccurate monitoring.

- Assessing learning is difficult because conditions that appear to create difficulties and slow the acquisition process can enhance long-term retention and transfer (the misinterpreted-effort hypothesis).

- Many learning strategies are like cough syrup. Teachers are strongly advised to teach not only the knowledge, but why and how these various learning strategies actually work.

- Metacognitive monitoring accuracy improves as a result of spaced retrieval practice (see Chapter 9).

- The KBCP framework is a helpful model when adopting test-enhanced learning.

- Technology and the saturation of devices presents the opportunity to personalise learning.

- Personalised spaced retrieval is superior to other forms of massed and spaced practice.

- Personalised learning offers ongoing learner metrics and teaching insights and automated marking reduces teacher workload.

- If you only have time to read one paper on this topic: A. Kirk-Johnson, B. M. Galla and S. H. Fraundorf, Perceiving effort as poor learning: the misinterpreted-effort hypothesis of how experienced effort and perceived learning relate to study strategy choice. *Cognitive Psychology*, 115 (2019), article 101237.

- Also, Heitmann's series of papers (Heitmann et al., 2018, 2021, 2022) as a collection is hard to beat.

Case study: Addressing overconfidence when the students don't yet believe in test-enhanced learning

Ambra Caretta is an assistant head academic at an all-through independent school in Suffolk. She oversees teaching and learning and the professional development of teachers. As part of a new approach to continuing professional development, the school is focused on the science of learning and evidence-based practice.

The challenge

The school has highlighted the following concerns for our student body:

- Students lack independence with their learning. This makes the teacher the only source of information; spoon-feeding must cease and a better balance must be sought between curriculum content and contact time with students.

- Students are averse to taking risks. They believe they are not allowed to fail or make mistakes. Consequently, students are hesitant to offer opinions, have a go and move outside their comfort zone. This is reflected in classrooms and in their learning.

- There seems to be a lack of skills and strategies to learn. Students believe they know what is best and shy away from opportunities that are effortful.

The COVID-19 pandemic has certainly not helped with these problems, so I was keen to explore ways of supporting my students with their GCSE combined chemistry course. With tests due in October and January, I wanted my Year 11s to have a well-organised and effortful revision plan. Needless to say, after so many weeks with very little time spent reviewing their GSCE chemistry, the results were lower than expected in October (two grades down in some cases). 'I wanted to see how much I remembered without revision' was the common theme.

As we flicked through the paper, mark scheme in hand, it was clear that the students knew they had made mistakes and knew there were better answers. They were equally certain that they would do better next time, now that they had made a particular mistake and seen the correction. The sense of overconfidence was unnerving, but the students refused to accept that in some cases they just simply didn't hit the marking points and instead waffled on about incoherent ideas. They were adamant that their approach was working (especially the low prior-attaining students, who trusted their confidence in the topic over what they could produce on paper). They were deeply wedded to their preferred poorly performing strategies.

The plan

With eight more topics to study, covering new content in Year 11 without forgetting the previous taught units was always going to be challenging, especially post-online learning. The chemistry curriculum builds on itself, so most of the topics rely on previous knowledge at some point (e.g. electrolysis (Chapter 6) relies on students understanding the conductivity of ionic compounds (Chapter 3)). Unfortunately, the last time we had covered Chapter 3 was five months before starting electrolysis. Therefore, in every lesson I found myself spending 10-15 minutes revisiting and reteaching topics which should have been easily accessible to them. But this knowledge was not accessible; in fact, it was nowhere to be found in their memories.

This is when I came across RememberMore flashcards, which you can tailor to your specification and, importantly, tag content to specific areas such as bonding and structure, reactivity and the periodic table. I spent half-term writing content for each topic taught in Year 10, chronologically tagged and organised. The task was simple but effective. Every lesson was going to start with this knowledge and homework was going to be based around it too.

The overt routine was easily embedded. Lesson starter: six questions on the board from a selection of previous chapters with a timer, generally drawing on ideas required for the lesson ahead. The students wrote down the questions and answers. Next, I reveal the answers and ask for their confidence level. They show me with their hands how many questions they felt confident about. I don't take a record of this per se; this is more for them – to debunk their illusion of confidence. This routine quickly moved to oracy and covert responses in the first 10 minutes of the lesson, which involved covering up to 10-15 questions. With a routine in place they now knew what to expect.

The next step was to explain to the students why we were doing this activity. It was time to teach them about the strategy. We were practising our ability to recall information. In their pairs and groups they were sharing how they got to an answer and what set of information they had to connect to recall a specific item from their long-term memory. They were modelling their thinking out loud. This was as exciting and innovative to them as it was for me, and it gave me a real insight into how their brains were making sense of the information they were receiving. Importantly, it clearly showed them their ability to interpret information from the periodic table to reach the required answer.

To increase the level of ownership of this retrieval strategy, I gave them access to the RememberMore app. Now, chemistry was accessible anywhere and at any point – on the bus on the way home, at breakfast, during break time – and they could choose which topic to revise based on our mock test reflection. This was personalised spaced retrieval practice in action. They had the ability to rate their confidence level on each flashcard, and there was an easy-to-use teacher dashboard to track progress and time invested.

The weekly lesson starters, combined with a weekly homework via the app, doubled (and in some cases tripled) the exposure to the Year 10 content, and I watched my Year 11s growing in confidence week on week. During the lesson starter, I would hear, 'I know this one – I've seen this question/card before!' More recently, they weren't shocked when I mentioned fractional distillation (from Chapter 1) when discussing the refining process of crude oil (Chapter 9).

Some students decided that this learning strategy wasn't for them and believed it to be ineffective and 'too demanding'. They said things like:

- 'If I don't know the answer and I click to reveal answer, it doesn't necessarily teach me [but, of course, we know that it does] as I don't have to write anything out [and we know that learning is the residue of thinking, not writing].'

■ 'I don't find flashcards useful.' (What do they find useful? And is that approach actually useful, or just familiar and reassuring?)

After requesting at least an hour's worth of time spent on the app (equivalent to three pieces of homework), I let them choose to use alternative revision methods. (Note: Weekly homework consists of 10–15 minutes on the app and one exam question.)

The outcomes

On analysis, the amount of time spent on RememberMore shows a very good correlation with improved student outcomes in the second round of mock exams (two months later). Those who engaged less with this structured retrieval practice lacked detail in their answers and achieved a smaller gain between tests. This was primarily due to their inability to connect more than one marking point together to formulate an answer which was worthy of two or three marks (e.g. reactivity of alkali metals – nuclear charge, electron shielding, atomic radius). Their ideas were not easily retrievable.

An English as an additional language (EAL) student showed the largest improvement (a 50% improvement in score with over two-and-a-half hours of guaranteed revision on RememberMore over seven weeks). From our conversations post-mock, and from personal experience of being an EAL student myself, it was evident that the flashcard system gave context to key words and therefore improved her ability and confidence to answer questions, even in unfamiliar contexts.

Interestingly, low prior-attaining students made a greater commitment to learning than the assigned homework allocation (20% increase on average). Those who chose not to engage with this structured retrieval practice (and scored poorly) have been advised to give it another go, as their progress was not as significant as some others. That is the point, of course: students do not always engage in what is good for them. Spaced retrieval through successive relearning is like cough medicine.

After-action review

With such positive feedback from my Year 11s, I shared the RememberMore app with my Year 10s too. It is now a key part of the class and homework routine, and the students enjoy the competitive element of its games-based format. Above-and-beyond effort is rewarded with academic points. Even the most sceptical of students in this class has now been converted: by engaging with the app at home, he realised that he could retrieve information more quickly when completing the lesson starter. The demonstrable strengths of the learning strategy have enabled him to buy into it with confidence.

What's next?

After a successful year of using RememberMore, and seeing the students' confidence grow, monitoring has become more accurate and two more departments are using the app to support spaced retrieval practice. Biology, business and economics, and soon psychology will also be able to monitor students' progress and tailor their teaching based on the data the dashboard provides. As a school, our strategic focus for the next two years will be the science of learning, cognitive overload, the illusion of competence and structured reflection.

Year 12 chemistry students were excited to know that we would use RememberMore again this year after a successful trial last year. Their belief and commitment have been secured. What's more, they are spreading the excitement among other classes who are new to it. Some Year 10 students have so far have clocked up more than one- and a half hours over the last three weeks, despite the app asking for 30 minutes of homework, and the new academic year has only just begun.

My takeaways

- Build a class routine which is effortful; make the students struggle without knocking their confidence.

- Make more of the insights on the RememberMore teacher dashboard to highlight topics that the students are not mastering as easily. Prioritise these flashcards as your lesson starters.

- Explain the forgetting curve, and both how and why personalised retrieval practice is one of the most effective uses of students' time when it comes to self-study and homework.

- Track and show them their results.

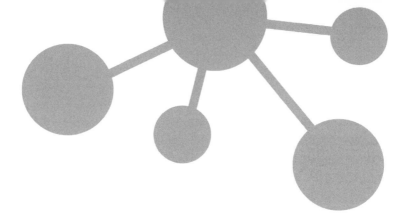

Chapter 9

Testing, motivation and achievement

The historic Roediger et al. (2011) paper offered us 'Ten benefits of testing and their applications to educational practice', citing many of the most recognised studies and researchers from the field at the point of publication. The 10 recommendations include that testing aids later retrieval, organises and plugs gaps in knowledge, potentiates and transfers to new information, improves metacognitive monitoring, blocks interference, motivates pupils and informs teachers. All have been highlighted in this book in some form or fashion, but allow me to expand on and add to the wealth of evidence.

Testing and test expectancy

Expectation of any kind of test enhances the processing of studied material. It is an important motivator driving pupils to commit more effort to prepare for subsequent tests (Szpunar et al., 2007; Agarwal and Roediger, 2011; Yang et al., 2019). The research also suggests that telling pupils the type of test format they should expect and the target learning goal can benefit their learning.

In addition:

- Learners make more notes when they are frequently tested (Szpunar et al., 2013) and frequent tests drive learners to allocate more time to learning (Yang et al., 2017).

- Experiencing retrieval practice makes pupils (76%) 'less anxious regarding upcoming tests and exams for classes in which retrieval practice was implemented' (Agarwal et al., 2014: 136) and helps inoculate against stress (Smith et al., 2016).

- A preannounced quiz encourages pupils to read the assigned textbook material and prepare better before class (Heiner et al., 2014).

- Frequent tests induce high test expectancy, which in turn boosts test performance (Weinstein et al., 2014).

- Frequent tests reduce task-unrelated thoughts (mind wandering – thoughts that are not related or irrelevant to the task to which you are trying to pay attention) while watching lecture videos (Jing et al., 2016).

- Quizzing within a course enhances not only the learning of specifically tested information but also the learning of non-tested conceptually related information (Bjork et al., 2014).

- Class quizzes increase attendance (Schrank, 2016).

It is hard not to see the value of testing and frequent, lesson-by-lesson quizzing.

Backward and forward effects of testing

We have discussed the power of the backward effect of testing – that is, retrieval practice of previously studied information (compared to restudy). Nothing new there.

But a growing body of research reveals that there is also a forward effect of testing. The retrieval of previously studied information can enhance the learning of subsequently presented new but conceptually related information, and also the learning of information that is not necessarily related to the previously tested material.

Szpunar et al. (2008) asked participants to study five lists of words in anticipation of a final cumulative recall test. Prior to the experiment, they were told to expect different activities that may follow the presentation of each single list: solving maths problems, restudying words from a 'just studied' list or the immediate free recall of words from a 'just studied' list. The experimenter pretended that the activities were determined randomly, but they were not. Each activity differed between experimental groups, and the participants passed through the same activities – maths, restudy or immediate recall testing – after studying lists 1–4.

Critically, all the participants were tested immediately on the fifth list. Two striking results emerged. Participants who had been tested immediately on lists 1–4 recalled about twice as many items on test 5 than the two non-tested groups. In addition, they showed notably fewer 'prior-list intrusions' than did participants in the two other groups.

What does this tell us? These results indicate a beneficial forward effect of recall testing. This would seem to be a retrieval-specific effect which is not restricted to the learning of words but generalises to the learning of various kinds of materials.

What is going on here?

Both encoding and retrieval explanations have been put forth to account for the forward effect of testing. These get pretty heavy, pretty quickly.

Suffice to say here that retrieval explanations suggest that recall testing between the study of a list (of information or facts) promotes 'contextual list segregation', enhancing list differentiation and reducing interference between lists. This allows participants to use context cues specific to each list, and thus create more focused memory searches. (I did warn you.)

Encoding explanations suggest that recall testing of prior non-target materials improves encoding of the subsequently studied target material. That testing induces a reset of the encoding process, making the encoding of the later lists as effective as the encoding of the earlier lists.

Although less frequently reported, there is some very interesting research on the forward effect of testing – also known as potentiated learning or pre-testing (Latimier et al., 2019; Yang et al., 2019; Todd et al., 2021).

Indeed, Carpenter et al. (2018: 34) state: 'Studies have shown that prequestions – asking students questions before they learn something – benefit memory retention.' So, interim low-stakes tests during a study phase can be used profitably to enhance the learning of new information regardless of whether it is from the same or a different domain. Pre- and interim tests induce greater test expectancy; hence, pupils are more likely to want to exert more effort towards encoding new information. Moreover, pre-tests induce pupils to exert more effort to retrieve the subsequently studied information. The recommendation is that teachers should use this knowledge to their (and their pupils') advantage – which brings us to motivation.

On motivation

Learning requires motivation, but motivation does not necessarily lead to learning.

Nuthall (2007: 35)

Motivation is not a personality trait or characteristic. Kriegbaum et al. (2018) reviewed the relative importance of intelligence and motivation as predictors of school achievement in a meta-analysis of 74 studies (80,145 learners). The results show that both intelligence (0.44) and motivation (0.27) contribute substantially to the prediction of school achievement. I doubt this will surprise anyone.

Now, considering both cognitive and motivational perspectives, and the comparative effectiveness of testing, spaced and interleaved practice, and insights from McDaniel and Einstein's (2020) KBCP framework, Bjork and Bjork (2020: 479) report that 'there is important research to be carried out on how motivational factors influence and interact with learning strategies'. It is hard to disagree.

Furthermore, Finn (2020) points out that pupils' memories of their past academic experiences and achievements, or lack thereof, provide a basis for their expectations and goals. Such expectations and goals, in turn, can heavily influence both pupils' effort to learn and their selection of learning procedures. From that standpoint, research on achievement motivation and on metacognition becomes highly relevant.

Most recently, Higham et al. (2021) report that recall of university course material at the end of a semester was better for relearning compared to restudying. Perhaps more importantly, increased recall during relearning sessions was associated with further learning benefits, including improved metacognition, increased self-reported sense of mastery, increased attentional control and reduced anxiety. The students also found successive relearning to be enjoyable and valuable. But it does not end there.

The Goldilocks effect

One aspect of testing that I find intriguing is the interaction between desirable difficulties and pupils' self-efficacy and sense of achievement. By now, I hope, you will be familiar with the fact that manipulations that increase initial acquisition difficulty and enhance delayed memory performance are referred to as 'desirable difficulties' (Bjork and Bjork, 2011).

Teachers and scholars have long understood that there is something of a sweet spot when it comes to learning. Sometimes referred to as the Goldilocks effect, it promotes just the right amount of success to produce better learning outcomes.

When assessing pupils' individual work and oral responses to class discussions, Rosenshine (2012) found that the most effective fourth-grade maths teachers had a pupil success rate of 82%. The least effective maths teachers only had success rates of 73% – that is, their questions were more accessible to the pupils. Thus, his seventh principle of instruction is obtaining a high success rate – he recommended aiming for an 80% success rate, meaning that pupils are being challenged but not so much that they don't succeed.

More recently, researchers at the University of Arizona reported on the 'Eighty Five Percent Rule for optimal learning':

> *In many situations we find that there is a sweet spot in which training is neither too easy nor too hard, and where learning progresses most quickly. We find that the optimal error rate for training is around 15.87% or, conversely, that the optimal training accuracy is about 85%. We show theoretically that training at this optimal difficulty can lead to exponential improvements in the rate of learning.*
>
> *Wilson et al. (2019)*

So, what level of difficulty is 'just right'? Back to Bjork and Bjork (2020: 476), who are succinct in their summation: 'The level of difficulty that is optimal … will vary with the degree of a learner's prior learning.'

Not so easy, then, when you have 30-plus unique learners, each with different prior knowledge and motivations. Is this a signpost for employing aspects of personalised learning? And we should not forget Eglington and Pavlik's (2020) intriguing research and conclusions from Chapter 6: that the learning gains and costs for correct and incorrect trials can be quite different and that content difficulty for individual pupils is highly relevant to optimising practice scheduling, particularly when time is limited.

Where the rubber hits the road

Having iteratively introduced and refined a spaced retrieval practice routine for encoding (learning) and maintenance (remembering/relearning) to numerous classes to date, and received feedback from teachers nationally and internationally across phrases, the observations and feedback are just too consistent to be ignored.

Test-enhanced learning promotes routined, independent, purposeful and meaningful learning (not assessment of learning), which directs and focuses pupil attention. If self-assessment is included as part of that routine, pupils also develop their metacognitive monitoring capabilities and challenge their metacognitive beliefs. Test-enhanced learning (specifically spaced retrieval practice) is demanding and requires effortful practice, with deferred but long-term durable learning gains. Forearmed with this knowledge, and adopting McDaniel and Einstein's (2020) KBCP framework and borrowing from our recommendations, teachers across phases, subjects and sectors report consistently encouraging experiences.

Predictably, after 9–12 episodes of testing (influenced by your subject's curriculum allocation, which will impact on the spacing), knowledge becomes more accessible – that is, more retrievable – to pupils. Weekly scores creep up. Pupils experience tangible success. Success begets motivation. That motivation begets a greater commitment to testing in class. At this point, I would say that the success–motivation–success cycle had kicked in. More pupils contribute to the lesson; notably, class discussions become richer. More time is invested in homework to support the daily quizzing. More questions are asked in the same time allocation (or even less time) and fewer corrections are required.

It was the consistency of the teacher reports – that test-enhanced learning with high success rates and self-assessment (low-stakes) at the eighth, ninth or tenth cycle led to a deeper commitment to learning in lessons and homework – that increased my professional interest in the relationship between motivation and achievement.

Why low-stakes quizzing? As outlined in Chapter 2, the research is unclear. What the pupils often want to know is whether or not the quiz grade counts for anything. 'When they [eighth-grade pupils] received a negative answer, their interest in the material dropped noticeably' (Liming and Cuevas, 2017: 122). Now, there is a motivational conundrum to solve.

Our solution: at the end of each term we include a quiz score from the full deck of cards studied. In some cases that is a deck of 400 or more flashcards.

The results have been quite breathtaking. The vast majority of pupils score over 50%, some score 70–80% and a few score over 80%. That is, they are able to recall 320 items of knowledge from a 12-week unit of study. As I say, breathtaking.

Motivation and achievement

The impact of achievement on self-concept is greater than the impact of self-concept on achievement.

Daniel Muijs[1]

This comment from a conversation with Professor Daniel Muijs, an expert in the field of educational and teacher effectiveness, has always stuck with me. We might also consider his remark that 'a lack of motivation is a logical response to repeated failure' to be a common sentiment. Up until recently, I held a relatively traditional perspective on motivation and achievement: motivated pupils achieve. And who doesn't want to teach motivated pupils, right?

Pekrun et al. (2017: 1653) attempted to challenge the traditional one-direction correlational model on motivation with a reciprocal (two-way) model highlighting 'the importance of emotions for students' achievement and of achievement for the development of emotions'. Motivation directs behaviour towards achievement and therefore is known to be an important

---

1   D. Muijs, interview with author (2018).

determinant of academic success. However, achievement motivation is not a single construct and subsumes factors such as motivational beliefs, task value and achievement goals.

The researchers reported a 'reciprocal effects model of emotion and achievement' (Pekrun et al., 2017: 1653), where positive emotions (enjoyment and pride) positively predicted subsequent end-of-year maths grades, and grades in turn positively predicted the development of positive emotions. Likewise, maths-related negative emotions (anger, anxiety, shame, hopelessness, boredom) were negative predictors of subsequent maths grades, and grades in turn were a negative predictor for the development of negative emotions.

These findings were consistent for seven discrete emotions, four time intervals, two different measures of achievement (grades and test scores) and three school tracks (or groupings), while controlling for gender, intelligence and critical demographic background variables.

Interestingly, Pekrun et al. (2017) also suggested that these results were mediated by pupils' perceptions of competence and control over achievement, again pointing to the importance of developing their metacognitive monitoring and control capabilities. Remember: 'emotions indeed have an influence on adolescents' achievement, over and above the effects of general cognitive ability and prior accomplishments' (Pekrun et al., 2017: 1660).

The effects of emotions on adolescents' academic achievement 'represent a true causal influence of students' emotion experiences' (Pekrun et al., 2017: 1661), with success generally increasing perceived control, thus enhancing positive emotions, and failure expected to decrease control, leading to negative emotions.

Therefore, how do we strengthen adolescents' positive emotions (and minimise their negative emotions)? Providing pupils with opportunities to experience success and mastery over competition goals may help to promote positive emotions and prevent negative emotions (Pekrun et al., 2014). Self-assessed, high-success spaced retrieval practice with confidence-based assessment would be a strong candidate. Using hints has been recommended. You could always ask your pupils!

In perhaps the most extensive study of this effect, Agarwal et al. (2014) surveyed 1,408 middle and high school pupils who had experienced classroom-based retrieval practice programmes. The key findings were that 92% of pupils viewed the classroom retrieval practice activities positively, believing that retrieval practice helped them to learn, and 72% said that frequent retrieval practice helped them to feel less nervous about classroom exams.

Cogliano et al. (2019: 117) also observed: 'Students perceived retrieval practice as helpful for retaining and retrieving information over time, for monitoring their comprehension, and for cueing important information for subsequent restudy.'

Does the answer lie in plain sight?

According to the expectancy-value theory (Wigfield and Eccles, 2000), expectations of success and task value are shaped by a combination of factors. Wigfield and Eccles' (2000) research has demonstrated that expectations for success and task value are distinct constructs and that expectations for success tend to predict learners' later task value – that is, learners tend to value the domains in which they feel competent.

And that makes sense: pupils are more likely to be motivated in a task if they expect to do well and they value the activity. We appreciate those tasks where we have situational confidence and have experienced success in the past or are experiencing success now. Together, expectations for success and task value have been shown to predict learner effort (motivation) and performance on learning tasks and tests.

Takeaways

- Testing is inherently good for learning, both directly and indirectly.
- Testing improves metacognitive monitoring accuracy and retrieval practice enhances learner confidence, all of which has clear links to motivation for learning.
- Testing has both forward and backward effects.
- Pre-testing or potentiated learning induces pupils to exert more effort to retrieve the subsequently studied information. Use this knowledge to your (and your pupils') advantage.
- Pre-testing or potentiated learning can support assessment of prior learning, identifying gaps in knowledge and sparking a sense of curiosity (see Chapter 5).

- Work out the success sweet spot for your pupils. Remember, the optimal failure rate for learning could be as low as 10-20%.

- Motivation and achievement have a reciprocal relationship.

- Learning is emotional and emotions influence adolescents' achievement, over and above the effects of general cognitive ability and prior accomplishments.

- The motivational conundrum to solve is making it count but not too much.

- If you only have time to read one paper on this topic: M. L. Rivers, Metacognition about practice testing: a review of learners' beliefs, monitoring, and control of test-enhanced learning. *Educational Psychology Review*, 33(3) (2021): 823-862.

- Although, as I recommended the Rivers (2021) paper in Chapter 7, you might also try: R. Pekrun, S. Lichtenfeld, H. W. Marsh, K. Murayama and T. Goetz, Achievement emotions and academic performance: longitudinal models of reciprocal effects. *Child Development,* 88(5) (2017): 1653-1670.

Case study: Deadpool teaches the classics (and now geography)

Ben Windsor is assistant head of faculty for humanities, and prior to this was head of a small classics department at a state academy school which had a high proportion of pupil premium students.

The first challenge

Being a relatively junior teacher (at that point) in charge of a department containing one member of staff with two GCSE subjects, my interest in retrieval practice (I had not stumbled upon successive relearning at this point) started on the back of necessity. The vast amount of examined content to teach, not only in history (which I taught part-time) but also ancient history and Latin, and the modest curriculum allocation meant that time was precious. I also knew that retrieval was both effective and efficient or 'low cost, high profit'.

Success in each of these subjects demands a deep knowledge of the source material, with the higher marks attained by those students who can make links between factual knowledge and apply facts as a springboard into complex thoughts regarding causes, effects, changes and continuities in the material. The sheer weight of content presented an almost insurmountable challenge.

In teaching Latin, particularly vocabulary, but also in the teaching of the Latin literature unit, the challenge included getting students to know and retain the quotes of various authors (in Latin), their translations, any techniques used therein and the intertextuality with other pieces. To put it simply, the weight of declarative knowledge content was greater than the allocation of curriculum time.

What we did

As the students became more au fait with retrieval practice as a whole, it quickly became apparent that the number of exposures they had to information greatly improved retrieval strength. This manifested in the speed and clarity of retrieved information from the learners as well as heightened intertextual links when writing about literature.

Classroom discussions yielded more contributions in general, from a wider group of students, while negative classroom behaviours manifested less. Building confidence through success quickly translated to student motivation, empowerment and agency. The students wanted to quiz; the students asked to quiz. However, it was not only the students who benefited: as a teacher, a heightened emphasis on my own routines and pedagogy underpinned my professional confidence to push forwards.

A second challenge

Now, 12 months on, with my career running firmly in the modern humanities, I am tasked with overseeing the teaching and learning of humanities in general and geography in particular. While being a fast learner, and quickly learning the source material of the AQA geography GCSE, I also put into practice what I had learned regarding retrieval and successive relearning, applying the pedagogical lessons to a new context with much the same success

The new challenge would be seeing a Year 10 group starting their GCSE up to and including their assessment in Year 11. I was determined to hit the ground running.

What we did

From the moment these students saw me at the beginning of the academic year, we focused on retrieval: pre-testing knowledge, relearning content from lessons and spaced learning with RememberMore. It was our very first class activity. It will be our last too.

More broadly, the department adopted a renewed pedagogical focus on testing and relearning. The school-wide vision – the overall improvement of grades, the empowerment of the individual in their own learning and the reduction of poor classroom behaviours – further supported our department goals.

Students were informed of the why (basic cognitive science, how memory and learning work, how successive relearning strengthens learning and memory processes) as well as the how. The additional buy-in was tangible. This was also linked to our department's growing sense of confidence in using retrieval and the improving day-to-day behaviours of classes (improved attention and fewer behaviour referrals).

The plan was to begin retrieving the knowledge almost as soon as it was learned, building up and accumulating subject knowledge by testing over a period of time. Both more traditional knowledge organisers and RememberMore decks draw on the exact same knowledge, creating two arms to the same body of knowledge – a mirror image of the other, directing students to the precise knowledge we want them to know and remember.

The topics learned would begin to be interleaved with one another, providing testing on all topics while making use of appropriate spacing. For example, at the beginning of each lesson Year 10 geographers are quizzed on tectonics, weather hazards, climate change, tropical rainforests and cold environments. By the time we reach the end of the teaching content, each class will have reviewed the entire course content. Encoding new knowledge was steady, even slow, but frequent relearning fostered a high degree of student agency and empowered the learners.

Self-assessment is core to our approach across the department; we do not check the students' self-marking. The expectation is for total honesty. We regularly tell our learners that they gain nothing by being dishonest and would forego the opportunity to see where they could improve.

Without question, this approach fosters student agency. Students accepted the idea of self-marking instantly and were pleased at the opportunity. Before long, they were ready to self-mark without explicit instruction; most teachers in the department reported this cultural change after only four or five lessons.

When corrective feedback was offered, it became an effective springboard for elaborative questioning – and yet more student agency and more motivation, as the students now wanted to showcase what else they knew and could remember around the questions being posed. Class discussions could be invigorated by pitching 'why' or 'how' questions in response to factual recall questions.

Self-perceptions of success continue on leaving the classroom, and so students are encouraged to use the same processes and protocols in their own self-directed learning and directed homework. A high proportion of our learners also use the RememberMore app. Where this is the case, I can clearly see which learners go above and beyond via the dashboard, and I reward them handsomely.

The outcomes

There are few things more effective when seeking to foster autonomy and motivation in learners than carefully celebrating their wins. Allowing the students to share their scores on two successive rounds of testing provides motivation, allowing them to see real, in-the-moment gains and upturns in knowledge acquisition. The gains are in knowing more, in knowing what they don't know confidently yet, in greater focus during lessons (as they expect to be tested), in building classrooms rich in how and why questions, and in fostering trustful classrooms.

All of this began to take effect in a noticeable way. It became evident that learners had to achieve some degree of success to enable them to self-motivate more effectively, particularly those students who found it difficult to self-motivate or felt insecure or disenfranchised in their learning.

Engagement with low-stakes testing has been palpable. In each lesson, the students are itching for a piece of quantitative data which shows they are improving or, more valuable yet, how and where they can improve.

There is a more focused and motivated classroom climate, and since the learners are given timely corrective feedback, there is also psychological security. This, in turn, affects learner confidence, which ultimately feeds back into application in class.

Therefore, there are not just the direct benefits of the testing effect (even getting answers wrong has an important impact on learning) and the valuable exercise of addressing misconceptions and correcting errors. There is also the indirect effect on students' motivation, metacognitive skills (know thyself) and agency. We have since whittled this down to a formula:

- Two parts psychological security (since the correct answers are always provided).
- Two parts student agency (self-marking and assessment and access to learning materials outside of class).
- One part low-stakes testing.

All of this means that my students, like the Marvel anti-hero Deadpool, are able to apply 100% maximum effort in a tight spot. The only difference is that they put in such effort all the time, with significant correlation between their latest assessment data and the time logged using RememberMore.

Elsewhere, the roll-out of these approaches to Year 7 has also yielded some interesting results, particularly in that many of our Year 7 students are now accessing higher-level content issued on the platform simply because they feel it is best for their learning. They have even started to enjoy it!

All in all, I have gained many new insights into teaching and learning and student motivation in my foray into cognitive science and successive relearning. First and foremost, as educators, we must do what we can to place the responsibility and ability to achieve success in the hands of the learners. Using RememberMore not only provides the direct benefit of a ready-to-go, portable means by which to review course content, but it also works indirectly as a vehicle for motivation and student autonomy. It has sharply increased engagement by providing a tool and framework from which the students can work to make positive steps in their own learning.

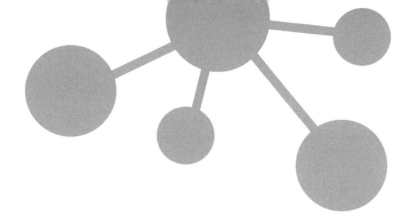

Conclusion

Ten years and still learning

Back in 2011, I encountered the research of Dr Jeffrey Karpicke via a Purdue University press release (Patterson Neubert, 2011; see also Karpicke and Blunt, 2011). At the time, I added a note to the blog post: 'One to follow up on. Testing promotes learning. If the practice of testing promotes learning, how can we make testing part of learning?'

I did go on to follow up. I casually read research papers that explored the impact of retrieval practice on learning, spacing, interleaving and, to a lesser extent, test-enhanced learning. After returning from teaching overseas in 2019, I found myself back in the classroom teaching English full-time. This opportunity reignited my interest in testing as a part of learning. I spent six months writing and reflecting on all that I had read, road-tested and discussed with researchers and fellow test-enhanced learning practitioners before I stumbled on successive relearning and subsequently personalisation. Of course, with an interest in test-enhanced learning comes curriculum design, defining and sequencing the substantive knowledge, and designing flashcard questions. Notably, the benefits of metacognition and motivation has commandeered the later part of the edventure, with my current professional interest focused on learning efficiencies, lowering failure rates and the use of self-assessment.

So, after nearly three years exploring how best to incorporate the benefits of test-enhanced learning, how has my teaching pedagogy evolved? First and foremost, I employ McDaniel and Einstein's (2020) KBCP framework! By taking the time to explain to my pupils why and how I am investing in quizzing and assessments, and more recently self-assessment, I am ready and accepting of the fact that the majority of them will be loath to take their cough syrup or eat their spinach without good reason. Next, I manage failure rates and spotlight successes in an effort to develop their belief and commitment for quizzing. I plan our quizzing very deliberately (daily, weekly, as homework, as revisions, as post-assessment review). Finally, I employ self-assessment to leverage the logistical, pedagogical, metacognitive and affective benefits of test-enhanced learning.

With a deeper understanding of cognitive architecture, memory, remembering and forgetting, I am fastidious about pupils being attentive and being precise about what I ask them to attend to. Attention is everything. The fact that most quizzing is 'independent learning' inherently helps to establish robust routines that demand every pupil's full attention. I am also insistent that pupils pay attention to one another: 'Next, I'm going to ask an important question. [Pause] Following that, I'm going to select three pupils for their considered response. The *fourth* pupil needs to be ready with their opinion on which pupils' answer was the best and why.'

As I have developed a deeper understanding of the two distinct phases of encoding (learning) and maintenance (remembering/relearning), I am more deliberate in what I select to teach. I now teach less, and I actually expect the pupils to learn and remember less. When introducing new knowledge, I am even more selective, more reductive and more prescriptive about what pupils are expected to attend to. And, as I told the *SecEd* (2022) podcast on memory, I never expect to teach something just once.

I see test-enhanced learning as teaching. I quiz cumulatively (self-assessed) in every lesson, not solely for teaching and relearning but to offer opportunities to experience success and for metacognitive monitoring. As Kirby and Helen advise:

Consistent routines build retrieval opportunities into every lesson (not just at the start).

Kirby Dowler

Lesson routines to help make the habits stick.

Helen Webb

I quiz (peer or teacher marked) every week, knowing that the act of assessing your own judgement of learning is one of the most effective ways to deepen a memory trace. I set an assessment in every teaching cycle. I now recognise and use the spacing opportunities afforded to me by my teaching timetable to promote spaced retrieval practice, which includes using personalised spaced retrieval as homework. I recognise and promote the value of sleep with my pupils. I see teaching as much more of a process and much less of an event.

I aim to use personalised spaced retrieval to promote acquisition of key knowledge ahead of the learning – for example, learning character names or contextual information about the text we are about to study. I will never forget that first experience of teaching *Othello*.

I also sometimes utilise testing for learning, particularly pre-testing to spark curiosity and interest in a topic, as well as priming future learning moments.

I know that relearning is super-efficient. Investing in testing for learning for encoding, through retrieval practice at the start of the unit, can be pedestrian, but I know I need to persist. Relearning rapidly accelerates learning, and success has a significant impact on pupils' motivation. Using self-assessment in class empowers pupils and offers significant metacognitive benefits too.

Promoting and forewarning about upcoming end-of-unit or end-of-year tests provides a very valid reason for pupils to direct their attention to your teaching in the first place. I often remind pupils of this too.

As for the actual use of test-enhanced learning and retrieval practice, I am more aware of the different modes of recall, the power of cues and hints to underpin pupils' success and how to manipulate the level of difficulty of retrieval prompts. Item difficulty is a factor. Difficult-to-learn information is reviewed at shorter time intervals and is tagged so that it can be accessed separatley or accumulatively.

I have learned that, in the early stages of learning, the shallow question or flashcard banks with high repetition and high success rates build confidence and motivation, which pays a weighty dividend in the long run.

When pupils acquire and retain knowledge, the way they interact and think about learning evolves and the climate in class changes. So, when new knowledge surfaces in lessons, notice it. Celebrate it.

One notable change is how I employ homework – moving from general learning tasks and activities to personalised spaced retrieval practice flash-cards. Homework commitment is measured in time invested. Every minute counts. The personalisation of retrieval practice and the efficiency of relearn-ing – its impact on motivation – is tangible. The term retrieval is misleading as it implies a terminal strategy. Testing *is*, and informs, learning, so pre-test, test during teaching and post-test after, are all important. In 2011 I wrote: 'Testing promotes learning. If the practice of testing promotes learning, how can we make testing part of learning? In 2022: 'Test before you learn. Test as you learn. Learn as you test.'[1]

Eight steps to test-enhanced learning

1 Explicitly define the knowledge to be learned. Teach less and plan to reteach content. Teacher knowledge is at the heart of test-enhanced learning.

2 Design your own testing routine and stick to it. Routines build habits. Teacher expertise is at the heart of test-enhanced learning.

3 Design with potentiation, encoding (learning) and maintenance (remembering/relearning) in mind. Test before you learn. Test as you learn. Learn as you test.

4 Lead the approach. Teach the pupils why testing is such a powerful approach for learning and preparation for assessments and examinations.

5 Design for low failure rates. Learning is emotional and emotions influence adolescents' achievement, over and above the effects of general cognitive ability and prior accomplishments. The optimal error rate could be as low as 15% (Wilson et al., 2019) or even lower (Eglington and Pavlik, 2020). Plan for 85% success, especially during encoding.

6 Testing and self-assessment develops metacognitive monitoring and enhances metacognition accuracy (Rivers, 2021), directing more informed study decisions and contributing to positively affective classrooms.

7 Testing as homework, or self-directed testing, can be very effective.

---

1 See https://www.kristianstill.co.uk/wordpress/2011/01/28/links-for-2011-01-28/.

8   The most efficient retrieval schedule is a personalised one, accounting for the learner's rates of forgetting and prior knowledge (Latimier et al., 2021). Use tools that support personalised spaced retrieval practice.

Kathleen McDermott (2021: 609) observes: 'If the eventual goal is to be able to retrieve … knowledge from memory, perhaps practicing retrieval of that information would be a better way to learn. Indeed, retrieval practice is one of the most effective ways of solidifying new knowledge, although this fact is underappreciated by most learners (and teachers).' Together, we can address this.

Glossary

attention	the primary gatekeeper of learning and relearning. It is the ability to direct, maintain and selectively focus on a specific stimulus.
cognitive load	the amount of information requiring our attention; the demands on the working memory of processing information.
declarative knowledge	the part of the subject where the pupils understand each discipline as a tradition of enquiry with its own distinctive pursuit of truth.
dual coding	the presentation and combination of words with visuals.
elaboration	adding details to memories and integrating new information with existing knowledge.
elaborative interrogation	a questioning method prompting learners to offer an explanation for an explicitly stated fact (their answer).
encoding	the process by which information moves from short-term to long-term memory.
forward testing effect	the finding that the retrieval of previously studied information can enhance the learning of subsequently presented new but conceptually related information.
interference	what happens when previously learned information competes or interferes with what is being learned and then retrieved.
interleaving/interleaved practice	involves switching between topics (e.g. ABAB), with learners forced to select an appropriate strategy for each topic.

maintenance	the process by which information in long-term is periodically accessed, remembered or relearned.
metacognition	learners' understanding and regulation (and self-regulation) of their own learning process, including their beliefs and perceptions about learning, monitoring the state of their knowledge and controlling their learning activities.
mind wandering	when thoughts that are unrelated or irrelevant to the task you are trying to pay attention to distract you.
motivation	(within test-enhanced learning) focused on the reciprocal effects of emotion and achievement on a learner's testing experience.
personalisation	where retrieval practice is adapted to meet the needs of each learner.
potentiated learning	the learning gains from asking pupils questions before they are taught new information.
relearning	the process of retrieving a target from a cue, previously successfully retrieved, at a spaced or distributed interval.
restudying	the general studying of previously taught material. Retrieval and restudying are commonly combined in research studies.
retrieval	accessing learned information held in long-term memory. In most retrieval research, it is the process of retrieving the target from a cue, often referred to as testing, test-enhanced learning or retrieval practice (quizzing).
schema	an interconnected network of related memories which we use to make sense of our world.

spacing or distributed practice	the deliberate act of separating encoding, relearning or retrieval tasks.
storage	securing newly acquired information into memory and maintaining it.
studying	presenting the cue and target for a period of time to allow participants to encode that association. (It is often quite a short period of time; four seconds is typical.)
substantive knowledge	the subject knowledge and explicit vocabulary used to learn about the content.
successive relearning	alternating between retrieval practice with corrective feedback until a certain level of retrieval success has been met and then relearning that material in subsequent sessions to a certain level of retrieval success.
testing effect/test-enhanced learning	the direct and indirect learning gains secured through retrieval practice.
transfer	where a learner's mastery of knowledge or skills in one context enables them to apply that knowledge or skill in a different context.
valley of disappointment	the period of investment where teachers and pupils feel discouraged, having put in hours of effortful practice and experienced nominal results preceding accelerated benefits.

References

Adesope, O. O., Trevisan, D. A. and Sundararajan, N. (2017). Rethinking the use of tests: a meta-analysis of practice testing. *Review of Educational Research*, 87(3): 659–701. https://doi.org/10.3102/0034654316689306.

Agarwal, P. K. (2021). I've said it before and I'll say it a million times more: the first time students retrieve shouldn't be on a midterm or final exam. Twitter post (8 December, 8:22pm). Available at: https://mobile.twitter.com/PoojaAgarwal/status/1468677482668826627.

Agarwal, P. K. (2022). Powerful teaching: unleash the science of learning [video]. Keynote presentation at SXSW EDU Conference, Austin, TX, 11–20 March. Available at: https://www.youtube.com/watch?v=OUl0mMVbkAc.

Agarwal, P. K. and Bain, P. M. (2019). *Powerful Teaching: Unleash the Science of Learning*. San Francisco, CA: Jossey-Bass.

Agarwal, P. K., D'Antonio, L., Roediger III, H. L., McDermott, K. B. and McDaniel, M. A. (2014). Classroom-based programs of retrieval practice reduce middle school and high school students' test anxiety. *Journal of Applied Research in Memory and Cognition*, 3(3): 131–139. https://doi.org/10.1016/j.jarmac.2014.07.002.

Agarwal, P. K., Finley, J. R., Rose, N. S. and Roediger III, H. L. (2017). Benefits from retrieval practice are greater for students with lower working memory capacity. *Memory*, 25(6): 764–771. https://doi.org/10.1080/09658211.2016.1220579.

Agarwal, P. K., Nunes, L. D. and Blunt J. R. (2021). Retrieval practice consistently benefits student learning: a systematic review of applied research in schools and classrooms. *Educational Psychology Review*, 33(4): 1409–1453. https://doi.org/10.1007/s10648-021-09595-9.

Agarwal, P. K. and Roediger III, H. L. (2011). Expectancy of an open-book test decreases performance on a delayed closed-book test. *Memory*, 19(8): 836–852. https://doi.org/10.1080/09658211.2011.613840.

Anderson, M. C. and Neely, J. H. (1996). Interference and inhibition in memory retrieval. In E. L. Bjork and R. A. Bjork (eds), *Memory*. San Diego, CA: Academic Press, pp. 237–313.

Andrade, H. G. (2019) .A critical review of research on student self-assessment. *Frontiers in Education*, 4: article 87. https://doi.org/10.3389/feduc.2019.00087.

Ariel, R., Dunlosky, J. and Bailey, H. (2009). Agenda-based regulation of study-time allocation: when agendas override item-based monitoring. *Journal of Experimental Psychology: General*, 138(3): 432–437. https://doi.org/10.1037/a0015928.

Ariel, R. and Karpicke, J. D. (2018). Improving self-regulated learning with a retrieval practice intervention. *Journal of Experimental Psychology: Applied*, 24(1): 43–56. https://doi.org/10.1037/xap0000133.

Ausubel, D. P. (1968). *Educational Psychology: A Cognitive View*. New York: Holt, Rinehart and Winston.

Baddeley, A. D. (2001) Is working memory still working? *American Psychologist*, 56(11): 851–864. https://doi.org/10.1037/0003-066x.56.11.851

Baddeley, A. D. (2003). Working memory: looking back and looking forward. *Nature Reviews Neuroscience*, 4(10): 829–839. https://doi.org/10.1038/nrn1201.

Baddeley, A. D. (2022). Working memory is a mental space that allows us to temporarily hold and manipulate information consciously for a limited time period. Twitter post (9 April, 8:18am). Available at: https://twitter.com/EvidenceInEdu/status/1512691346922000390.

Bahrick, H. P. (1979). Maintenance of knowledge: questions about memory we forgot to ask. *Journal of Experimental Psychology: General*, 108(3): 296–308. https://doi.org/10.1037/0096-3445.108.3.296.

Bahrick, H. P., Bahrick, L. E., Bahrick, A. S. and Bahrick, P. E. (1993). Maintenance of foreign language vocabulary and the spacing effect. *Psychological Science*, 4(5): 316–321. https://doi.org/10.1111/j.1467-9280.1993.tb00571.x.

Bahrick, H. P. and Hall, L. K. (2005). The importance of retrieval failures to long-term retention: a metacognitive explanation of the spacing effect. *Journal of Memory and Language*, 52(4): 566–577. https://doi.org/10.1016/j.jml.2005.01.012.

Barenberg, J. and Dutke, S. (2019). Testing and metacognition: retrieval practise effects on metacognitive monitoring in learning from text. *Memory*, 27(3): 269–279. https://doi.org/10.1080/09658211.2018.1506481.

Bertilsson, F., Stenlund, T., Wiklund-Hörnqvist, C. and Jonsson, B. (2021). Retrieval practice: beneficial for all students or moderated by individual differences? *Psychology Learning and Teaching*, 20(1): 21–39. https://doi.org/10.1177/1475725720973494.

Birnbaum, M., Kornell, N., Bjork. E. L. and Bjork, R. A. (2013). Why interleaving enhances inductive learning: the roles of discrimination and retrieval. *Memory and Cognition*, 41(3): 392–402. https://doi.org/10.3758/s13421-012-0272-7.

Biwer, F., oude Egbrink, M. G. A., Aalten, P. and de Bruin, A. B. H. (2020). Fostering effective learning strategies in higher education: a mixed-methods study. *Journal of Applied Research in Memory and Cognition*, 9(2): 186–203. https://doi.org/10.1016/j.jarmac.2020.03.004.

Bjork, E. L. and Bjork, R. A. (2011). Making things hard on yourself, but in a good way: creating desirable difficulties to enhance learning. In M. A. Gernsbacher, R. W. Pew, L. M. Hough and J. R. Pomerantz (eds), *Psychology and the Real World: Essays Illustrating Fundamental Contributions to Society*. New York: Worth Publishers, pp. 56–64.

Bjork, E. L., Little, J. L. and Storm, B. C. (2014). Multiple-choice testing as a desirable difficulty in the classroom. *Journal of Applied Research in Memory and Cognition*, 3(3): 165–170. https://doi.org/10.1016/j.jarmac.2014.03.002.

Bjork, R. A. (1994). Memory and metamemory considerations in the training of human beings. In J. Metcalfe and A. P. Shimamura (eds), *Metacognition: Knowing About Knowing*. Cambridge, MA: MIT Press, pp. 185–205.

Bjork, R. A. (2011). On the symbiosis of remembering, forgetting and learning. In A. S. Benjamin (ed.), *Successful Remembering and Successful Forgetting: A Festschrift in Honor of Robert A. Bjork*. New York: Psychology Press, pp. 1–22.

Bjork, R. A. (2015). Forgetting as a friend of learning. In D. S. Lindsay, C. M. Kelley, A. P. Yonelinas and H. L. Roediger III (eds), *Remembering: Attributions, Processes, and Control in Human Memory: Papers in Honour of Larry L. Jacoby*. New York: Psychology Press, pp. 15–28.

Bjork, R. A. and Bjork, E. L. (1992). A new theory of disuse and an old theory of stimulus fluctuation. In A. F. Healy, S. M. Kosslyn and R. M. Shiffrin (eds), *From Learning Processes to Cognitive Processes: Essays in Honor of William K. Estes*, vol. 2. Hillsdale, NJ: Erlbaum, pp. 35–67.

Bjork, E. and Bjork, R. (2011). Making things hard on yourself, but in a good way: Creating desirable difficulties to enhance learning. In: M. Gernsbacher, R. Pew, L. Hough et al. (eds) *Psychology and the Real World: Essays Illustrating Fundamental Contributions to Society.* New York: Worth, pp. 55–64.

Bjork, R. A. and Bjork, E. L. (2019). Forgetting as the friend of learning: implications for teaching and self-regulated learning. *Advances in Physiology Education*, 43(2): 164–167. https://doi.org/10.1152/advan.00001.2019.

Bjork, R. A. and Bjork, E. L. (2020). Desirable difficulties in theory and practice. *Journal of Applied Research in Memory and Cognition*, 9(4): 475–479. https://doi.org/10.1016/j.jarmac.2020.09.003.

Bjork, R. A., Dunlosky, J. and Kornell, N. (2013) .Self-regulated learning: beliefs, techniques, and illusions. *Annual Review of Psychology*, 64: 417–444. https://doi.org/10.1146/annurev-psych-113011-143823.

Black, P. and Wiliam, D. (1998). Assessment and classroom learning. *Assessment in Education: Principles, Policy & Practice*, 5(1): 7–74. https://doi.org/10.1080/0969595980050102.

Bol, L. and Hacker, D. J. (2001). A comparison of the effects of practice tests and traditional review on performance and calibration. *Journal of Experimental Education*, 69(2): 133–151. https://doi.org/10.1080/00220970109600653.

Buchin, Z. L. and Mulligan, N. W. (2022). Retrieval-based learning and prior knowledge. *Journal of Educational Psychology* [advance online publication]. https://doi.org/10.1037/edu0000773.

Butler, A. C., Godbole, N. and Marsh, E. J. (2013). Explanation feedback is better than correct answer feedback for promoting transfer of learning. *Journal of Educational Psychology*, 105(2): 290–298. https://doi.org/10.1037/a0031026.

Butler, A. C., Karpicke, J. D. and Roediger III, H. L. (2008). Correcting a metacognitive error: feedback increases retention of low-confidence correct responses. *Journal of Experimental Psychology: Learning, Memory, and Cognition*, 34(4): 918–928. https://doi.org/10.1037/0278-7393.34.4.918.

Carpenter, S. K. (2017). Spacing effects on learning and memory. In J. H. Byrne (ed.), *Learning and Memory: A Comprehensive Reference*, 2nd edn. Cambridge, MA: Academic Press, pp. 465–485.

Carpenter, S. K., Cepeda, N. J., Rohrer, D., Kang, S. H. K. and Pashler, H. (2012). Using spacing to enhance diverse forms of learning: review of recent research and implications for instruction. *Educational Psychology Review*, 24(3): 369–378. https://doi.org/10.1007/s10648-012-9205-z.

Carpenter, S. K., Rahman, S. and Perkins, K. (2018). The effects of prequestions on classroom learning. *Journal of Experimental Psychology: Applied*, 24(1): 34–42. https://doi.org/10.1037/xap0000145.

Cepeda, N. J., Coburn, N., Rohrer, D., Wixted, J. T., Mozer, M. C. and Pashler, H. (2009). Optimizing distributed practice: theoretical analysis and practical implications. *Experimental Psychology*, 56(4): 236–246. https://doi.org/10.1027/1618-3169.56.4.236.

Cepeda, N. J., Pashler, H., Vul, E., Wixted, J. T. and Rohrer, D. (2006). Distributed practice in verbal recall tasks: a review and quantitative synthesis. *Psychological Bulletin*, 132(3): 354–380. https://doi.org/10.1037/0033-2909.132.3.354.

Cepeda, N. J., Vul, E., Rohrer, D., Wixted, J. T. and Pashler, H. (2008). Spacing effects in learning: a temporal ridgeline of optimal retention. *Psychological Science*, 19(11): 1095-1102. https://doi.org/10.1111/j.1467-9280.2008.02209.x.

Chan, J. C. K. (2009). When does retrieval induced forgetting and when does it induce facilitation? Implications for retrieval inhibition, testing effect, and text processing. *Journal of Memory and Language*, 61(2): 153-170. https://doi.org/10.1016/j.jml.2009.04.004.

Chan, J. C. K., McDermott, K. B. and Roediger III, H. L. (2006). Retrieval-induced facilitation: initially nontested material can benefit from prior testing of related material. *Journal of Experimental Psychology: General*, 135(4): 553-571. https://doi.org/10.1037/0096-3445.135.4.553.

Chen, O., Paas, F. and Sweller, J. (2021). Spacing and interleaving effects require distinct theoretical bases: a systematic review testing the cognitive load and discriminative-contrast hypotheses. *Educational Psychology Review,* 33(4): 1499-1522. https://doi.org/10.1007/s10648-021-09613-w.

Chew, S. L. (2021). An advance organizer for student learning: choke points and pitfalls in studying. *Canadian Psychology/Psychologie canadienne*, 62(4): 420-427. https://doi.org/10.1037/cap0000290.

ChildWise (2020). *The Monitor Report 2020*. Norwich: ChildWise.

Christodoulou, C. (2013). *Seven Myths About Education*. Abingdon and New York: Routledge.

Christodoulou, D. (2022). I love Anki! Planning to blog more about it soon … Twitter post (17 February, 3:40pm). Available at: https://twitter.com/daisychristo/status/1229430512479035393.

Clark, R., Kirschner, P. and Sweller, J. (2012). Putting students on the path to learning: the case for fully guided instruction. *American Educator* (spring): 6-11. Available at: https://www.aft.org/sites/default/files/periodicals/Clark.pdf.

Clear, J. (2018). *Atomic Habits: An Easy and Proven Way to Build Good Habits and Break Bad Ones*. London: Random House.

Cogliano, M., Kardash, C. M. and Bernacki, M. L. (2019). The effects of retrieval practice and prior topic knowledge on test performance and confidence judgments. *Contemporary Educational Psychology*, 56: 117-129. https://doi.org/10.1016/j.cedpsych.2018.12.001.

Colbran, S., Gilding, A., Colbran, S., Oyson, M. and Nauman, S. (2015). The impact of student-generated digital flashcards on student learning of constitutional law. *The Law Teacher*, 51(1): 69-97. https://doi.org/10.1080/03069400.2015.1082239.

Couchman, J. J., Miller, N. E., Zmuda, S. J., Feather, K. and Schwartzmeyer, T. (2016). The instinct fallacy: the metacognition of answering and revising during college exams. *Metacognition and Learning*, 11(2): 171-185. https://doi.org/10.1007/s11409-015-9140-8.

Coutinho, M. V. C., Papanastasiou, E., Agni, S., Vasko, J. M. and Couchman, J. J. (2020). Metacognitive monitoring in test-taking situations: a cross-cultural comparison of college students. *International Journal of Instruction*, 13(1): 407-424. https://doi.org/10.29333/iji.2020.13127a.

Cowan, N. (2001). The magical number 4 in short-term memory: a reconsideration of mental storage capacity. *Behavioral and Brain Sciences*, 24(1): 87-114. https://doi.org/10.1017/S0140525X01003922.

De Jonge, M. O. (2014). *A Test of the Efficiency of Study and a Study on the Efficacy of Tests*. Erasmus University Rotterdam. Available at: https://repub.eur.nl/pub/51530.

De Jonge, M. O., Tabbers, H. K., Pecher, D. and Zeelenberg, R. (2012). The effect of study time distribution on learning and retention: a Goldilocks principle for presentation rate. *Journal of Experimental Psychology: Learning, Memory, and Cognition*, 38(2): 405–412. https://doi.org/10.1037/a0025897.

Dedrick, R. F., Rohrer, D. and Stershic, S. (2016). Content analysis of practice problems in 7th grade mathematics textbooks: blocked vs. interleaved practice. Presentation at the Annual Meeting of the American Educational Research Association, Washington, DC, 4 September.

Diekelmann, S. and Born, J. (2010). The memory function of sleep. *Nature Reviews: Neuroscience*, 11(2): 114–126. https://doi.org/10.1038/nrn2762.

Dobson, J. L. and Linderholm, T. (2015). Self-testing promotes superior retention of anatomy and physiology information. *Advances in Health Sciences Education: Theory and Practice*, 20(1): 149–161. https://doi.org/10.1007/s10459-014-9514-8.

Donoghue, G. and Hattie, J. (2021). A meta-analysis of ten learning techniques. *Frontiers in Education*, 6: article 5812161. Available at: https://www.frontiersin.org/articles/10.3389/feduc.2021.581216/full.

Dunlosky, J. (2013). Strengthening the student toolbox: study strategies to boost learning. *American Educator* (fall): 12–21. Available at: https://www.aft.org/sites/default/files/periodicals/dunlosky.pdf.

Dunlosky, J. and Metcalfe, J. (2009). *Metacognition*. Thousand Oaks, CA: SAGE Publications.

Dunlosky, J. and O'Brien, A. (2022). The power of successive relearning and how to implement it with fidelity using pencil and paper and web-based programs. *Scholarship of Teaching and Learning in Psychology*, 8(3): 225–235. https://doi.org/10.1037/stl0000233.

Dunlosky, J. and Rawson, K. A. (eds) (2019). *The Cambridge Handbook of Cognition and Education*. Cambridge: Cambridge University Press.

Dunlosky, J., Rawson, K. A., Marsh, E. J., Nathan, M. J. and Willingham, D. T. (2013). Improving students' learning with effective learning techniques: promising directions from cognitive and educational psychology. *Psychological Science in the Public Interest*, 14(1): 4–58. https://doi.org/10.1177/1529100612453266.

Earl, L. M. (2012). *Assessment As Learning: Using Classroom Assessment to Maximize Student Learning*. Thousand Oaks, CA: Corwin Press.

Ebbinghaus, H. (1885). *Über das Gedächtnis: Untersuchungen zur experimentellen Psychologie*. Leipzig: Duncker & Humblot.

Eglington, L. G. and Pavlik Jr, P. I. (2020). Optimizing practice scheduling requires quantitative tracking of individual item performance. *npj Science of Learning*, 5: article 15. https://doi.org/10.1038/s41539-020-00074-4.

Einstein, G. O., Mullet, H. G. and Harrison, T. L. (2012). The testing effect: illustrating a fundamental concept and changing study strategies. *Teaching of Psychology*, 39(3): 190–193. https://doi.org/10.1177/0098628312450432.

Emeny, W. G., Hartwig, M. K. and Rohrer, D. (2021). Spaced mathematics practice improves test scores and reduces overconfidence. *Applied Cognitive Psychology*, 35(4): 1082–1089. https://doi.org/10.1002/acp.3814.

Enders, N., Gaschler, R. and Kubik, V. (2021). Online quizzes with closed questions in formal assessment: how elaborate feedback can promote learning. *Psychology Learning and Teaching*, 20(1): 91–106. https://doi.org/10.1177/1475725720971205.

Endres, T., Carpenter, S., Martin, A. and Renkl, A. (2017). Enhancing learning by retrieval: enriching free recall with elaborative prompting. *Learning and Instruction*, 49: 13–20. https://doi.org/10.1016/j.learninstruc.2016.11.010.

Endres, T., Kranzdorf, L., Schneider, V. and Renkl, A. (2020). It matters how to recall – task differences in retrieval practice. *Instructional Science*, 48: 699–728. https://doi.org/10.1007/s11251-020-09526-1.

Ericsson, K. A. and Kintsch, W. (1995). Long-term working memory. *Psychological Review*, 102(2): 211–245. https://doi.org/10.1037/0033-295X.102.2.211.

Eysenck, M. W., Hunt, E., Ellis, A. and Johnson-Laird, P. N. (1994). *The Blackwell Dictionary of Cognitive Psychology*. Oxford: Blackwell.

Fazio, L. K. and Marsh, E. J. (2019). Retrieval-based learning in children. *Current Directions in Psychological Science*, 28(2): 111–116. https://doi.org/10.1177/0963721418806673.

Finn, B. (2020). Exploring interactions between motivation and cognition to better shape self-regulated learning. *Journal of Applied Research in Memory and Cognition*, 9(4): 461–467. https://doi.org/10.1016/j.jarmac.2020.08.008.

Finn, B. and Tauber, S. K. (2015). When confidence is not a signal of knowing: how students' experiences and beliefs about processing fluency can lead to miscalibrated confidence. *Educational Psychology Review*, 27(4): 567–586. https://doi.org/10.1007/s10648-015-9313-7.

Firth, J., Rivers, I. and Boyle, J. (2021). A systematic review of interleaving as a concept learning strategy. *Review of Education*, 9(2): 642–684. https://doi.org/10.1002/rev3.3266.

Flavell, J. H. (1979). Metacognition and cognitive monitoring: a new area of cognitive-developmental inquiry. *American Psychologist*, 34(10): 906–911. https://doi.org/10.1037/0003-066X.34.10.906.

Freeman, S., Eddy, S. L., McDonough, M., Smith, M. K., Okoroafor, N., Jordt, H. and Wenderoth, M. P. (2014). Active learning increases student performance in science, engineering, and mathematics. *Proceedings of the National Academy of Sciences of the United States of America*, 111(23): 8410–8415. https://doi.org/10.1073/pnas.1319030111.

Freemark, S. (2014). Studying with quizzes helps make sure the material sticks [interview with Henry Roediger III and Mark McDaniel], *Mindshift* (16 October). Available at: https://www.kqed.org/mindshift/37752/studying-with-quizzes-helps-make-sure-the-material-sticks.

Furst, E. (2018). Reconsolidation: the 'life' of a memory trace (December). Available at: https://sites.google.com/view/efratfurst/reconsolidation?pli=1.

Graham, S., Hebert, M. and Harris, K. R. (2015) Formative assessment and writing: a meta-analysis. *Elementary School Journal,* 115(4): 523–547. https://doi.org/10.1086/681947

Griffin, T., Wiley, J. and Thiede, K. (2008). Individual differences, rereading, and self-explanation: concurrent processing and cue validity as constraints on metacomprehension accuracy. *Memory and Cognition*, 36(1): 93–103. https://doi.org/10.3758/mc.36.1.93.

Grimaldi, P. J. and Karpicke, J. D. (2014). Guided retrieval practice of educational materials using automated scoring. *Journal of Educational Psychology*, 106(1): 58–68. https://doi.org/10.1037/a0033208https://doi.org/10.1037/a0033208.

Gupta, M. W., Pan, S. C. and Rickard, T. C. (2022). Prior episodic learning and the efficacy of retrieval practice. *Memory and Cognition*, 50: 722–735. https://doi.org/10.3758/s13421-021-01236-4.

Hacker, D. J. and Bol, L. (2019). Calibration and self-regulated learning: making the connections. In J. Dunlosky and K. A. Rawson (eds), *The Cambridge Handbook of Cognition and Education*. Cambridge: Cambridge University Press, pp. 647–677.

Harackiewicz, J. M., Canning, E. A., Tibbetts, Y., Priniski, S. J. and Hyde, J. S. (2016). Closing achievement gaps with a utility-value intervention: disentangling race and social class. *Journal of Personality and Social Psychology*, 111(5): 745–765. https://doi.org/10.1037/pspp0000075.

Hartwig, M. K. and Dunlosky, J. (2012). Study strategies of college students: are self-testing and scheduling related to achievement? *Psychonomic Bulletin and Review*, 19(1): 126–134. https://doi.org/10.3758/s13423-011-0181-y.

Hausman, H. and Kornell, N. (2014). Mixing topics while studying does not enhance learning. *Journal of Applied Research in Memory and Cognition*, 3(3): 153–160. https://doi.org/10.1016/j.jarmac.2014.03.003.

Heiner, C. E., Banet, A. I. and Wieman, C. (2014). Preparing students for class: how to get 80% of students reading the textbook before class. *American Journal of Physics*, 82(10): 989–996. https://doi.org/10.1119/1.4895008.

Heitmann, S., Grund, A., Berthold, K., Fries, S. and Roelle, J. (2018). Testing is more desirable when it is adaptive and still desirable when compared to note-taking. *Frontiers in Psychology*, 9, article 2596. https://doi.org/10.3389/fpsyg.2018.02596.

Heitmann, S., Grund, A., Fries, S., Berthold, K. and Roelle, J. (2022). The quizzing effect depends on hope of success and can be optimized by cognitive load-based adaptation. *Learning and Instruction*, 77: article 101526. https://doi.org/10.1016/j.learninstruc.2021.101526.

Heitmann, S., Obergassel, N., Fries, S., Grund, A., Berthold, K. and Roelle, J. (2021). Adaptive practice quizzing in a university lecture: a pre-registered field experiment. *Journal of Applied Research in Memory and Cognition*, 10(4): 603–620. https://doi.org/10.1037/h0101865.

Higham, P. A., Zengel, B., Bartlett, L. K. and Hadwin, J. A. (2021). The benefits of successive relearning on multiple learning outcomes. *Journal of Educational Psychology*, 114(5): 928–944. https://doi.org/10.1037/edu0000693.

Holt, N. and Lewis R. (2015). *AQA Psychology*. Carmarthen: Crown House Publishing.

Hui, L., de Bruin, A. B. H., Donkers, J. and van Merriënboer, J. J. G. (2021). Does individual performance feedback increase the use of retrieval practice? *Educational Psychology Review*, 33: 1835–1857. https://doi.org/10.1007/s10648-021-09604-x.

Hulleman, C. S., Kosovich, J. J., Barron, K. E. and Daniel, D. (2017) .Making connections: replicating and extending the utility-value intervention in the classroom. *Journal of Educational Psychology*, 109(3): 387–404. https://doi.org/10.1037/edu0000146.

Janes, J., Dunlosky, J., Rawson, K. and Jasnow, A. (2020). Successive relearning improves performance on a high stakes exam in a difficult biopsychology course. *Applied Cognitive Psychology*, 34(5): 1118–1132. https://doi.org/10.1002/acp.3699.

Jenkins, J. (1979). Four points to remember: a tetrahedral model of memory experiments. In L. S. Cermak and F. I. M. Craik (eds), *Levels of Processing in Human Memory*. Hillsdale, NJ: Erlbaum, pp. 429–446.

Jing, H. G., Szpunar, K. K. and Schacter, D. L. (2016). Interpolated testing influences focused attention and improves integration of information during a video-recorded lecture. *Journal of Experimental Psychology: Applied*, 22(3): 305-318. https://doi.org/10.1037/xap0000087.

Kang, S. H. K. (2016a). Spaced repetition promotes efficient and effective learning: policy implications for instruction. *Policy Insights from the Behavioral and Brain Sciences*, 3(1): 12-19. https://doi.org/10.1177/2372732215624708 .

Kang, S. H. K. (2016b). Spacing study sessions enhances learning [video] (13 February). Available at: https://www.youtube.com/watch?v=BLS4rylubBM.

Kang, S. H. K., McDermott, K. B. and Roediger III, H. L. (2007). Test format and corrective feedback modulate the effect of testing on memory retention. *European Journal of Cognitive Psychology*, 19(4-5): 528-558. https://doi.org/10.1080/09541440601056620.

Karpicke, J. D. (2009). Metacognitive control and strategy selection: deciding to practice retrieval during learning. *Journal of Experimental Psychology: General*, 138(4): 469-486. https://doi.org/10.1037/a0017341.

Karpicke, J. D. (2017). Retrieval-based learning: a decade of progress. In J. H. Byrne (ed.), *Learning and Memory: A Comprehensive Reference*. Cambridge, MA: Academic Press, pp. 487-514.

Karpicke, J. D. and Aue, W. R. (2015). The testing effect is alive and well with complex materials. *Educational Psychology Review*, 27(2): 317-326. https://doi.org/10.1007/s10648-015-9309-3.

Karpicke, J. D. and Blunt, J. R. (2011). Retrieval practice produces more learning than elaborative studying with concept mapping. *Science*, 331(6018): 772-775. https://doi.org/10.1126/science.1199327.

Karpicke, J. D., Blunt, J. R. and Smith, M. A. (2016). Retrieval-based learning: positive effects of retrieval practice in elementary school children. *Frontiers in Psychology*, 7(350): 1-8. http://dx.doi.org/10.3389/fpsyg.2016.00350.

Karpicke, J. D., Butler, A. C. and Roediger III, H. L. (2009). Metacognitive strategies in student learning: do students practise retrieval when they study on their own? *Memory*, 17(4): 471-479. https://doi.org/10.1080/09658210802647009.

Karpicke, J. D. and Roediger III, H. L. (2008). The critical importance of retrieval for learning. *Science*, 319(5865): 966-968. https://doi.org/10.1126/science.1152408.

Karpicke, J. D. and Roediger III, H. L. (2010). Is expanding retrieval a superior method for learning text materials? *Memory and Cognition*, 38: 116-124. https://doi.org/10.3758/MC.38.1.116.

Khanna, M. M. (2015). Ungraded pop quizzes: test-enhanced learning without all the anxiety. *Teaching of Psychology*, 42(2): 174-178. https://doi.org/10.1177/0098628315573144.

Kirk-Johnson, A., Galla, B. M. and Fraundorf, S. H. (2019) Perceiving effort as poor learning: the misinterpreted-effort hypothesis of how experienced effort and perceived learning relate to study strategy choice. *Cognitive Psychology*, 115: article 101237. https://doi.org/10.1016/j.cogpsych.2019.101237.

Kirschner, P. A. (2022) The more you know, the better you learn and the more you learn, the easier it gets! Twitter post (16 September, 4:35pm). Available at: https://twitter.com/P_A_Kirschner/status/1570798652964376577.

Kirschner, P. A., Sweller, J. and Clark, R. E. (2006) Why minimal guidance during instruction does not work: an analysis of the failure of constructivist, discovery, problem-based, experiential, and inquiry-based teaching. *Educational Psychologist*, 41(2): 75–86. https://doi.org/10.1207/s15326985ep4102_1.

Kluger, A. N. and DeNisi, A. (1996). The effects of feedback interventions on performance: a historical review, a meta-analysis, and a preliminary feedback intervention theory. *Psychological Bulletin*, 119(2): 254–284. https://doi.org/10.1037/0033-2909.119.2.254.

Köhler, W. (1947) .*Gestalt Psychology: An Introduction to New Concepts in Modern Psychology*. New York: Liveright.

Koriat, A. (2008). Easy comes, easy goes? The link between learning and remembering and its exploitation in metacognition. *Memory and Cognition*, 36(2): 416–428. https://doi.org/10.3758/MC.36.2.416.

Koriat, A. and Bjork, R. A. (2005). Illusions of competence in monitoring one's knowledge during study. *Journal of Experimental Psychology: Learning, Memory, and Cognition*, 31(2): 187–194. https://doi.org/10.1037/0278-7393.31.2.187

Kornell, N. (2009). Optimising learning using flashcards: spacing is more effective than cramming. *Applied Cognitive Psychology,* 23(9): 1297–1317. https://doi.org/10.1002/acp.1537.

Kornell, N. and Bjork, R. A. (2007). The promise and perils of self-regulated study. *Psychonomic Bulletin and Review*: 14, 219–224. https://doi.org/10.3758/BF03194055.

Kornell, N. and Bjork, R. A. (2008) .Learning concepts and categories: is spacing the 'enemy of induction'? *Psychological Science*, 19(6): 585–592. https://doi.org/10.1111/j.1467-9280.2008.02127.x.

Kornell, N. and Bjork, R. A. (2009). A stability bias in human memory: overestimating remembering and underestimating learning. *Journal of Experimental Psychology: General*, 138(4): 449.

Kornell, N., Klein, P. J. and Rawson, K. A. (2015). Retrieval attempts enhance learning, but retrieval success (versus failure) does not matter. *Journal of Experimental Psychology: Learning, Memory, and Cognition*, 41(1): 283–294. https://doi.org/10.1037/a0037850.

Kornell, N. and Metcalfe, J. (2006) Study efficacy and the region of proximal learning framework. *Journal of Experimental Psychology: Learning, Memory, and Cognition*, 32(3): 609–622. https://doi.org/10.1037/0278-7393.32.3.609.

Kornell, N., Rhodes, M. G., Castel, A. D. and Tauber, S. K. (2011) The ease-of-processing heuristic and the stability bias: dissociating memory, memory b.eliefs, and memory judgments. *Psychological Science*, 22(6): 787–794. https://doi.org/10.1177/0956797611-407929.

Krasne, S., Stevens, C. D., Kellman, P. J. and Niemann, J. T. (2020). Mastering electrocardiogram interpretation skills through a perceptual and. adaptive learning module. *AEM Education and Training*, 5(2): e10454. https://doi.org/10.1002/aet2.10454.

Kriegbaum, K., Becker, N. and Spinath, B. (2018). The relative importance of intelligence and motivation as predictors of school achievement: a meta-analysis. *Educational Research Review*, 25: 120–148. https://doi.org/10.1016/j.edurev.2018.10.001.

Kroneisen, M. and Kuepper-Tetzel, C. E. (2021). Using day and night – scheduling retrieval practice and sleep. *Psychology Learning and Teaching*, 20(1): 40–57. https://doi.org/10.1177/1475725720965363.

Latimier, A., Peyre, H. and Ramus, F. (2021). A meta-analytic review of the benefit of spacing out retrieval practice episodes on retention. *Educational Psychology Review*, 33: 959-987. https://doi.org/10.1007/s10648-020-09572-8.

Latimier, A., Riegert, A., Peyre, H., Ly, S. T., Casati, R. and Ramus, F. (2019). Does pre-testing promote better retention than post-testing? *npj Science of Learning*, 4: article 15. https://doi.org/10.1038/s41539-019-0053-1.

Leahy, W., Hanham, J. and Sweller, J. (2015). High element interactivity information during problem solving may lead to failure to obtain the testing effect. *Educational Psychology Review*, 27(2): 291-304. https://doi.org/10.1007/s10648-015-9296-4.

Leger, D., Beck, F., Richard, J. B. and Godeau, E. (2012). Total sleep time severely drops during adolescence. *PLOS One*, 7(10): e45204. https://doi.org/10.1371/journal.pone.0045204.

Leitner, S. (1972). *So lernt man lernen: Der Weg zum Erfolg*. Freiburg: Herder.

Liming, M. C. and Cuevas, J. (2017). An examination of the testing and spacing effects in a middle grade social studies classroom. *Georgia Educational Researcher*, 14(1): article 4. https://doi.org/10.20429/ger.2017.140104.

Lindsey, R. V., Mozer, M. C., Cepeda, N. J. and Pashler, H. (2009). Optimizing memory retention with cognitive models. In A. Howes, D. Peebles and R. Cooper (eds), *Proceedings of the 9th International Conference on Cognitive Modeling*. Manchester: ICCM. Available at: https://iccm-conference.neocities.org/2009/proceedings/cd/papers/257/paper257.pdf.

Lindsey, R. V., Shroyer, J. D., Pashler, H. and Mozer, M. C. (2014). Improving students' long-term knowledge retention through personalized review. *Psychological Science*, 25(3): 639-647. https://dx.doi.org/10.1177/0956797613504302.

Lyle, K. B., Bego, C. R., Hopkins, R. F., Hieb, J. L. and Ralston, P. A. (2020) .How the amount and spacing of retrieval practice affect the short- and long-term retention of mathematics knowledge. *Educational Psychology Review*, 32(1): 277-295.

MacLeod, C. M. (2011). I said, you said: the production effect gets personal. *Psychonomic Bulletin and Review*, 18: 1197-1202. https://doi.org/10.3758/s13423-011-0168-8.

MacLeod, C. M., Gopie, N., Hourihan, K. L., Neary, K. R. and Ozubko, J. D. (2010). The production effect: delineation of a phenomenon. *Journal of Experimental Psychology: Learning, Memory, and Cognition*, 36(3): 671-685. https://doi.org/10.1037/a0018785.

Mayer, R. E. (2014). Cognitive theory of multimedia learning. In R. E. Mayer (ed.), *The Cambridge Handbook of Multimedia Learning*. New York: Cambridge University Press, pp. 43-71.

Mazza, S., Gerbier, E., Gustin, M.-P., Kasikci, Z., Koenig, O., Toppino, T. C. and Magnin, M. (2016). Relearn faster and retain longer: along with practice, sleep makes perfect. *Science, Technology and Society*, 27(10): 46-65. https://doi.org/10.1177/0956797616659930.

McClelland, J. L. (2013) Incorporating rapid neocortical learning of new schema-consistent information into complementary learning systems theory. *Journal of Experimental Psychology: General*, 142(4): 1190-1210. https://doi.org/10.1037/a0033812.

Mccrea, P. (2019) *Learning: What Is It, And How Might We Catalyse It?* London: Ambition Institute. Available at: https://www.ambition.org.uk/research-and-insight/learning-what-is-it.

McDaniel, M. A. and Einstein, G. O. (2020) Training learning strategies to promote self-regulation and transfer: the knowledge, belief, commitment, and planning framework.

Perspectives on Psychological Science, 15(6): 1363–1381. https://doi.org/10.1177/1745-691620920723.

McDaniel, M. A., Einstein, G. O. and Een, E. (2021). Training college students to use learning strategies: a framework and pilot course. *Psychology Learning and Teaching*, 20(3): 364–382. https://doi.org/10.1177/1475725721989489.

McDaniel, M. A. and Little, J. L. (2019). Multiple-choice and short-answer quizzing on equal footing in the classroom: potential indirect effects of testing. In J. Dunlosky and K. A. Rawson (eds), *The Cambridge Handbook of Cognition and Education*. Cambridge: Cambridge University Press, pp. 480–499.

McDermott, K. B. (2021). Practicing retrieval facilitates learning. *Annual Review of Psychology*, 72: 609–633. https://doi.org/10.1146/annurev-psych-010419-051019.

McIntyre, S. H. and Munson, J. M. (2008). Exploring cramming: student behaviors, beliefs, and learning retention in the principles of marketing course. *Journal of Marketing Education*, 30(3): 226–243. https://doi.org/10.1177/0273475308321819.

Melton, A. W. (1963). Implications of short-term memory for a general theory of memory. *Journal of Verbal Learning and Verbal Behavior*, 2(1): 1–21. https://doi.org/10.1016/S0022-5371(63)80063-8.

Mettler, E., Massey, C. and Kellman, P. J. (2016). A comparison of adaptive and fixed schedules of practice. *Journal of Experimental Psychology: General*, 145(7): 897–917. https://doi.org/10.1037/xge0000170.

Miller, G. A. (1956). The magical number seven, plus or minus two: some limits on our capacity for processing information. *Psychological Review*, 63(2): 81–97. https://doi.org/10.1037/h0043158.Miller, T. M. and Geraci, L. (2011). Training metacognition in the classroom: the influence of incentives and feedback on exam predictions. *Metacognition and Learning*, 6(3): 303–314. https://doi.org/10.1007/s11409-011-9083-7.

Moreira, B. F. T., Pinto, T. S. S., Starling, D. S. V. and Jaeger, A. (2019). Retrieval practice in classroom settings: a review of applied research. *Frontiers in Psychology*, 4: article 5. http://dx.doi.org/10.3389/feduc.2019.00005.

Mould, K. (2022). Making sense of metacognition and self-regulation. Keynote session at the SecEd and Headteacher Update Conference: Metacognition – Practical Strategies for the Classroom, London, 23 September.

Mozer, M. C. and Lindsey, R. V. (2017) .Predicting and improving memory retention: psychological theory matters in the big data era. In M. Jones (ed.), *Big Data in Cognitive Science*. Abingdon and New York: Routledge, pp. 34–64.

Mozer, M. C., Pashler, H., Cepeda, N., Lindsey, R. and Vul, E. (2009). Predicting the optimal spacing of study: a multiscale context model of memory. In Y. Bengio, D. Schuurmans, J. Lafferty, C. Williams and A. Culotta (eds), *Advances in Neural Information Processing Systems*, vol. 22. La Jolla, CA: NIPS Foundation, pp. 1321–1329.

Mughal, A. (2021). *Think! Metacognition-Powered Primary Teaching*. Thousand Oaks, CA: SAGE Publications.

Mullet, H. G., Butler, A. C., Verdin, B., von Borries, R. and Marsh, E. J. (2014). Delaying feedback promotes transfer of knowledge despite student preferences to receive feedback immediately. *Journal of Applied Research in Memory and Cognition*, 3(3): 222–229. https://doi.org/10.1016/j.jarmac.2014.05.001.

Nazari, K. B. and Ebersbach, M. (2019). Distributed practice in mathematics: recommendable especially for students on a medium performance level? *Trends in Neuroscience and Education*, 17: article 100122. https://doi.org/10.1016/j.tine.2019.100122.

Nietfeld, J. L., Cao, L., and Osborne, J. W. (2005). Metacognitive monitoring accuracy and student performance in the postsecondary classroom. *The Journal of Experimental Education*, 74(1): 7-28.

Nunes, L. D. and Karpicke, J. D. (2015). Retrieval-based learning: research at the interface between cognitive science and education. In R. A. Scott and S. M. Kosslyn (eds), *Emerging Trends in the Social and Behavioral Sciences*. New York: John Wiley & Sons, pp. 1-16.

Nuthall, G. (2007). *The Hidden Lives of Learners*. Wellington: NZCER Press.

Pan, S. C. and Rickard, T. C. (2018). Transfer of test-enhanced learning: meta-analytic review and synthesis. *Psychological Bulletin*, 144(7): 710-756. https://doi.org/10.1037/bul0000151.

Pan, S. C., Schmitt, A. G., Bjork, E. L. and Sana, F. (2020). Pretesting reduces mind wandering and enhances learning during online lectures. *Journal of Applied Research in Memory and Cognition*, 9(4): 542-554. https://doi.org/10.1016/j.jarmac.2020.07.004.

Pashler, H., Bain, P., Bottge, B., Graesser, A., Koedinger, K., McDaniel, M. and Metcalfe, J. (2007). *Organizing Instruction and Study to Improve Student Learning. IES Practice Guide*. Washington, DC: National Center for Education Research, Institute of Education Sciences and US Department of Education. Available at: https://files.eric.ed.gov/fulltext/ED498555.pdf.

Pashler, H., Cepeda, N. J., Wixted, J. T. and Rohrer, D. (2005). When does feedback facilitate learning of words? *Journal of Experimental Psychology: Learning, Memory, and Cognition*, 31(1): 3-8. https://doi.org/10.1037/0278-7393.31.1.3

Patterson Neubert, A. (2011). Research finds practicing retrieval is best tool for learning. *Purdue University News Service* [press release] (20 January). Available at: https://www.purdue.edu/newsroom/research/2011/110120KarpickeScience.html.

Paul, A. M. (2015). A new vision for testing. *Scientific American*, 313(2): 54-61. Available at: https://www.scientificamerican.com/article/researchers-find-that-frequent-tests-can-boost-learning.

Pavlik Jr, P. I. and Anderson, J. R. (2005). Practice and forgetting effects on vocabulary memory: an activation-based model of the spacing effect. *Cognitive Science*, 29(4): 559-586. https://doi.org/10.1207/s15516709cog0000_14.

Pavlik Jr, P. I. and Anderson, J. R. (2008). Using a model to compute the optimal schedule of practice. *Journal of Experimental Psychology: Applied*, 14(2): 101-117. https://doi.org/10.1037/1076-898X.14.2.101.

Pekrun, R., Cusack, A., Murayama, K., Elliot, A. J. and Thomas, K. (2014). The power of anticipated feedback: effects on students' achievement goals and achievement emotions. *Learning and Instruction*, 29: 115-124. https://doi.org/10.1016/j.learninstruc.2013.09.002.

Pekrun, R., Lichtenfeld, S., Marsh, H. W., Murayama, K. and Goetz, T. (2017). Achievement emotions and academic performance: longitudinal models of reciprocal effects. *Child Development*, 88(5): 1653-1670. https://doi.org/10.1111/cdev.12704.

Perry, T., Lea, R., Jørgensen, C. R., Cordingley, P., Shapiro, K. and Youdell, D. (2021). *Cognitive Science Approaches in the Classroom: A Review of the Evidence*. London: Education Endowment Foundation. Available at: https://educationendowmentfoundation.org.uk/education-evidence/evidence-reviews/cognitive-science-approaches-in-the-classroom.

Peterson, L. and Peterson, M. (1959). Short-term retention of individual verbal items. *Journal of Experimental Psychology: General*, 58(3): 193–198. https://doi.org/10.1037/h0049234.

Putnam, A. L. and Roediger III, H. L. (2013). Does the response mode affect amount recalled or the magnitude of the testing effect? *Memory and Cognition*, 41: 36–48. https://doi.org/10.3758/s13421-012-0245-x.

Pyc, M. A. and Rawson, K. A. (2012). Are judgments of learning made after correct responses during retrieval practice sensitive to lag and criterion level effects? *Memory and Cognition*, 40(6): 976–988. https://doi.org/10.3758/s13421-012-0200-x.

Rawson, K. A. (2014). The power of relearning: if at first you do succeed, try, try again. Presentation at the McMaster Conference on Education & Cognition, McMaster University, Hamilton, ON. Available at: https://www.youtube.com/watch?v=5kDxNyygdXQ.

Rawson, K. A. (2014). The power of relearning: if at first you succeed, try, try again [video] (12 July). Available at: https://www.youtube.com/watch?v=5kDxNyygdXQ.

Rawson, K. A. and Dunlosky, J. (2011). Optimizing schedules of retrieval practice for durable and efficient learning: how much is enough? *Journal of Experimental Psychology: General*, 140(3): 283–302. https://doi.org/10.1037/a0023956.

Rawson, K. A. and Dunlosky, J. (2012). When is practice testing most effective for improving the durability and efficiency of student learning? *Educational Psychology Review*, 24(3): 419–435. https://doi.org/10.1007/s10648-012-9203-1.

Rawson, K. A. and Dunlosky, J. (2022). Successive relearning: an underexplored but potent technique for obtaining and maintaining knowledge. *Current Directions in Psychological Science*, 31(4): 362–368. https://doi.org/10.1177/09637214221100484.

Rawson, K. A., Dunlosky, J. and Janes, J. L. (2020). All good things must come to an end: a potential boundary condition on the potency of successive relearning. *Educational Psychology Review,* 32: 851–871. https://doi.org/10.1007/s10648-020-09528-y.

Rawson, K. A., Dunlosky, J. and Sciartelli, S. M. (2013). The power of successive relearning: improving performance on course exams and long-term retention. *Educational Psychology Review*, 25(4): 523–548. https://www.jstor.org/stable/43546826.

Rawson, K. A., Vaughn, K. E., Walsh, M. and Dunlosky, J. (2018). Investigating and explaining the effects of successive relearning on long-term retention. *Journal of Experimental Psychology: Applied*, 24(1): 57–71. https://doi.org/10.1037/xap0000146.

Rickard, T. C. and Pan, S. C. (2018). A dual memory theory of the testing effect. *Psychonomic Bulletin and Review*, 25(3): 847–869. https://doi.org/10.3758/s13423-017-1298-4.

Rivers, M. L. (2021). Metacognition about practice testing: a review of learners' beliefs, monitoring, and control of test-enhanced learning. *Educational Psychology Review*, 33(3): 823–862. https://doi.org/10.1007/s10648-020-09578-2.

Roediger III, H. L. (2008). Relativity of remembering: why the laws of memory vanished. *Annual Review of Psychology*, 59: 225–254. https://doi.org/10.1146/annurev.psych.57.102904.190139.

Roediger III, H. L. and Butler, A. C. (2011). The critical role of retrieval practice in long-term retention. *Trends in Cognitive Sciences*, 15(1): 20–27. https://doi.org/10.1016/j.tics.2010.09.003.

Roediger III, H. L. and Karpicke, J. D. (2006). The power of testing memory: basic research and implications for educational practice. *Perspectives on Psychological Science*, 1(3): 181–210. https://doi.org/10.1111/j.1745-6916.2006.00012.x.

Roediger III, H. L. and Karpicke, J. D. (2011). Intricacies of spaced retrieval: a resolution. In A. S. Benjamin (ed.), *Successful Remembering and Successful Forgetting: A Festschift in Honor of Robert A. Bjork*. New York: Psychology Press, pp. 23-47.

Roediger III, H. L., Putnam, A. L. and Smith, M. A. (2011). Ten benefits of testing and their applications to educational practice. *Psychology of Learning and Motivation*, 55: 1-36. https://doi.org/10.1016/B978-0-12-387691-1.00001-6.

Rohrer, D. (2012). Interleaving helps students distinguish among similar concepts. *Educational Psychology Review*, 24: 355-367. https://doi.org/10.1007/s10648-012-9201-3.

Rohrer, D., Dedrick, R. F., Hartwig, M. K. and Cheung, C. N. (2019). A randomized controlled trial of interleaved mathematics practice. *Journal of Educational Psychology*, 112(1): 40-52. https://doi.org/10.1037/edu0000367.

Rohrer, D., Dedrick, R. F. and Stershic, S. (2015). Interleaved practice improves mathematics learning. *Journal of Educational Psychology*, 107(3): 900-908. https://doi.org/10.1037/edu0000001.

Rosenshine, B. (2012). Principles of instruction: research-based strategies that all teachers should know. *American Educator* (spring): 12-39. Available at: https://www.aft.org/sites/default/files/periodicals/Rosenshine.pdf.

Rowland, C. A. (2014). The effect of testing versus restudy on retention: a meta-analytic review of the testing effect. *Psychological Bulletin*, 140(6): 1432-1463. https://doi.org/10.1037/a0037559.

Sadler, P. (2006). The impact of self- and peer-grading on learner learning. *Educational Assessment*, 11(1): 1-31. https://doi.org/10.1207/s15326977ea1101_1.

Sadler, P. M. and Good, E. (2006). The impact of self- and peer-grading on student learning. *Educational Assessment*, 11: 1-31. https://doi.org/10.1207/s15326977ea1101_1.

Samani, J. and Pan, S. C. (2021). Interleaved practice enhances memory and problem-solving ability in undergraduate physics. *npj Science of Learning*, 6: article 32. https://doi.org/10.1038/s41539-021-00110-x.

Sana, F. and Yan, V. X. (2022) Interleaving retrieval practice promotes science learning. *Psychological Science,* 33(5): 782-788. https://doi.org/10.1177/09567976211057507.

Sana, F., Yan, V. X. and Carvalho, P. F. (2022). On rest-from-deliberate-learning as a mechanism for the spacing effect: commentary on Chen et al. (2021). *Educational Psychology Review*, 34: 1843-1850. https://doi.org/10.1007/s10648-022-09663-8.

Sanchez, C. E., Atkinson, K. M., Koenka, A. C., Moshontz, H. and Cooper, H. (2017). Self-grading and peer-grading for formative and summative assessments in 3rd through 12th grade classrooms: a meta-analysis. *Journal of Educational Psychology*, 109(8): 1049-1066. https://doi.org/10.1037/edu0000190.

Schrank, Z. (2016). An assessment of student perceptions and responses to frequent low-stakes testing in introductory sociology classes. *Teaching Sociology,* 44(2): 118-127. https://doi.org/10.1177/0092055X15624745.

Schwieren, J., Barenberg, J. and Dutke, S. (2017). The testing effect in the psychology classroom: a meta-analytic perspective. *Psychology Learning and Teaching*, 16(2): 179-196. https://doi.org/10.1177/1475725717695149.

Sealy, C. (2019). The importance of students asking 'why?' *TES* (11 October). Available at: https://www.tes.com/magazine/archived/importance-students-asking-why.

SecEd (2022). A teacher's guide to retrieval practice, *SecEd Podcast* (episode 52, March). Available at: https://www.sec-ed.co.uk/podcasts/knowledge-bank/the-seced-podcast-a-teachers-guide-to-retrieval-practice-memory-spaced-learning-metacognition-motivation-feedback-testing-pedagogy-classroom-lesson-planning-homework-knowledge-retention-revision-exams-teaching-school.

Sense, F., Behrens, F., Meijer, R. R. and Grimaldi, H. (2016). An individual's rate of forgetting is stable over time but differs across materials. *Topics in Cognitive Science*, 8(1): 305–321. https://doi.org/10.1111/tops.12183.

Seo, E. H. (2012). Cramming, active procrastination, and academic achievement. *Social Behavior and Personality*, 40(8): 1333–1340. https://doi.org/10.2224/sbp.2012.40.8.1333

Sherrington, T. (2020). Re-reading Nuthall's *Hidden Lives of Learners*: insights from a classic [blog]. *TeacherHead* (15 February). Available at: https://teacherhead.com/2020/02/15/re-reading-nuthalls-hidden-lives-of-learners-insights-from-a-classic.

Siedlecka, M., Paulewicz, B. and Wierzchoń, M. (2016). But I was so sure! Metacognitive judgments are less accurate given prospectively than retrospectively. *Frontiers in Psychology*, 7: article 218. https://doi.org/10.3389/fpsyg.2016.00218.

Smith, A., Floerke, V. and Thomas, A. (2016). Retrieval practice protects memory against acute stress. *Science*, 354(6315): 1046–1048. https://doi.org/10.1126/science.aah5067.

Smith, M. A., Roediger III, H. L. and Karpicke, J. D. (2013). Covert retrieval practice benefits retention as much as overt retrieval practice. *Journal of Experimental Psychology: Learning, Memory, and Cognition*, 39(6): 1712–1725. https://doi.org/10.1037/a0033569.

Sobel, H. S., Cepeda, N. J. and Kapler, I. V. (2011). Spacing effects in real-world classroom vocabulary learning. *Applied Cognitive Psychology*, 25: 763–767. https://doi.org/10.1002/acp.1747.

Soderstrom, N. C. and Bjork, R. A. (2015). Learning versus performance: an integrative review. *Perspectives on Psychological Science*, 10(2): 176–199. https://doi.org/10.1177/1745691615569000.

Son, L. K. and Kornell, N. (2008). Research on the allocation of study time: key studies from 1890 to the present (and beyond). In J. Dunlosky and R. A. Bjork (eds), *Handbook of Metamemory and Memory*. New York: Psychology Press, pp. 333–351.

Song, D. (2016). Student-generated questioning and quality questions: a literature review. *Research Journal of Educational Studies and Review*, 2(5): 58–70.

Sotola, L. K. and Crede, M. (2021). Regarding class quizzes: a meta-analytic synthesis of studies on the relationship between frequent low-stakes testing and class performance. *Educational Psychology Review*, 33: 407–426. https://doi.org/10.1007/s10648-020-09563-9.

Still, K. (2021). Why and how we should be using retrieval practice and spaced learning. *SecEd* (1 December). Available at: https://www.sec-ed.co.uk/best-practice/why-and-how-we-should-be-using-retrieval-practice-and-space-learning-feedback-metacognition-interleaving-memory-revision-assessment-teaching-pedagogy.

Stobart, G. (2008) *Testing Times: The Uses and Abuses of Assessment*. Abingdon and New York: Routledge.

Storm, B. C., Bjok, R. A. and Storm, J. C. (2010). Optimizing retrieval as a learning event: when and why expanding retrieval practice enhances long-term retention. *Memory and Cognition*, 38(2): 244–253. https://doi.org/10.3758/MC.38.2.244.

Swanson, H. L. (1999). What develops in working memory? A life span perspective. *Developmental Psychology*, 35(4): 986-1000. https://doi.org/10.1037//0012-1649.35.4.986.

Sweller, J. (1988). Cognitive load during problem solving: effects on learning. *Cognitive Science*, 12(2): 257-285. https://doi.org/10.1016/0364-0213(88)90023-7.

Sweller, J. (2016). Story of a research program. *Education Review*, 23: 1-18. https://doi.org/10.14507/er.v23.2025.

Sweller, J. (2017). Cognitive load theory: without an understanding of human cognitive architecture, instruction is blind, researchED Melbourne [video] (3 July). Available at: https://www.youtube.com/watch?v=gOLPfi9Ls-w.

Sweller, J., van Merrienboer, J. and Paas, F. (1998). Cognitive architecture and instructional design. *Educational Psychology Review*, 10(3): 251-296. https://doi.org/10.1023/a:1022193728205.

Szpunar, K. K., Jing, H. G. and Schacter, D. L. (2014). Overcoming overconfidence in learning from video-recorded lectures: implications of interpolated testing for online education. *Journal of Applied Research in Memory and Cognition*, 3(3): 161-164. https://doi.org/10.1016/j.jarmac.2014.02.001.

Szpunar, K. K., Khan, N. Y. and Schacter, D. L. (2013). Interpolated memory tests reduce mind wandering and improve learning of online lectures. *Proceedings of the National Academy of Sciences of the United States of America*, 110(16): 6313-6317. https://doi.org/10.1073/pnas.1221764110.

Szpunar, K. K., McDermott, K. B. and Roediger III, H. L. (2007). Expectation of a final cumulative test enhances long-term retention. *Memory and Cognition*, 35(5): 1007-1013. https://doi.org/10.3758/BF03193473.

Szpunar, K. K., McDermott, K. B. and Roediger III, H. L. (2008). Testing during study insulates against the buildup of proactive interference. *Journal of Experimental Psychology: Learning, Memory, and Cognition*, 34(6): 1392-1399. https://doi.org/10.1037/a0013082.

Tabibian, B., Upadhyay, U., De, A., Zarezade, A., Schölkopf, B. and Gomez-Rodriguez, M. (2019). Enhancing human learning via spaced repetition optimization. *Proceedings of the National Academy of Sciences of the United States of America*, 116(10): 3988-3993. https://doi.org/10.1073/pnas.1815156116.

Taraban, R., Maki, W. and Rynearson, K. (1999) Measuring study time distributions: implications for designing computer-based courses. *Behavior Research Methods, Instruments, and Computers*, 31: 263-269. https://doi.org/10.3758/BF03207718.

Tauber, S. K., Witherby, A. E., Dunlosky, J., Rawson, K. A., Putnam, A. L. and Roediger III, H. L. (2018). Does covert retrieval benefit learning of key-term definitions? *Journal of Applied Research in Memory and Cognition*, 7(1): 106-115. https://doi.org/10.1016/j.jarmac.2016.10.004.

TES (2021). How to build a better learner: an interview with John Dunlosky, *TES Podcast*, September. Available at: https://player.captivate.fm/episode/73284499-6c30-419f-ae2d-b03897f6b12b.

Thai, K. P., Krasne, S. and Kellman, P. J. (2015). Adaptive perceptual learning in electrocardiography: the synergy of passive and active classification. In *Proceedings of the 37th Annual Conference of the Cognitive Science Society*. Austin, TX: Cognitive Science Society. Available at: https://cogsci.mindmodeling.org/2015/papers/0404/paper0404.pdf.

Tishauser, J. (2019). Graham Nuthall: educational research at its best, *researchED* (26 February). Available at: https://researched.org.uk/2019/02/26/graham-nuthall-educational-research-at-its-best.

Todd, K., Therriault, D. J. and Angerhofer, A. (2021). Improving students' summative knowledge of introductory chemistry through the forward testing effect: examining the role of retrieval practice quizzing. *Chemistry Education Research and Practice*, 22(1): 175–181. https://doi.org/10.1039/D0RP00185F.

Toppino, T. C., Phelan, H. A. and Gerbier, E. (2018). Level of initial training moderates the effects of distributing practice over multiple days with expanding, contracting, and uniform schedules: evidence for study-phase retrieval. *Memory and Cognition*, 46(6): 969–978. https://doi.org/10.3758/s13421-018-0815-7.

Tullis, J. G., Finley, J. R. and Benjamin, A. S. (2013). Metacognition of the testing effect: guiding learners to predict the benefits of retrieval. *Memory and Cognition*, 41(3): 429–442. https://doi.org/10.3758/s13421-012-0274-5.

Urhahne, D. and Wijnia, L. (2021). A review on the accuracy of teacher judgments. *Educational Research Review*, 32: article 100374. https://doi.org/10.1016/j.edurev.2020.100374.

van Dongen, E. V., Thielen, J-W., Takashima, A., Barth, M. and Fernández, G. (2012) .Sleep supports selective retention of associative memories based on relevance for future utilization. *PLOS One,* 7(8): e43426. https://doi.org/10.1371/journal.pone.0043426.

Van Gog, T. and Sweller, J. (2015). Not new, but nearly forgotten: the testing effect decreases or even disappears as the complexity of learning materials increases. *Educational Psychology Review*, 27(2): 247–264. https://doi.org/10.1007/s10648-015-9310-x.

Van Kesteren, M., Krabbendam, L. and Meeter, M. (2018). Integrating educational knowledge: reactivation of prior knowledge during educational learning enhances memory integration. *npj Science of Learning*, 3: article 11. https://doi.org/10.1038/s41539-018-0027-8.

Van Rijn, H., van Maanen, L. and van Woudenberg, M. (2009). Passing the test: improving learning gains by balancing spacing and testing effects. In A. Howes, D. Peebles and R. P. Cooper (eds), *Proceedings of the 9th International Conference on Cognitive Modeling*. Manchester: ICCM. Available at: https://iccm-conference.neocities.org/2009/proceedings/cd/papers/200/paper200.pdf.

Vaughn, K. E., Dunlosky, J. and Rawson, K. A. (2016). Effects of successive relearning on recall: does relearning override the effects of initial learning criterion? *Memory and Cognition*, 44(6): 897–909. https://doi.org/10.3758/s13421-016-0606-y.

Vaughn, K. E., Fuegen, K., Goddard, P. and Krull, D. S. (2021) .The influence of self-testing websites on college exam performance. *Scholarship of Teaching and Learning in Psychology* [advance online publication]. https://doi.org/10.1037/stl0000258.

Vaughn, K. E., Hausman, H. and Kornell, N. (2017). Retrieval attempts enhance learning regardless of time spent trying to retrieve. *Memory*, 25(3): 298–316. https://doi.org/10.1080/09658211.2016.1170152.

Vaughn, K. E. and Kornell, N. (2019). How to activate students' natural desire to test themselves. *Cognition Research*, 4, article 35. https://doi.org/10.1186/s41235-019-0187-y.

Weinstein, Y., Gilmore, A. W., Szpunar, K. K. and McDermott, K. B. (2014). The role of test expectancy in the build-up of proactive interference in long-term memory. *Journal of*

Experimental Psychology: Learning, Memory, and Cognition, 40(4): 1039–1048. https://doi.org/10.1037/a0036164.

Wigfield, A. and Eccles, J. S. (2000). Expectancy-value theory of achievement motivation. *Contemporary Educational Psychology*, 25(1): 68–81. https://doi.org/10.1006/ceps.1999.1015.

Wiliam, D. (2015). Feedback for learning: make time to save time. *LSi Dylan Wiliam Center* (6 January). Available at: https://www.dylanwiliamcenter.com/2015/01/06/feedback-for-learning-make-time-to-save-time.

Wiliam, D. (2017). I've come to the conclusion Sweller's Cognitive Load Theory is the single most important thing for teachers to know. Twitter post (26 January, 6:16pm). Available at: https://twitter.com/dylanwiliam/status/824682504602943489?lang=en-GB.

Wiliam, D. (2018). Memories are made of this. *TES* (28 January). Available at: https://www.tes.com/magazine/archive/memories-are-made.

Wiliam, D. (2022). Research into practice: the case of classroom formative assessment. In S. Gorard (ed.), *Getting Evidence into Education*. Abingdon and New York: Routledge, pp. 119–135.

Willingham, D. T. (2003). Ask the cognitive scientist: Students remember … what they think about. *American Educator* (summer). Available at: https://www.aft.org/periodical/american-educator/summer-2003/ask-cognitive-scientist-students-rememberwhat.

Willingham, D. T. (2007) Critical thinking: why is it so hard to teach? *American Educator* (summer): 8–19. Available at: https://www.aft.org/sites/default/files/periodicals/Crit_Thinking.pdf.

Willingham, D. T. (2008). Ask the cognitive scientist: what will improve a student's memory. *American Educator* (winter): 17–25. Available at: https://www.aft.org/sites/default/files/periodicals/willingham_0.pdf.

Willingham, D. T. (2009). *Why Don't Students Like School? A Cognitive Scientist Answers Questions About How the Mind Works and What It Means for the Classroom*. San Francisco, CA: Jossey-Bass.

Willingham, D. T. (2017). A mental model of the learner: teaching the basic science of educational psychology to future teachers. *Mind, Brain, and Education*, 11(4): 166–175. https://doi.org/10.1111/mbe.12155.

Willingham, D. T. (2021). Ask the cognitive scientist: why do students remember everything that's on television and forget everything I say? *American Educator* (summer). Available at: https://www.aft.org/ae/summer2021/willingham.

Wilson, R. C., Shenhav, A., Straccia, M. and Cohen, J. D. (2019). The Eighty Five Percent Rule for optimal learning. *Nature Communications,* 10: article 4646. https://doi.org/10.1038/s41467-019-12552-4 .

Wiseheart, M., Küpper-Tetzel, C. E., Weston, T., Kim, A. S. N., Kapler, I. V. and Foot-Seymour, V. (2019). Enhancing the quality of student learning using distributed practice. In J. Dunlosky and K. A. Rawson (eds), *The Cambridge Handbook of Cognition and Education*. Cambridge: Cambridge University Press, pp. 550–583.

Wisniewski, B., Zierer, K. and Hattie, J. (2020). The power of feedback revisited: a meta-analysis of educational feedback research. *Frontiers in Psychology*, 10: article 3087. https://doi.org/10.3389/fpsyg.2019.03087.

Yan, V. X., Bjork, E. L. and Bjork, R. A. (2016). On the difficulty of mending metacognitive illusions: a priori theories, fluency effects, and misattributions of the interleaving benefit. *Journal of Experimental Psychology: General*, 145(7): 918-933. https://doi.org/10.1037/xge0000177.

Yan, V. X., Eglington, L. G. and Garcia, M. A. (2020) Learning better, learning more: the benefits of expanded retrieval practice. *Journal of Applied Research in Memory and Cognition*, 9(2): 204-214. https://doi.org/10.1037/h0101849.

Yan, V. X. and Sana, F. (2021) The robustness of the interleaving benefit. *Journal of Applied Research in Memory and Cognition*, 10(4): 589-602. https://doi.org/10.1037/h0101863.

Yang, C., Chew, S. J., Sun, B. and Shanks, D. R. (2019). The forward effects of testing transfer to different domains of learning. *Journal of Educational Psychology*, 111(5): 809-826. https://doi.org/10.1037/edu0000320.

Yang, C., Luo, L., Vadillo, M. A., Yu, R. and Shanks, D. R. (2021). Testing (quizzing) boosts classroom learning: a systematic and meta-analytic review. *Psychological Bulletin*, 147(4): 399-435. https://doi.org/10.1037/bul0000309.

Yang, C., Potts, R. and Shanks, D. R. (2017). The forward testing effect on self-regulated study time allocation and metamemory monitoring. *Journal of Experimental Psychology: Applied*, 23(3): 263-277. http://dx.doi.org/10.1037/xap0000122.

Zepeda, C. D., Martin, R. S. and Butler, A. C. (2020) Motivational strategies to engage learners in desirable difficulties. *Journal of Applied Research in Memory and Cognition*, 9(4): 468-474. https://doi.org/10.1016/j.jarmac.2020.08.007.

Zerr, C. L., Berg, J. J., Nelson, S. M., Fishell, A. K., Savalia, N. K. and McDermott, K. B. (2018). Learning efficiency: identifying individual differences in learning rate and retention in healthy adults. *Psychological Science*, 29(9): 1436-1450. https://doi.org/10.1177/0956797618772540.

About the author

Kristian Still is a former headteacher and currently deputy head academic at Boundary Oak School in Fareham. A school leader by day, together with his co-creator Alex Warren, a full-time senior software developer, Kritian built RememberMore, a philanthropic project, offering free personalised spaced retrieval practice resources to teachers and pupils.

Visit www.remembermore.app and www.classroom.remembermore.app for more information.

Visit www.kristianstill.co.uk/wordpress to keep up to date on his adventures.

Neuroscience for Teachers
Applying research evidence from brain science
Richard Churches, Eleanor Dommett and Ian Devonshire
ISBN: 978-178583183-6

Neuroscience for Teachers expertly unpacks, in an easy-to-read and instantly useable way, what every teacher needs to know about the brain and how we really learn – and what that suggests for how they should teach.

Packed with examples and research-informed tips on how to enhance personal effectiveness and improve classroom delivery, this book provides accessible, practical guidance supported by the latest research evidence on the things that will help your learners to learn better.

Laid out in an easy-to-use format, each chapter features: 'Research Zones' highlighting particular pieces of research with a supplementary insight into the area being explored; 'Reflection' sections that give you something to think about, or suggest something you might try out in the classroom; and concluding 'Next steps' that outline how teachers might incorporate the findings into their own practice. The authors have also included a glossary of terms covering the book's technical vocabulary to aid the development of teachers' literacy in the field of neuroscience.

Suitable for LSAs, NQTs, teachers, middle leaders, local authority advisers and anyone working with learners.

Cognitive Load Theory
A handbook for teachers
Steve Garnett
ISBN: 978-178583501-8

In *Cognitive Load Theory: A handbook for teachers*, Steve Garnett brings clarity to the complexity surrounding CLT and provides a user-friendly toolkit of techniques to help teachers optimise their pupils' learning.

Cognitive load theory (CLT) is rapidly becoming education's next 'big thing'.

It is natural, therefore, that teachers will want to know more about it and, more importantly, understand how they can embed it in their classroom teaching.

Written by author and international teacher trainer Steve Garnett, this invaluable handbook offers a complete yet concise summary of what CLT involves and how it can impact on pupil performance.

Steve covers a wide range of teaching strategies to help teachers avoid overloading their pupils' working memories, and empowers them with the tools to get their pupils learning more effectively – particularly when learning new content.

He talks you through the 14 effects that can 'clutter' working memory – for example, the split-attention effect, redundancy effect, and expertise reversal effect – and shares a diverse collection of figures and diagrams as examples of how teachers can optimise their delivery of content to students. Furthermore, he also explores the 'cognitive architecture' of the brain and how a better understanding of it can inform and improve teachers' practice.

Suitable for teachers, department heads, school leaders and anyone with a responsibility for improving teaching and learning.